Symbolic Communities

Studies of Urban Society

Albert Hunter *Symbolic Communities*

The Persistence and Change of Chicago's Local Communities

With a Foreword by Morris Janowitz

The University of Chicago Press

Chicago and London

To Annie

THE UNIVERSITY OF CHICAGO PRESS, CHICAGO 60637
THE UNIVERSITY OF CHICAGO PRESS, LTD., LONDON

© *1974 by The University of Chicago*
All rights reserved. Published 1974
Phoenix edition 1982
Printed in the United States of America
89 88 87 86 85 84 83 82   2 3 4 5 6

International Standard Book Number: 0-226-36080-6 (cloth);
0-226-36081-4 (paper)
Library of Congress Catalog Card Number: 74-75612

Contents

Illustrations

Tables

Foreword

In the decade of the 1920s, the Chicago "school" of urban sociology developed its main intellectual outlines. It strove for a delicate mixture of descriptive details, presented with humanistic concern, and quantitative indicators, reflective of social change, plus a reasoned search for broader generalizations which would not become separated from social reality. These elements have continued to appear and reappear in sociological endeavors in a variety of formats, although formalistic theorizing and standardized survey research have become the more typical work of sociologists.

It is particularly noteworthy that there is an old-fashioned element in the contemporary practitioner of the Chicago school of urban sociology. He is a person who seeks to collect his own data wherever possible, using a variety of sources. After he grapples with his particular subject for a number of years, he prepares a monograph of which he is the sole author. Albert Hunter's *Symbolic Communities* conforms to this mold as he seeks to give a more precise quantitative basis to his description and analysis of persistence and change in Chicago's local communities. It is more than half a century later that Hunter returns explicitly to the themes of W. I. Thomas which inspired Robert E. Park and Ernest Burgess to examine in detail the ecology, institutions, and norms of the variety of neighborhoods and local communities in a particular urban metropolis. The result of his efforts is that the fusion of social history and sociology has become more of an intellectual reality.

But intellectual traditions are not made to survive or flourish by repeating the procedures of the past giants, as is often done by academic disciples. Hunter had the opportunity for only one interview with Ernest Burgess. But he had the advantage of taking as his point of departure Burgess's written

formulations about local communities, not the imagery and
the mythography that surround a once-creative intellectual
circle, although he has the same fierce attraction to the vi-
tality of the urban metropolis which so often characterizes
"urban sociologists."

Continuity requires a powerful element of intellectual distance. As he laboriously explored the neighborhoods of Chicago, Hunter knew he had the responsibility of replicating the
essential data which had been collected and analyzed fifty
years ago. Sociologists all too often neglect their historical
obligation. But he also had the imagination to drastically alter
both his orientation and his research procedures to encompass
the merging realities of a city vastly transformed. Thus Hunter's penetrating achievement rests in good measure on the
conscious balance of efforts which enabled him to probe and
analyze persistence and change.

Not for a moment does he overlook the central historical
assumption on which his analysis rests. The transformation of
the social fabric of the metropolis—the changed character of
neighborhood and local communities—is related to the increase
in the scale of organization. In essence, the underlying issue is
not mere growth in numbers, for the population base has not
increased, but rather changes in organizational scale.

The increase in scale is taken for granted, but it has its
origin in both the technology and the political norms which
create a mass society in which the demand becomes dominant
that economic, welfare, and legal rights should be universal.
This increase in scale does not produce uniformity or homogeneity in the social organization of metropolitan life. On the
contrary, it produces a greater degree of differentiation in social groupings, a greater degree of interdependence, and a
more complex social order. Moreover, the essential implication is that the greater degree of interdependence does not
insure integration and coordination in the urban metropolis.
In the absence of effective voluntaristic and political initia-
tive, the structure within the metropolitan community becomes fragmented and disarticulated.

Concretely, Hunter takes as his point of departure the well-
known seventy-five local community areas of Chicago charted
by Ernest Burgess in the 1920s. He is fully aware of the arbi-

trary definitions which were imposed. The more elaborate and multifaceted picture of Chicago neighborhoods and communities which he presents for the 1960s reflects not only the process of change but a deeper and richer mode of study, one rooted in the long-standing ecological, institutional, and normative dimensions of analysis.

First, in his ecological perspective he is not searching for the survival of the zonal format. The ecological elements lead him to examine the patterns of change which are generated in the central city and extend outward in a sequential pattern throughout the city. His statistical analysis focuses on the key variables of economic position, family status, and race in order to characterize the structure of the local community. Obviously the major transformation has been the central significance of racial expansion. But the ecological analysis already acknowledges the emerging new transition in which higher income and new types of family groups relocate at the core of the central city.

Second, by means of extensive participant observation and field interviews, he probes the residents' perceptions of the boundaries and symbolic meanings of their local communities. The residential community—the social block, the neighborhood, and the local community area—defines a central axis of life-space and self-respect. Hunter is aware that a cartographic representation with fixed boundaries presents only a partial picture of the images in men's minds. Each individual maintains, with various degrees of clarity, a hierarchy of images. But the essential point is that with the increased scale of organization in the metropolitan community, the residents' perceptions of their home areas have become more elaborate, more narrow, and more delimited. At the same time, an important minority of the residents holds more than one point of reference and sees itself in both a particular locality and a larger section of the city.

In the setting of extensive geographical and social mobility, it is striking that more than 40 percent of the respondents made use of geographical points of reference which were extant when Burgess mapped his local community areas. Moreover, attachment and identification of local areas reflect less societal-wide social status—occupation and race—and more local social status—in particular length of residence, number of children, and patterns of daily behavior. Persons who are of long residence and who have children are the most attached to their local communities.

Third, at the institutional level Hunter has focused on voluntary associations—particularly voluntary associations with geographical referents. Although he does not encompass political party organization, he presents an analysis which extends beyond case studies and highlights the overall structure of local voluntary associations. Again, under the impact of growth of organizational scale, these voluntary associations are structured in two directions. There is a pattern of strong articulation of voluntary associations with the smallest "natural" geographical units on the one hand; and on the other hand there is a definite trend toward the development of roof organizations, federations, and even "regional" alliances to link the local units to the realities of large-scale administrative organization of government and economic enterprise. One can speak of the emergence of a hierarchical structure in community organization.

A central empirical finding is that the black community displays similar patterns with regard to the perceived boundaries of the local community and the structure of voluntary associations. One can add that for the limited minority of blacks who reside in integrated and biracial communities, on the Near North Side and Near South Side of Chicago, the patterns of internal differentiation and linkages to the large metropolis are indeed elaborate and complex.

The mode of analysis Hunter offers helps to explain the persistence of powerful local attachments and community-based strivings for power. He points out the limitations of the Gemeinschaft-Gesellschaft approach—the folk-urban formulation of urbanization and industrialization. The model he offers stands in contradistinction to that of the postindustrial society in which the individual is linked to the larger polity essentially or even exclusively by his occupation and the interest groups which occupations and professions generate. The realities of the neighborhood and the local community as he charts them rest on the emergence, persistence, and transformation of a variety of ascriptive solidarities and communal forms based on age groups, residential defense, ethnic-religious definitions, and life-styles. To explore the continual regrouping of these "social worlds" of the metropolis is to help explain the fragmentation of social and institutional relations.

There is no reason to believe that a clearer and more accurate ethnography, even a quantitative ethnography, of the social fabric of the metropolis will produce a more effective basis for institution building—especially for institution building in the political arena to overcome the extensive fragmentation. But Hunter's volume belongs to the tradition that asserts that effective sociological analysis per se is a relevant contribution to the efforts of collective problem-solving, because a clearer understanding of social reality serves to stir the visions of men and women.

Morris Janowitz
The University of Chicago

Acknowledgments

A general debt is owed to the early researchers at the University of Chicago, especially Ernest W. Burgess and Robert E. Park, whose work stands as a backdrop for these current efforts. Also, a debt is owed to the residents of Chicago themselves, who are being observed in Robert Park's "laboratory" by yet another generation of graduate students.

This study was carried out from 1966 to 1968 while I was a fellow at the Center for Social Organization Studies at the University of Chicago. It was supported by the Russell Sage Foundation and the Ford Foundation's urban sociology grant to the Department of Sociology. The research problem was collectively defined, and my own efforts benefited from a number of initial field studies of selected local communities carried out by fellow graduate students in the Center. Among them were Charles Derber, Charles Goldsmid, William Kornblum, Sidney Kronus, Harvey Molotch, Howard Rotblat, and Daniel Willick. Among the "faculty" of the Center I thank David Street for his encouragement and advice, and I especially thank Gerald Suttles, who patiently listened to my early formulations of the problem, read several drafts of the manuscript, and offered many valuable comments and insights from his own research. Above all I would like to thank Morris Janowitz, director of the Center, who provided financial support, moral encouragement, and intellectual stimulation both during this research and throughout my graduate-school years. Without him this book simply would not be.

Other colleagues who listened to or read my struggling attempts for clarity and offered valuable advice include Brian J. L. Berry, John Brewer, Vernon Dibble, and Hubert "Bob" O'Gorman. There are others too numerous to mention who aided in direct and indirect ways, and to them and those mentioned above, my thanks.

Finally, to Ann Grice Hunter, who coded, encouraged, and comforted without complaint through the years of this research, and to Allyson and Andrew, who grew up with it, thank you.

Symbolic Communities

Introduction

THE PROBLEM OF COMMUNITY

This is yet another study of local urban communities, and of the city of Chicago. Like the bride on her wedding day, it has elements that are old, borrowed, and new. It arises from the old tradition of the Chicago school of urban sociology, it borrows in both theory and methods from developments occurring in sociology since that time, and it presents a somewhat new empirical emphasis upon the symbolic culture and sentiments of community.

The problem of community is both sociological and social. The social problems arising from the transformations of Western society in the eighteenth and nineteenth centuries led to the development of sociology as a discipline and to its early concern with the generic concepts of community and society. The continuing urbanization of the world's population has kept "community" a central concept within social theory and a central problem in social life. Therefore, to understand the variety of meanings attached to the concept we will study it where it is perhaps most problematic, within the small local areas and neighborhoods of a large industrial urban center, the city of Chicago.

In studying Chicago's local communities I will rely upon a number of distinct sets of data, utilize a variety of research methods, and focus upon several distinct meanings or dimensions of community. My data range from personal observations to census material to structured questionnaires. My methods include fieldwork and participant observation, correlation and factor analysis, and cross-tabulation of a sample survey. My theoretical focus is on the ecological, cultural, and social dimensions of community. This, then, is the purpose of my research: by using a variety of methods and data, to study the structure and change of Chicago's local urban communities—their ecology, their symbolic culture, and their social structure.

CONCEPTS OF COMMUNITY AND COMMUNITY CHANGE

There are two basic dimensions to the definition of "community" which emerges from the literature—the ecological and the normative.[1] Ecological, of course, refers to the selective spatial distribution of populations and functions and to interaction mediated through the spatial and physical environment. The normative may be further subdivided to include, first, normative social interaction and resulting social structure and, second, the cultural and symbolic elements of community—shared collective representations and moral sentiments. Although different writers may leave out or selectively emphasize one or more of these three elements, they are found in the most widely accepted definitions of community.

The specification of these different elements suggests that perhaps it is best to approach the study of community in general, and of local urban communities specifically, in a more differentiated manner, fully recognizing the importance of each. Such an approach leaves as a variable the extent and degree to which community is present, and it is preferable to a conception which forces a false dichotomy. Rather than asking whether "community" does or does not exist, we should approach the problem by asking whether this or that element of community is present and to what degree. This approach in fact reflects some of the more multidimensional conceptions of community contained in the literature. For example even Ernest Burgess, who was often criticized for his emphasis upon the ecological dimension, says, "the study of social forces in a local area should assume that the neighborhood or the community is the resultant of three main types of determining influences: first, ecological forces; second, cultural forces; and third, political forces." Further defining these forces, he adds, "the ecological forces are those which have to do with the process of competition and the consequent distribution and segregation by residence and occupation"; and "local culture includes those sentiments, forms of conduct, attachments, and ceremonies which are characteristic of a locality, which have either originated in the area or have become identified with it"; and finally "political forces have to do with the more formal control of public opinion and law. Neighborhood work is concerned with political forces whenever social action is desired."[2]

The three empirical and theoretical orientations of this research, the ecological, symbolic-cultural, and social structural, have direct continuity with the orientations of the earlier Chicago school.

ECOLOGICAL THEORIES AND RESEARCH

The ecological approach to the study of community structure and change was first developed in this country during the twenties by Park and Burgess at the University of Chicago.[3] Borrowing extensively from plant and animal ecology, Spencerian sociology, and writings of Weber and Simmel, these early researchers began to compile a variety of data and to relate it to spatial distribution as indicating basic social and ecological processes.[4] On the one hand their research emphasized some general and persistent components of ecological structures—the configuration of the city as a "mosaic of little worlds," the relationship between "social" and "spatial" distance, and the resulting segregation of populations into functionally interdependent "natural community areas." On the other hand, they also recognized that natural processes were at work transforming this ecological structure, and these were summarized in Burgess's now classic concentric zone model of "The Growth of the City."[5] Their analysis of urban change also documented the disorganization and decline of local communities and neighborhoods. This disorganization was seen to be a consequence of ethnic assimilation as well as the continuing urbanization and industrialization of society.

Many researchers have built upon this twofold base, some emphasizing persistent ecological structure, others community change. For example "social distance," or stratification broadly conceived, has consistently shown a relationship to spatial distance. This is true whether social distance is measured by income, occupation, education, or ethnicity, or, even more recently, by the perception of these.[6] On the other hand, authors like Form and Hatt have emphasized community disorganization, and their studies call into question the existence of "natural community areas" in today's urban setting.[7]

A more recent analytical development for the study of urban ecological structure and change is social area analysis, or "factorial ecology." Since its first formulation by Shevky and Bell in the fifties a number of comparative replications have attested the generality of their three principal factors of ecological differentiation—economic, family, and racial-ethnic status.[8] Although its earliest formulation deemphasized the "spatial" and "natural area" distribution of these factors, more recent studies have explicitly related these to the earlier ecological models of the city by considering sectors, rings, and distance gradients.[9]

Both of these approaches emphasize not only ecological structure but processes of change in this structure. For the earlier Chicago school these were the processes of invasion, succession, and competition within the city's "natural areas," concentric zones, and sectors, whereas social area analysis relies upon the basic dynamic concept that an "increase in scale" produces the three factors of urban differentiation and homogeneous "social areas." One of the purposes of this study is to explore ecological change as well as ecological structure; furthermore, it attempts to empirically relate social area analysis to earlier ecological analyses of urban structure and change.

SYMBOLIC-CULTURAL THEORIES AND RESEARCH

The importance of the cultural and symbolic element of community has been widely recognized in social theory from Toennies's discussion of Gemeinschaft and Gesellschaft to Durkheim's emphasis upon "moral density" in the shift from mechanical to organic solidarity.[10] Even Park at Chicago stressed the "moral" as well as the "spatial" order of community.[11] But the symbolic-cultural dimension of local urban communities generally has not received as extensive empirical analysis as has the ecological. Undoubtedly this was in part due to the widespread belief that local communities and neighborhoods simply do not provide a clear cultural and symbolic basis of identification in today's highly complex urban setting.

More recently, however, a few writers have recognized the continuing persistence of collectively shared cultural and symbolic elements at the level of the urban community. Suttles's recent work in Chicago's West Side slum points out the importance of shared spatial identifications in producing a "segmented social order."[12] Similarly, the work of Kevin Lynch demonstrates the widespread though varying ability of people to define and identify local communities and neighborhoods.[13] Firey's earlier study of Boston's Beacon Hill also suggests that such symbolically defined local areas have unique local cultures which retain historical meaning and sentiment.[14]

In short, it appears that the spatial order itself may be a central and persistent component of the cultural and symbolic order of local urban communities. These findings suggest as a guiding proposition that for meaningful social action to take place individuals need some organizing principle, some "definition of the situation," which includes a spatial referent. Specifically, this proposition suggests that for local urban communities to operate as objects and arenas of meaningful social action their residents must possess some conceptual image of them. Furthermore, it suggests that these symbolic images must be shared or collective representations, and that individuals must have the means, varying needs, and abilities to draw on this local culture to define and delimit meaningful symbolic communities.

THEORIES AND RESEARCH ON LOCAL
PARTICIPATION AND SOCIAL STRUCTURE

Like the ecological and symbolic-cultural dimensions, the social structure of local urban communities has gone through a period of hypothesized decline, only to be resurrected in subsequent research. The early theorists, including Toennies, Durkheim, and Park, suggested that the increasing division of labor, the broadening scope of communication, and the proliferation of multifarious associations of interest were resulting in a social structure in which local forms of social organization would be truncated, if not entirely eclipsed. These new forms of social organization were expected to crosscut and diminish the common cultural and spatial elements of community, reducing the significance of the local area as an arena of normatively structured social action. This trend of an increasing scale of social organization eclipsing that of the local community was documented by several researchers who looked at the social structure of whole communities—for example, the Lynds in Middletown, Warner in Yankee City, and Vidich and Bensman in Springdale.[15] The only local social structures seen as remaining viable were those centering on the daily needs of the family—primarily shopping and child-rearing.

It was therefore noteworthy when in the fifties empirical studies of local urban communities began to document the persistence of local forms of social organization. Janowitz's study of the local community press pointed to one persistent form of local social structure that related directly to the retail function and yet provided a communication mechanism for social and cultural integration of the local area.[16] Similarly, studies by Zimmer and Hawley, Axelrod, and others pointed to the persistence of informal social circles of participation at the local level in addition to participation in more highly organized voluntary associations.[17] This new body of research is perhaps best summarized in Scott Greer's *The Emerging City*, in which he expands upon Janowitz's concept of the "community of limited liability."[18] This perspective holds that local orientation and participation are still to be found in the modern urban setting, but that they are somewhat attenuated and variable and are generally less binding than they once were. Greer suggests that the "inclusive spatial group"—organizationally represented by community voluntary associations—is a viable form of social organization alternative and complementary to the more currently dominant "exclusive membership group."

In short, these studies and theories suggest that the social structure of the local community is becoming more formally organized. If individuals *choose* to become involved locally—and it appears that this is above all a voluntaristic act—they will find themselves participating in highly structured and goal-oriented organizations.

One purpose of this study, then, will be to discover who does choose to become involved in these local community groups, the degree and nature of their involvement, and the structures and goals of the organizations they join.

THREE EMPIRICAL APPROACHES TO ANALYZING THE
STRUCTURES OF LOCAL URBAN COMMUNITIES

An Ecological Approach

To study the ecological structure of Chicago's local communities, and changes in this structure, the research draws upon recent developments in "social area analysis," or "factorial ecology." In all, seven factor analyses are computed upon nine selected census variables for Chicago's seventy-five community areas for the years 1930 to 1960.[19] It should be noted that these areas were initially delimited by Burgess and his students in the twenties as "natural areas," and that this research is explicitly concerned with relating the "natural areas" of the Chicago school and the "social areas" of factorial ecology.[20]

From the four factor solutions made upon data from 1930, 1940, 1950, and 1960, three principal factors of urban segregation consistently emerge—economic status, family status, and racial-ethnic status. Despite the major uniformities in ecological structure observed across these four points in time, there are changes in the overall ecological structure of Chicago which suggest increasing differentiation. To understand these changes we will assess the relative and changing importance of economic, family, and racial-ethnic status as dimensions of urban differentiation by seeing the relative explanatory power of each factor at the four different points in time. We will see, for example, that economic status is consistently the most important factor of segregation, while family status declines in importance and racial-ethnic status increases.

To further explicate these ecological changes I will then carry out three factor analyses based upon correlations among *differences* in the nine variables at two points in time. These solutions for 1930–40, 1940–50, and 1950–60 depict in effect the "structure of change" in contrast to the previous analysis of "change in structure." These three solutions are compared among themselves and also compared with the previous four static solutions. The overall results suggest that these factors of change are more variable from decade to decade than are the factors of structure, and they are important in highlighting or isolating the decade specific changes in ecological structure.

Subsequent analysis of these ecological data is based upon the factor scores of the community areas on each of the three factors. The position or score of each community on each factor is mapped, and by comparing the spatial distributions of these scores at four different points in time the changing ecological configuration of the city can be assessed.[21] By looking at concentric zones, sectors, and multiple nuclei, we will see that each dimension of economic, family, and racial-ethnic status exhibits a different spatial pattern, and that the spatial patterns of the dimensions are changing in different ways.

The final analysis of these ecological data will isolate sequential "stages" of community change by looking at simultaneous changes of communities along each of the dimensions of social area analysis. This will enable us to test a number of dynamic propositions about urban growth and local community succession that have not been adequately explored since their early formulation by Burgess in his seminal article "The Growth of the City."[22]

A Symbolic-cultural Approach

The guiding proposition of this section, extracted from the previously discussed theory and research, is that local communities develop local cultures that residents will draw on in orienting themselves to the local community, in varying degrees as their needs and interests require and as their abilities and opportunities allow. This section is based upon observations and interviews with more than eight hundred residents in all of Chicago's seventy-five community areas.[23] Since these areas were initially delimited by Burgess in the twenties, we will be able to make comparisons and analyze gross changes and uniformities in residents' perceptions of these local communities over this fifty-year period.

The analysis of these symbolically defined areas focuses upon two general elements—cognition and sentiment. The cognitive image of the local community is measured by variation in residents' ability to name the area and give its boundaries and in the size of the area defined. Sentiment, in turn, is measured by variation in expressions of attachment to the local area and in evaluations of it. These elements of cognition and sentiment are the primary dependent variables of this section of the research.[24]

Three sets of independent variables are explored by cross-tabulation as "explanations" of these variations in orientations toward local communities. First, general social statuses which the individual occupies—statuses which are normatively defined throughout the society—are hypothesized to structure local orientations and to produce variations in the degree of local attachment and the clarity of the cognitive image of the local area. Such general social statuses are exemplified by race and class. Similarly, we expect local cognitions and sentiments to vary with the positions an individual occupies in the social structure of the local community itself. Such local social statuses include membership in local voluntary associations, whether an individual works, shops, or worships inside or outside the local area, and the length of time he has lived there. All these statuses, both general and local, are postulated to include different normative elements which effectively structure a person's orientation to the local area.[25]

The third set of independent variables focuses upon the community itself. One would expect, for example, that the evaluation of the local area would depend not solely upon the social positions of individual residents, but also upon characteristics of the community. The primary independent variables used to characterize the communities in this analysis are the factor scores of the previous factor analysis for 1960. Consequently, economic, family, and racial-ethnic statuses of the community are related directly to the interview data on symbolic communities. These community characteristics are also used as controls in relating individual social statuses to local symbolic perceptions and in pointing out certain structural effects at different points in the analysis.[26]

A Social Organizational Approach

The third section of the study explores the social structure of the local community by focusing on several aspects of local voluntary associations. As a review of the literature shows, such explicitly organized local groups are one of the principal social structures operating at the level of the local community.[27] The guiding proposition of this section is that as the bases of local community social structure previously considered "natural," such as ethnicity and kinship, have declined in significance they have been replaced by a proliferation of purposively organized local community voluntary associations which serve to integrate members into the social structure and symbolic culture of the local community.

In an attempt to answer the question of who becomes involved, we will first use the interview data to assess the types and degree of participation in locally organized groups. Variations in participation are correlated with the same sets of variables used in the previous section, namely, general and local social statuses an individual occupies and characteristics of the community itself. We will then analyze in turn the impact which membership in such organizations has upon residents' cognitive, evaluative, and affective orientations to their local symbolic communities. Finally, we will explore the degree to which residents are "aware" of these local organizations, even though they may not be members, and analyze the correlates and consequences of such "awareness." We are interested in seeing, in short, the impact and importance such organizations have for the local community as a whole, beyond their involved membership.

However, since this study is interested not only in individual participation and its correlates but also in the organizational structure of the community itself, a summary analysis is made of data obtained in a survey of more than two hundred local community organizations throughout the city, and a more detailed analysis is made of fifteen of the larger groups.[28] By looking at gross differences in organizational goals and structure, and by relating these to characteristics of the communities in which they operate, I will describe the different forms this "voluntaristic" dimension of community assumes in different areas of the city. For although the significance of local voluntary organizations in the social structure of the local community has been well documented, the different forms (goals and structures) such organizations exhibit have yet to be explored.[29] We will see, for example, that such groups range from local block clubs that are essentially neighborhood primary groups to powerful federated associations covering large sectors of the city.

I am taking the perspective that the structure and change of cities can be analyzed in part by looking at their local neighborhoods and communities. This means that local communities are viewed as objects for analysis in their own right, but also as part of a larger, functionally integrated whole. As Burgess said, "in the study of the growth of the city it is found that the life of any neighborhood is determined, in the long run, not altogether by the forces within itself, but even more by the total course of city life. To think of the neighborhood or the community in isolation from the city is to disregard the biggest fact about the neighborhood."[30] Therefore, to understand a city's local communities we must consider the ecological, cultural, and social forces operating within the larger context.

The dynamics of all three dimensions can be, and have been described in terms of a single general concept—"increase in scale."[31] An increase in scale for the ecological realm has meant the inclusion of small, relatively isolated and independent communities into a larger societal system of functionally interdependent metropolitan communities. This in turn has meant increasing levels of ecological organization such as were documented by Bogue.[32] He saw these large-scale communities as being composed of a dominant central city surrounded by smaller subdominant cities, which in turn set the conditions of existence for subinfluent smaller communities surrounding them. Although such an increase in scale has implied a fusion of previously isolated entities, it has also meant a differentiation of function, a "division of labor," as communities become more functionally specific and interdependent.

In the symbolic-cultural realm the increase in scale has been described by many "mass society" theorists. One such group of theorists sees a cultural decline to the lowest common denominator—a loss of specific and refined symbolic meanings—as the technology of mass society, especially the mass media, creates a larger system of shared but debased cultural symbols.[33] In short, there is a fusion or inclusion within a larger and commonly shared symbol system, but one which is markedly inferior to its more varied predecessors.

With respect to the symbols of community, for example, such writers found a ready target in the proliferation of homogeneous cracker-box suburban developments with tacked-on names like "Fair Elms," "Forest View," or "Meadow Brook." Such names were seen to symbolize a desired but debased dream. They were symbols of community which could not convey the distinctiveness and the varied but rich reality of a "Back of the Yards," a "Gold Coast," or a "Skid Row."

Mass-society theorists having a more positive orientation to the phenomenon see the same processes at work but evaluate their consequences differently. Edward Shils, for example, sees the "inclusiveness" of mass society as leading to a greater involvement of the "periphery" with the "center," and to inclusion of the masses in the central values of the society.[34] Such a dispersion of central values need not mean debasement, but may include increased involvement, commitment, and symbolic identification with the collective whole. To the citizens of "Fair Elms," "Forest View," and "Meadow Brook" it may mean a greater share of societal values and a long-desired life-style. Although to an outsider these communities may all seem alike, undoubtedly the residents are able to name, bound, and differentiate their seemingly similar locales. Even though the distinctions may not be as great as those between a "Gold Coast" and a "Skid Row," they may be no less meaningful to the residents and to the collective social life within each community.

Both groups of theorists see a decline in local community sentiment and attachment, although for different reasons. The first group sees it as the result of a general "alienation," and the second sees a superseding allegiance and sentiment toward the collective whole displacing more parochial attachments.

Consequently, an increase in scale may lead to the dialectic of fusion and differentiation with respect to cultural symbols and sentiments of community just as it does in the ecological realm.

The implications of an "increase in scale" for local community social structure are usually expressed in two ways: in shifting forms of social interaction and in changing patterns of institutional structure and functional utilization.

Shifting forms of social interaction in the urban arena were a consistent focus of the Chicago school and were perhaps summarized best in Louis Wirth's "Urbanism as a Way of Life."[35] The shift from primary to secondary relationships and its correlated institutional and functional differentiation are jointly described in the following passage:

> Characteristically, urbanites meet one another in highly
> segmental roles. They are, to be sure, dependent upon more
> people for the satisfactions of their life-needs than are
> rural people and thus are associated with a greater number
> of organized groups, but they are less dependent upon
> particular persons, and their dependence upon others is
> confined to a highly fractionalized aspect of the other's
> round of activity. This is essentially what is meant by
> saying that the city is characterized by secondary rather than
> primary contacts.

Institutional differentiation becomes possible, and perhaps necessary, as societies increase in scale and scope both socially and territorially. The consequence for the individual actor is that his set of roles becomes increasingly diverse and segmented as he attempts to fulfill his functional "life-needs." The individual becomes involved within more narrowly circumscribed and formally defined roles, as opposed to knowledge of and interaction with "particular persons." It may even mean a clearer delimiting of "neighbor" as a distinctly circumscribed role, a role recently analyzed by Suzanne Keller.[36] Such a role may include occasional chats over the backyard fence, but to be a "good" neighbor one must often still, as Robert Frost says, maintain the fence.

The increase in scale also brings a greater dependence upon and involvement in secondary, as opposed to primary, groups. Such formal groups may be either the nonspatial membership group based upon interest or the inclusive local membership group based upon space. The latter groups retain a tenuous definition in terms of a local area and are often seen as the structural embodiment of local solidarity, even though they may not include all who consider themselves members of the community. In addition, such groups are seen to represent a move away from the intimate primary contacts with friends and kin.

In short, increase in scale has meant a fusion in the increased contact and interaction with greater numbers of people, but it has also meant that this interaction increasingly takes place within highly segmented roles and formally organized groups. This is seen to result from institutional and functional differentiation and to cause the small community to lose its ability to meet the daily "life-needs" of its residents.[37]

In the following chapters I will present findings that trace some of the implications of this general increase in scale, with its dialectic of differentiation and fusion. In part 1 we will consider its impact upon the ecological structure of Chicago's local communities and the resulting changes in that structure; in part 2 we will trace its impact upon the symbolic culture and sentiments of local communities as expressed by residents; and in part 3 we will focus upon local community organizations by looking at residents' participation in them, and at the effect that increase in scale has upon their structure and functioning. Finally, in the concluding chapter I will summarize the findings and attempt a synthesis of these three empirical and theoretical approaches, which I hope will capture the complexity of the phenomenon under study—the meanings of community in an urban setting.

Part One   *Ecology*

One

*The Ecological
Structure and Change
of Local Communities*

This chapter will explore the ecological dimension of Chicago's local communities. As I mentioned in the Introduction, the ecological approach to the study of community emphasizes the community as an "object" to be studied in and of itself. Even though this orientation implies what some have called a "macro" or a "holistic" approach, it does not mean that ecological communities are not seen as being composed of smaller units and entities. Human ecologists have long viewed the city as a supraorganism, similar to a biological community, in which different units are functionally related through activities carried out within a particular position or "functional niche."[1] For the city as a whole, these functional niches or positions have often been defined in terms of local communities and neighborhoods. Some local areas, such as the Loop, were focal points, where administrative and commercial activities dominated. Other areas had other functions —industrial areas for manufacturing and employment, bright-light districts for entertainment and vice, and a variety of residential areas ranging from tenement slums to elite mansions. From this perspective, then, the city is a functionally integrated whole made up of interdependent local community areas engaged in symbiosis, cooperation, competition, and conflict. The positions define ecological structure, and their interrelationships define ecological process.

ECOLOGICAL STRUCTURE AND ECOLOGICAL PROCESS

To describe and analyze ecological structure and process, early researchers relied extensively upon the territorial or spatial arrangement of these different "functional niches." Structure and process were operationalized by mapping the location of different functions, and ecological relationships were analyzed

19

by noting variations in spatial relationships. Space or territorial distance was not assumed to be an independent factor;
rather, space was seen primarily as affecting the communication and transportation of goods and people.[2] Proximity in
physical space heightened the probability of interaction between functional niches. However, early studies quickly
pointed out that social space and physical space are independent dimensions. Zorbaugh's *The Gold Coast and the
Slum* was significant precisely because it showed the anomaly
of close physical proximity and extreme social distance.[3]

However, a related significance which early human ecologists attributed to space was derived principally from economics.[4] Space was seen as a scarce commodity, with different
locations having different values. As a result, space, or more
specifically location, was a market commodity subject to the
laws of supply and demand and to economic competition.
For example, the scarcity of land located at the city's center
would drive up both rents and building heights, since those
who required the land for their activities would value it most
highly, compete for it, and develop it intensively. The central
focal point provided the minimum aggregate travel distance
to all points within the city and therefore was most valuable
to commercial, financial, and administrative functions requiring extensive coverage of a general clientele. To industry and
manufacturing, proximity to an immediate general market
was less significant, and therefore they did not compete for
central land, perhaps considering closeness to waterways or
other lines of transportation more important to the shipment
of goods and materials.

As a result of these different functional needs and different
capacities to afford specific locations, different areas of the
city would come to be associated with particular activities,
or "niches." In short, the spatial arrangement and composition of local communities would reflect the ecological structure and processes of the city as a whole.[5]

This model of ecological structure and process had two
important implications for local community areas. First, it
was in large part the underpinning of the "natural areas"
defined by Park and Burgess—the "natural" alluding to an
area's ecological rather than normative formation, within

which the norms of a local social structure and a local culture would develop. Second, it meant that any local area was part of a larger ecological whole and could be understood only in this context. Conversely, it also meant that to know the ecology of a city one would have to know the composition and inter-relationships of these smaller local areas.

It was with this perspective that Burgess sent his students into the neighborhoods and local communities of Chicago during the twenties and thirties. Out of this research emerged on the one hand the delimiting of local community areas and on the other hand the concentric zone model of the city. Whereas the former emphasized similarity in the spatial structure of exclusive neighborhoods with similar residential and local activities, the latter emphasized the process of urban growth and its implications for different areas and the resulting dynamics of local community change. The growth of cities and the related changes in their local communities were seen to result from both centripetal and centrifugal forces. As the centripetal force of urbanization continued to draw people and functions into urban areas, centrifugal expansion of cities would occur in successive waves outward from the central core. As the central business district expanded into nearby areas, these would change function from residential and local activities to serving citywide commercial and administrative needs. Outlying residential areas in turn would experience a succession of more centrally displaced populations, and as a result areas would come to occupy different ecological positions or niches within the city.

In general, an inverse relationship was posited between social class and distance from the central business district. The centrally located slums, or "gray areas," were those areas being allowed to deteriorate in speculation that they would soon change from residential use to a more valuable commercial function. Beyond these slums were the working-class residential areas and beyond them the commuting zones of the middle class. Of course the model also allowed for aberrations, such as the presence of elite residential areas near the center of the city along the lakefront.

It was the presence of such elite residential patterns that led Homer Hoyt to expound his sector model of the city.[6]

He found that rather than being situated on a peripheral ring at an ever greater distance from the center of the city, elite or high-rent areas tended to cluster along particular sectors. As a city grew the high-rent areas would continue to expand outward as Burgess suggested, but they would remain within a particular wedge-shaped sector. When one overlays the Burgess and Hoyt models, one has a configuration of sectors and zones intersecting to produce smaller areas—areas more similar to the "natural areas" first proposed by Park and Burgess. It is this joint model which Berry and Reese used in their recent analysis of the ecology of Calcutta and Chicago.[7]

A third model, developed by Harris and Ullman, also addressed itself to the ecological structure of cities and the functional composition of different local areas.[8] They proposed a "multinucleate" model in which there were no concentric zones or sectors, but rather multiple nodes of dominant functions, such as large commercial, financial, or industrial institutions or other noneconomic institutions like hospitals and universities. These in turn would affect the location of surrounding activities. Therefore the dominants would set the pattern and other functional activities would locate at various points surrounding them. For example, the elite would avoid proximity to noisy, smoking factories, and consequently the residential areas near them, being less valued, would become the location of poorer and working-class families. Similarly, bright-light and entertainment districts would locate near central business districts to draw shoppers and employees for evening entertainment. Although this model may adequately describe the structure of a number of cities at a given point in time, it is less valuable ecologically than the Burgess and Hoyt models for analyzing the growth of cities and changes in their local areas.

INCREASE IN SCALE AND SOCIETAL DIFFERENTIATION

A more recent development in analysis of the ecological structure of cities is "factorial ecology," deriving from the early work of Eshref Shevky and his students called "social area analysis."[9] Relying upon census variables and using census tracts as the areal units, social area analysis attempted to discern a small number of underlying dimensions or factors that would account for the segregation patterns of a large number of selected variables. The segregation patterns of certain variables were found to be closely correlated with the segregation patterns of others, and these intercorrelated variables were seen to indicate a more general, underlying dimension. The three most common factors for American cities were found to be economic status, life-style or family status, and racial-ethnic status. Economic status emerges as a factor because such variables as occupation, income, value of dwelling unit, and education are seen to be highly correlated in their spatial distribution. Similarly, percentage married, percentage females employed, percentage children, and percentage single-family dwelling units in an area are seen to be highly correlated, and they make up the life-style or family-status factor. Finally, percentage foreign-born and percentage black are seen to be highly correlated on the racial-ethnic factor. Not only are variables of a given factor highly correlated with one another, but they are relatively uncorrelated with variables composing the other factors. In short, it appears that economic, family, and racial-ethnic status are relatively independent dimensions of ecological segregation.

To explain the emergence of these three independent dimensions of ecological segregation Shevky relied upon the general concept of "increase in scale." He argued that with the increase in scale of modern industrial urban society these three factors separate out as independent bases of social differentiation. This social differentiation is then reflected in ecological segregation or "social areas." Although he and his associates deemphasized the areal properties of their data, forcing the distinction between "social" and "natural" areas, later researchers related the three factors directly to the earlier spatial structures of Burgess and Hoyt. For example, Anderson and Egeland found that family status varies principally by concentric ring, but economic status varies principally by sector.[10]

The more recent developments in "factorial ecology" rely on a larger number of variables and lay greater stress upon the factor structures that emerge for a city or a given sample of cities. Also, a greater emphasis is given to the spatial distribution of these factors by census tracts or, conversely, to

the distribution of census tracts in the factor space. The recent
work of Brian J. L. Berry, for example, attempts to place this
factor structure into a more theoretical model closer to earlier discussions of human ecology.[11] Berry sees the factors of
economic, family, and racial-ethnic status as three principal
locational decisions confronting potential residents. Where
can I afford to live? What kind of life-style do I want—family-
and home-oriented or other? And finally, In what racial or
ethnic area do I want, or am I allowed, to live? The independence of the three dimensions means in part that the
answer to any one of these questions is increasingly less dependent upon how one answers the other two. In short, increasing social differentiation means that one has a greater
choice of where to live, which results in increased ecological
differentiation.

Some, like Wendell Bell in his article "The City, the Suburb, and a Theory of Social Choice," have argued that this
increased variety in choice of location means an increased
voluntarism consonant with modern, rational industrial society.[12] Other writers, such as William Form, have alluded to
the persistence of larger structural constraints on individuals
confronted with locational decisions.[13]

These two ecological perspectives of Burgess and the Chicago school and of Shevky and social-area analysis, or factorial
ecology, have general similarities in spite of their many specific differences. These similarities are in fact defining orientations of human ecology itself. First is the concern with
establishing ecological structure, whether this structure is
defined in terms of functional niches and natural areas or in
terms of factor structures and social areas. Second is concern
with understanding the processes of change in ecological
structure, whether the change comes from the growth of cities
and results in functional succession through concentric zones
or whether it comes from a societal increase in scale and
results in finer social and ecological differentiation.

These two questions of ecological structure and ecological
change are the guiding focus of this section. Viewing the local
community areas of Chicago as "functional niches" and using
them as units of analysis, we will attempt to explore the
ecological structure of Chicago from 1930 to 1960. Also, we

will attempt to discern the processes of change in this structure over this thirty-year period.

METHODS

The basic unit of analysis for this ecological study is the community area as defined by Burgess and his students in the 1920s at the University of Chicago. At that time the city of Chicago was mapped into seventy-five exhaustive and mutually exclusive "natural areas." According to the editors of the *Local Community Fact Book . . . 1960*,

> When community area boundaries were delineated . . . the objective was to define a set of sub-areas of the city each of which could be regarded as having a history of its own as a community, a name, an awareness on the part of its inhabitants of community interests, and a set of local businesses and organizations oriented to the local community.[14]

By using these areas as the units of analysis, this study partially corrects the previously mentioned lack of correspondence between "social areas" and "natural areas." Although these areas were delineated more than forty years ago, we will see in later sections that for a large proportion of Chicago's residents they still operate as meaningful "symbolic communities" or "natural areas." More pragmatically, these areas were also selected as the units of analysis because for the three decades from 1930 to 1960, unlike census tracts, their boundaries remained constant, thus permitting valid comparisons over time.

The selection of variables to be included in the factor analysis was based, first, on closely approximating the variables used by Shevky and his colleagues in their "social area analysis"; second, the variables had to have comparability over the thirty-year period under study; and third, they had to be related to other empirical and theoretical findings about urban ecological structure and change.

Nine variables were finally selected for analysis. The variables relating to economic status were median years of schooling, median value of owner-occupied dwelling units, and, for 1930, percentage employed in the professional sector; for 1940–60 I used percentage professional, technical, and kindred workers. This last deviation from strict comparability over time was necessary because for 1930 I did not have an occupational classification, but I did have a classification by sector of employment. Similarly, income could not be included because data were not available for 1930. Median value of homes owned is an indirect measure of income and perhaps of its most significant "application" in the ecological distribution of social classes by residence. The variable of occupation has been shown, most clearly by the Duncans, to have significance for selectively segregating the urban population.[15] In addition, the study by Feldman and Tilly shows that the variables of education and income make related, though different, contributions to the ecological distribution of urban residents by occupation.[16] And finally, of course, the ecological segregation of social classes was an integral part of the Burgess concentric zone model.

The variables selected for family status were percentage of the population under five years of age (a substitute for the Shevky fertility ratio), percentage married, percentage females employed, and percentage single-family dwelling units in an area. The theoretical and empirical justification for selecting these variables comes from a variety of sources. Several of the earlier case studies of Chicago's local communities pointed to the selective residential segregation of both unmarried populations ("Bohemia," Skid Row, etc.) and of employed females. The selective distribution of different family structures was early shown by Mowrer in his analysis of family disorganization in Chicago in the 1920s.[17] This has continued to be recognized in more recent analyses, such as those by Young and Wilmott and by Adams.[18]

The two variables selected to measure racial-ethnic status were percentage black and percentage foreign-born. These variables have been shown to be significant for urban social structure by a variety of research methods and for different periods in time. Such ethnic segregation has been stressed in older case studies like Wirth's analysis of Chicago's Jewish ghetto in the 1920s and by more recent work such as Suttles's study of Chicago's multiethnic West Side community. To complement older quantitative studies of racial segregation like those by Frazier and Drake and Cayton's *Black Metrop-*

olis, we have recent quantitative studies by the Duncans and the Taeubers which show the persistence of racial segregation in American cities and also its independence from economic segregation.[19]

The factor model utilized in this analysis is the varimax method, a multiple-factor solution that rotates factors orthogonally. This results in a simple-factor structure which manifests both minimal and maximal loadings for the variables on a given factor. The output was in the form of cascading factor matrices, so that at various points in the following analysis reference will be made to three-, four-, and even six-factor solutions for the nine variables under consideration. I will also refer to the original correlation matrix of the nine variables when clarification is needed.[20]

Two sets of factor analyses will be performed upon the nine selected census variables. The first method, defined as an analysis of "change in ecological structure," is based upon a separate factor analysis for each of the four censuses from 1930 to 1960. The four resulting factor structures are then compared in an analysis of change in ecological structure. The factor solutions for this method are based upon correlations exemplified by

$$r_{xy}$$

where

$x =$ percentage under five years of age, 1930
$y =$ percentage foreign-born, 1930

The essential questions this method asks are "What is related to what?" and "How do these relationships change over time?"

The second set of factor analyses, defined as an analysis of "the structure of ecological change," is based upon the correlation of differences at two points in time of the nine variables. This produces three separate factor solutions, with each showing the structure of change taking place during one of the three decades. The factor solutions for this method are based upon correlations exemplified by

$$r_{(x_1 - x_2) \quad (y_1 - y_2)}$$

where

$x_1 =$ percentage under five years of age, 1930

$x_2 =$ percentage under five years of age, 1940
$y_1 =$ percentage foreign-born, 1930
$y_2 =$ percentage foreign-born, 1940

The essential question this method asks is "What is changing with what?"[21]

In addition, another method will be used which connects factorial ecology more closely to a spatial referent and to the Chicago school of ecology.

For each of the first four factor solutions a community area will be assigned a standardized score on each factor with a mean of zero and unit variance of plus one and minus one. These factor scores will then be categorized into four different rankings for each factor. Consequently, each community will have a score on each factor at four different points in time. The categorization is shown in the accompanying diagram.

| | *Factor Score* | | | |
Factor	**+1**	**0**		**−1**
Economic	High	Moderately high	Moderately low	Low
Family	High	Moderately high	Moderately low	Low
Racial-ethnic	High black	Mixed	Mixed	High foreign-born

The scores of each community on all three factors will be mapped for each decade, and changes in the spatial distributions of the three factors will be analyzed for this thirty-year period.

Finally, we will also attempt to discern general systemic changes in Chicago's ecology similar to the general concentric zone model of Burgess. This will be done by dichotomizing and cross-classifying the two dimensions of family and economic status, thereby setting up a four-position attribute space for two dimensions. Each community will occupy one of the four possible positions in this attribute space at time 1, and we will then analyze the probabilities of its moving to one of the other three positions over time.[22] By plotting most common or most probable stages of change on a map we will be able to test, and possibly further refine, the dynamic model of urban growth and resulting zonal succession which Burgess hypothesized would occur in Chicago's local communities.

FACTOR STRUCTURE AND CHANGE

The Four-Factor Solutions

In the original factor solutions, three factors were isolated for 1930 and four for the remaining three censuses. The 1930 factor solution is essentially the same as that of Shevky and Bell, with all the variables loading highest on their expected factor and having small loadings on the other factors (for this analysis, a loading of less than .4 is considered small).

For 1940, however, the picture becomes more complex. From the same variables and the same factor model, four factors result. One again has the first three factors of economic, family, and ethnic status, but in addition a fourth factor appears, with single-family dwelling units loading highest on it and with a moderate but inverse loading of percentage females employed. This suggests that for 1940 the distribution of single-family dwelling units within Chicago's communities has become, compared with 1930, less associated with the distribution of the other variables under consideration. The isolation of a fourth factor with single-family dwelling units loading highest on it is also true of the factor solutions for 1950 and 1960. In contrast to 1940, however, in 1950 and 1960 no other variables have even a moderate loading on this factor.

Throughout the four periods, then, the distribution of single-family dwelling units becomes less associated with the distribution of the other variables throughout the city. This result is probably due to the continuing metropolitan growth of Chicago, including both the continuing movement of families into single-family homes in suburbs beyond the city limits and the increasing number of multiple-family dwelling units being built within the central city. This is not to suggest that community areas within the central city do not differ in their proportions of single-family homes; rather, the mixture of housing types in an area appears to be decreasingly related to its economic, family, and ethnic composition. Whereas in 1930 areas characterized as having a large number of single-family homes were also likely to have a large percentage married and children under five and a small percentage females employed, in 1960 this was not as likely. Housing type, in short, has become less indicative of the other characteristics of local communities within the central city.

The Three-Factor Solutions

For greater comparability in the rest of this analysis, I will refer to the three-factor solutions for 1940, 1950, and 1960. The reader should keep in mind, however, the above findings about housing type.

In looking at the three-factor solutions, the most striking impression is the general similarity over the four time periods (tables 1–4). For all four solutions, the same two variables load

TABLE 1

Factorial Ecology of Chicago, 1930

	Factor Matrix		
Factor	Family	Economic	Racial-Ethnic
Sum of squares	3.174	2.972	1.628
Variance explained (%):			
9 factors	35.3	68.3	86.4
3 factors	40.8	79.1	100.0

No.	Name	Communality	Family	Economic	Racial-Ethnic
4.	Married (%)	.849	−.914	.073	.101
5.	Female employed (%)	.944	.877	.243	.339
3.	Children under five (%)	.918	−.842	−.452	−.075
6.	Median school years	.911	−.067	.946	.105
9.	Single-family dwelling units (%)	.634	−.790	−.092	−.041
8.	Male professional (%)	.396	.250	.900	.091
7.	Median value home	.836	.306	.860	−.044
1.	Black (%)	.909	.246	−.180	.904
2.	Foreign-born (%)	.877	.131	−.450	−.811

SOURCE: Hunter, "Ecology of Chicago," pp. 431–33.
NOTE: Number of rotations for varimax convergence, 8.

TABLE 2
Factorial Ecology of Chicago, 1940

	Factor Matrix		
Factor	Economic	Family	Racial-Ethnic
Sum of squares	3.100	2.745	1.701
Variance explained (%):			
9 factors	34.4	64.9	83.8
3 factors	41.1	77.5	100.0

No.	Name	Communality	Economic	Family	Racial-Ethnic
8.	Male professional (%)	.917	.952	−.084	.058
6.	Median school years	.895	.944	.002	.058
7.	Median value home	.898	.874	.362	.052
5.	Female employed (%)	.791	.055	−.833	.307
4.	Married (%)	.726	.158	.831	.099
9.	Single-family dwelling units (%)	.693	.174	.813	−.047
3.	Children under five (%)	.790	−.537	.704	.078
1.	Black (%)	.932	−.182	−.221	.922
2.	Foreign-born (%)	.903	−.396	−.128	−.854

SOURCE: Hunter, "Ecology of Chicago," pp. 431–33.
NOTE: Number of rotations for varimax convergence, 8.

highest on a given factor. This suggests a marked stability in the relationships among these six variables over the four periods. Upon closer inspection, however, one also sees certain variations that suggest processes at work transforming the ecological structure of the city.

The percentage of total variance explained decreases over the four periods, from 86.4 percent in 1930 to 75.9 percent in 1960. This decrease in explained variance is also reflected in the communality of the variables. In 1930 four of the nine variables had a communality above .9, but in 1960 none of them does. This means that the relationships among the variables selected for this analysis are becoming weaker and suggests that, over time, the city's local communities are becoming more varied in their composition and the city as a whole is becoming more ecologically differentiated.

TABLE 3
Factorial Ecology of Chicago, 1950

Factor	Factor Matrix		
	Economic	Family	Racial-Ethnic
Sum of squares	2.967	2.770	1.801
Variance explained (%):			
9 factors	33.0	63.7	83.8
3 factors	39.4	76.1	100.0

No.	Name	Communality	Economic	Family	Racial-Ethnic
8.	Male professional (%)	.932	.961	.004	−.091
6.	Median school years	.870	.932	.046	.010
7.	Median value home	.825	.896	.150	.006
5.	Female employed (%)	.809	−.126	−.891	−.011
4.	Married (%)	.793	.028	.885	−.100
9.	Single-family dwelling units (%)	.701	.289	.772	−.146
3.	Children under five (%)	.789	−.416	.736	.272
2.	Foreign-born (%)	.907	−.179	−.078	−.932
1.	Black (%)	.912	−.259	−.162	.905

SOURCE: Hunter, "Ecology of Chicago," pp. 431–33.
NOTE: Number of rotations for varimax convergence, 7.

Changing Explanatory Power of the Three Factors

Another way of viewing changes reflected in the factor structures is to look at the percentage of nine-factor variance explained by each factor over the four time periods. This
enables one to analyze the relative importance of each factor
in accounting for the segregation of Chicago's population.
For 1930 one sees that the family-status factor accounted for
the most explained variance, followed by the economic-status
factor, and finally the segregation factor. This means that in
1930 family status was more important than the other two
factors in accounting for variations in the ecological distribution of population in the city. We should realize, however,
that four variables were selected for family status, three for
economic status, and two for segregation, and that the order
of explained variance is in part due to this discrepancy.

However, the order of the factors for later periods shows that percentage of explained variance is somewhat independent of the number of variables selected. From 1930, when family status accounted for the most variance (35.3 percent), there was a gradual decline; then between 1950 and 1960 its explanatory power decreased markedly (1950, 30.7 percent; 1960, 19.9 percent). In 1940, 1950, and 1960, economic status is the factor explaining most of the variance; and in general family status declines in explanatory power while the factor of racial-ethnic status increases most, going from 18.1 percent in 1930 to 25.6 percent in 1960. The economic-status factor is noteworthy for its relative stability throughout the three decades. Although its relative position shifted, this is mainly due to the changing significance of the other two factors. Over the four time periods, its percentage of nine-factor variance explained ranged narrowly, from 34.4 percent to 30.4 percent.

TABLE 4

Factorial Ecology of Chicago, 1960

	Factor Matrix		
Factor	Economic	Racial-Ethnic	Family
Sum of squares	2.737	2.307	1.784
Variance explained (%):			
9 factors	30.4	56.0	75.9
3 factors	40.1	73.9	100.0

No.	Name	Communality	Economic	Racial-Ethnic	Family
6.	Median school years	.866	.928	−.038	.061
8.	Male professional (%)	.855	.894	−.179	−.153
7.	Median value home	.768	.872	−.024	.086
2.	Foreign-born (%)	.873	−.051	−.932	−.028
1.	Black (%)	.883	−.210	.911	−.100
3.	Children under five (%)	.847	−.491	.680	.378
4.	Married (%)	.801	.021	−.202	.852
5.	Female employed (%)	.752	.125	−.105	−.852
9.	Single-family dwelling units (%)	.183	.114	.244	.331

SOURCE: Hunter, "Ecology of Chicago," pp. 431–33.
NOTE: Number of rotations for varimax convergence, 7.

Overall, these findings show that the variation in the ecological distribution of the city's population during this thirty-year period is accounted for decreasingly by family status and increasingly by economic status and racial-ethnic segregation.

This is in accord with the theories of Berry and Rees and of Abu-Lughod,[23] who hypothetize from their static studies of "less-modern" cities that as metropolitan growth develops economic status will emerge as a unique and predominant dimension of ecological segregation. The increasing significance of the racial-ethnic factor is of course due in large part to the growth of Chicago's black population and its continuing segregation in the South Side and West Side ghettos. The relative decline of family status as a basis of ecological segregation can be interpreted initially by the same developmental theory that points to a decreasing segregation based upon variations in family and kinship concerns, especially when compared with economic status.

The general decline in explanatory power of the family-status factor can be accounted for in part by the declining communality of the variable "percentage of single-family dwelling units." But another variable, percentage of children under five, also shifts its factor loadings and helps to account for both the decline of the family-status factor and the increasing importance of the racial-ethnic factor.

The most dramatic shift occurs in 1960, when percentage of children under five shifts its highest loading from the family-status factor to the racial-ethnic factor. The former loading is .378; the latter, .680. It also has a moderately high inverse loading on the economic-status factor (−.491). In short, the shifting loading of the percentage of children under five from the family-status to the ethnic-status factor partly accounts for the declining significance of the former and the increasing importance of the latter over these four time periods. This shifting relationship suggests that the racial and ethnic segregation of the city is associated with a segregation of children in the city. Furthermore, the relationships between children under five and the other variables of the family-status factor (especially percentage of females employed and percentage of single-family dwelling units) is declining.

The higher association of the percentage of children under five with the racial-ethnic factor in 1960 implies a relationship to both percentage black and percentage foreign-born. When we look at the zero-order correlations among these variables, a clearer picture emerges.

The correlation of percentage black with percentage children under five becomes increasingly positive over time, going from —.192 in 1930 to .665 in 1960. Contrarywise, the correlation between percentage foreign-born and percentage children under five shows an increasingly negative correlation (1930, .141; 1960, —.560). Furthermore, the correlation of percentage black and percentage foreign-born becomes increasingly negative over this period, going from —.520 in 1930 to —.733 in 1960.

These findings point out, therefore, that the distribution of population in Chicago is progressively a function of (a) the increasing segregation between foreign-born and black populations and (b) the differing age structures of these two populations. To a certain extent, then, in 1960 racial-ethnic status and family status are becoming more closely associated in the ecological segregation of the central city.

The explanation for this convergence is of course tied to the movement of young white families to Chicago's suburbs, as noted by Rees, leaving as a residual population within the city a central ghetto core of young black families surrounded by communities with an older ethnic population.[24]

The Structure of Ecological Change

The previous analysis is based upon correlations among variables at a single point in time, and the resulting factor structures for each time period are compared in the analysis of change. This section asks the question "What is changing with what?" Specifically, the analysis is based upon the correlation of differences in variables at two points in time. The results, therefore, depict the structure of ecological change and not simply ecological structure at a single point in time. The proposition of Shevky and Bell in their social area analysis that economic, family, and ethnic status are significant and distinct dimensions of urban ecological differentiation has been dem-

onstrated. If these are a result of a dynamic "increase in
scale" as hypothesized, one would expect these same factors to
emerge as the principal factors of change.

However, when one looks at the factor solutions for these
three decades, one sees structures emerging which are often
different from each other as well as from the four previous
static factor solutions. First, for each decade six rather than
three principal factors emerge (see table 5). This suggests that
changes in the variables under consideration are less highly
associated than is their ecological distribution at a single point
in time. However, since six factors for nine variables tells
little more than do the variables considered separately, two
simplified approaches to analyzing these results are suggested:
focusing attention upon the three principal factors of the

TABLE 5
The Structure of Change

A. Three Principal Factors of the Six-Factor Solutions for Each Decade

	Factor 1	Factor 2	Factor 3
1930–40: (89.1)[a] (53.5)[b]	(20.5)[c] + Children under five + Married	(18.7)[c] + Black + Foreign-born	(14.3)[c] − Male professional
1940–50: (91.1)[a] (56.2)[b]	(26.6) − Children under five + Foreign-born − Married − Black	(16.2) − Single-family dwelling units − Married + Black	(13.4) + Male professional − Black
1950–60: (92.7)[a] (56.6)[b]	(26.8) − Foreign-born + Black + Children under five	(17.5) + Schooling + Male professional	(14.3) − Female employed + Children under five

TABLE 5—Continued

B. Three Factors of the Three-Factor Solutions for Each Decade

	Factor 1	Factor 2	Factor 3
1930–40: (61.4)[a]	(23.9)[c] +Children under five +Married −Value of home −Schooling	(19.7)[c] +Black +Foreign-born	(17.6)[c] −Male professional −Single-family dwelling units +Value of home
1940–50: (65.6)[a]	(29.7) +Foreign-born −Children under five −Black −Married	(19.4) +Schooling +Male professional +Female employed +Value of home	(16.5) −Single-family dwelling units −Married +Black
1950–60: (66.4)[a]	(29.5) +Black −Foreign-born −Male professional +Married +Children under five	(20.7) −Female employed +Single-family dwelling units +Children under five	(16.2) +Schooling +Value of home

[a] Percentage of nine-factor variance explained by all factors.
[b] Percentage of nine-factor variance explained by these three factors.
[c] Percentage of nine-factor variance explained by each factor.
SOURCE: Hunter, "Ecology of Chicago," p. 439.

six-factor solutions, and looking at the three-factor solutions for each decade.

The three principal factors of the six-factor solution for 1930–40 show this to be the only period of change in which economic, family, and racial-ethnic status are isolated as clear and distinct factors of change as well as structure. Family status appears as the most significant factor of change, and economic status as the least significant. Racial and ethnic status are interesting in that change in percentage black and change in percentage foreign-born are positively associated for this period. This may be in part a function of the increasing percentage of Jewish immigrants settling predominately in areas simultaneously beginning to experience black invasion.

From the three-factor solution of change from 1930 to 1940, one sees that the three hypothesized factors of differentiation are less distinct. The principal factor is one which combines family and economic variables, which suggests that changes in these were highly associated during the period.

For the period from 1940 to 1950, the six-factor solution and the three-factor solution are in fairly close agreement, with the principal factor in both solutions combining family and ethnic variables. In fact, a second factor in both solutions also combines variables reflecting family and ethnic status. During this period, then, the structure of ecological change suggests that a combined family and racial-ethnic change predominates.

For the period from 1950 to 1960, the six-factor solution again approximates the simple structure, with distinct economic, family, and ethnic factors. There is one exception, which was also noted previously—the association of the change in percentage of children under five with changes in the percentage black and percentage foreign-born. The three-factor solution for the 1950s lends additional support to the association between changes in variables of family status and of racial-ethnic status. The principal factor of change again combines these two dimensions.

Two general findings emerge from these differing results. First, the structure of ecological change is much more variable and complex than the simple ecological structure found at a single point in time. The factors of ecological change appear unique for each decade, and yet the changes are taking place within a relatively well established and persistent ecological structure. Second, and related to this, these processes of change are highly variable from one decade to the next and appear to be dependent upon the historical context of each period.

The first method of analysis of change in ecological structure raised the question "What is related to what?" and from this emerged Chicago's ecological structure at four points in time. When we compared these structures and asked "How are the structures or relationships changing?" the findings did point to certain important changes; but the principal conclusion was the persistence and similarity of Chicago's ecological structure over time. In contrast, when we ask "What is changing with what?" using the second method, the structure of ecological change, we can more sensitively measure specific events or short-run processes of ecological change. In other words, both methods address themselves to ecological change, but given that the questions asked by each method are different, a different set of findings with different emphases will emerge. One emphasizes persistence; the other, variability and change.

SPATIAL STRUCTURE AND CHANGE

Let us now turn to an analysis of the spatial distribution of the three factors of economic, family, and racial--ethnic status. Specifically, we will look at the spatial distribution of factor scores for each of the seventy-five community areas and see how this spatial structure has changed over the thirty-year period from 1930 to 1960. (See maps 1–4.)

Racial-Ethnic Status

One of the more obvious changes in community scores on the racial-ethnic factor is an increase in the number of areas with a high percentage black. From the five areas of the South Side in 1930 the black ghetto expands to sixteen areas in 1960, with the inclusion of the West Side ghetto and its community areas as well as the Near North Side community. In 1930 Morgan Park, on the Far Southwest Side of the city, was the only black area with a high economic status. This is an older black settlement, separated from the old "Black Belt," which in 1960 shifts to a "mixed" status owing to the increasing percentage and concentration of blacks in other communities.

In 1960 there is also one isolated community area with a high percentage black which is separated from the contiguous black communities of the ghetto; and this area, Riverdale, shows the influence that public policy decisions have upon the changing status of community areas. In 1940 this com-

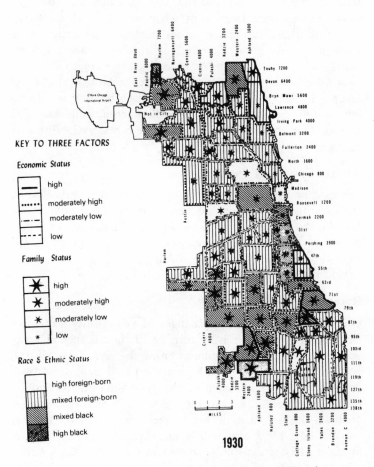

KEY TO THREE FACTORS

Economic Status

———	high
••••••	moderately high
—•—•—	moderately low
— — —	low

Family Status

✶	high
✶	moderately high
✶	moderately low
✶	low

Race & Ethnic Status

	high foreign-born
	mixed foreign-born
	mixed black
	high black

1930

MAP 1. Spatial distribution of economic, family, and racial-ethnic status, 1930.

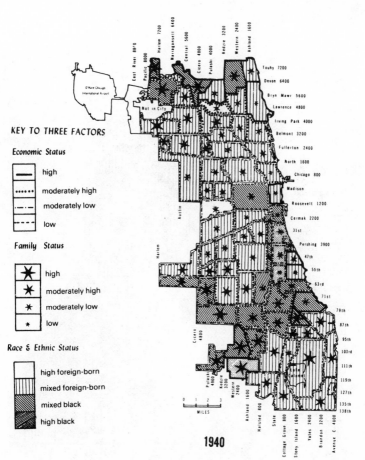

KEY TO THREE FACTORS

Economic Status

————— high

∙∙∙∙∙∙∙ moderately high

—∙—∙— moderately low

— — — low

Family Status

✸ high

✶ moderately high

✳ moderately low

∗ low

Race & Ethnic Status

☐ high foreign-born

▥ mixed foreign-born

▨ mixed black

◼ high black

1940

MAP 2. Spatial distribution of economic, family, and racial-ethnic status, 1940.

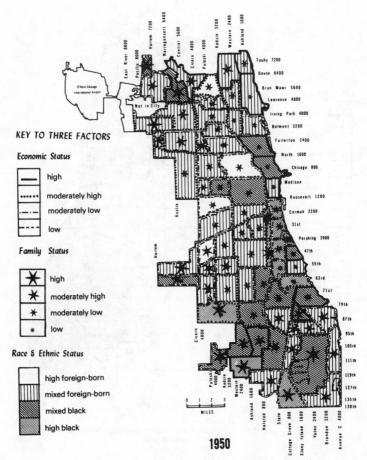

KEY TO THREE FACTORS

Economic Status

high

moderately high

moderately low

low

Family Status

high

moderately high

moderately low

low

Race & Ethnic Status

high foreign-born

mixed foreign-born

mixed black

high black

1950

MAP 3. Spatial distribution of economic, family, and
racial-ethnic status, 1950.

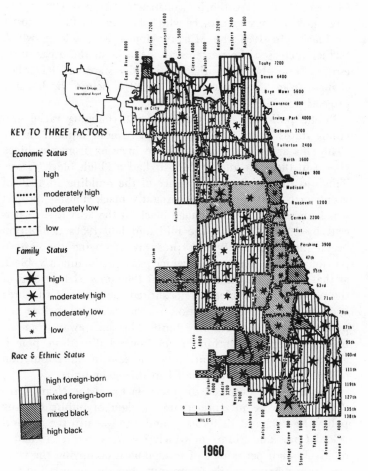

KEY TO THREE FACTORS

Economic Status

	high
	moderately high
	moderately low
	low

Family Status

✳	high
✱	moderately high
✶	moderately low
✳	low

Race & Ethnic Status

	high foreign-born
	mixed foreign-born
	mixed black
	high black

1960

MAP 4. Spatial distribution of economic, family, and racial-ethnic status, 1960.

munity was still a sparsely settled but old community of German and Russian stock. In 1930 and 1940 it had a "mixed" score on the ethnic and racial dimension. But in 1943–44 the Chicago Housing Authority constructed Altgeld Gardens, a large public housing project which became inhabited mostly by blacks. In 1954 the Murray Homes were added, which further increased the percentage of blacks in the area. Interestingly, one also notes that the family status of Riverdale changes from "moderately high" in 1940, before the housing projects, to "high" in 1950 and 1960.

Public policy is also evident in the changing racial and ethnic status of the community area Armour Square. In the 1930s this area began to experience invasion from the black ghetto to the east, and in 1950 it had a "high black" score. This was in part the consequence of the building in 1946 of Wentworth Gardens, a predominantly black housing project which increased the percentage black in the area to 46.9 percent by 1950. Then, in the mid and late 1950s demolition began for the Dan Ryan Expressway, removing the eastern portion of the community, which was predominantly black at that time. The result was that in 1960 only 31.4 percent of the population was black. This shifted the status of this area back to the "mixed" position it had occupied before the public housing projects were built. This shift away from the black pole of the continuum and toward the ethnic pole is also a function of the continuing increase in the population of Chinatown, which is situated in this community.

The changing status on the racial factor of the Near North Side can also be interpreted in the light of public housing policy. In 1930 and 1940 this community was still the classical "Gold Coast and Slum" of which Zorbaugh wrote. It had a relatively high percentage of foreign-born occupying the western, slum portion of the community, but this population was offset by the elite of Chicago who lived a few blocks east along the lakefront. As a consequence, the area had a "mixed foreign-born" factor score during these two decades. In 1942 the Chicago Housing Authority built the large housing project Frances Cabrini Homes in the western portion of the community. Since these buildings became occupied mostly by blacks, their percentage in the whole area climbed from 6.7

percent in 1940 to 20 percent in 1950. These homes were added to in 1958, and the percentage black rose to 30.6 percent by 1960. Over the years, then, the Near North Side went from "mixed foreign-born" status in 1930 and 1940 to "mixed black" status in 1950 and finally to "high black" status in 1960. To be sure, the Gold Coast population also expanded during these years with the building of such high-rise complexes as Sandburg Village. This has resulted in the anomaly of an area's experiencing an increasing influx of blacks into public housing, thereby raising its ethnic status to "high black," while at the same time its economic status climbed from moderately high in 1930 and 1940 to high in 1950 and 1960.

The most dramatic change in ethnic status is the shift of North Lawndale from "high foreign-born" in 1950 to a "high black" position in 1960. This shifting status has been documented in Lieberson's analysis of the ecological movement of Chicago's old Jewish ghetto originally studied by Wirth.[25] The ghetto was situated in the North Lawndale community, and in 1930 to 1950 this area had a "high foreign-born" status because of the persistence of foreign-born Jews. In the 1950s the area was invaded as the black ghetto of the West Side pushed outward, and the area went from 13.1 percent black in 1950 to 91.1 percent black in 1960. The flight of the Jews also affected the community areas into which they moved. For example, the areas of North Park and Albany Park, as well as West Rogers Park or West Ridge, all on the North Side of Chicago, shifted their positions toward a higher foreign-born status. In 1960 Albany Park and North Park both occupied "high foreign-born" positions, while West Rogers Park shifted to a "moderately high foreign-born" position.

Another anomaly is Hyde Park, on the South Side of the city. The effect of urban renewal as well as the continued presence of an institutional base—the University of Chicago —is clearly reflected in the fact that this area in 1960 was an isolated "mixed" area in a general region of "high black" status.[26]

The racial-ethnic status of the remaining community areas shows several broad spectrums of change as well as stability.

For example, on the Southwest Side along the southern branch of the Chicago River one sees a general persistence of mixed and high foreign-born areas, most clearly demonstrated in 1960 by Chicago Lawn and Brighton Park. On the Far Southwest Side and especially on the Northwest Side one sees a general increase in the number of areas scoring as mixed foreign-born. This general movement outward spatially and ecologically reflects the increasing dispersion of the ethnic factor in community areas throughout the city. This is undoubtedly because ethnic populations have migrated outward from their more centrally located communities of the 1930s. For example, the community area of West Town, which is the traditional entering point of immigrants, has a high foreign-born status in both 1930 and 1960. Occupied in previous periods by successive waves of ethnic groups, the old Wicker Park area of "Polonia" studied by Lopata is in the southeastern section of this community; today it is occupied by the newest foreign-born immigrants to this nation's cities—Mexicans and Puerto Ricans.[27] Consequently, the high foreign-born status of this community has been retained in spite of the outward movement of the older ethnic populations into the Northwest Side. This community clearly demonstrates the functional significance of this area to the city as a whole and the stability of this functional position in spite of intrinsic population changes.

Economic Status of Communities: Distribution and Changes

The distribution of economic status shows evidence of both the concentric and the sector theories of the city, but these are often interrupted so that isolated pockets appear on the maps of these distributions.

The distribution of areas with low economic status in 1930 showed two pockets: one was in a sector along the southwest branch of the Chicago River, and the second was less centrally located along the lakefront on the southeastern corner of the city. Both areas were heavily industrialized. Eleven areas scored low economic status in 1930 and six of these were along the more centrally located sector, while the other five were in the more peripheral industrial area of the Southeast

Side. By 1960 the distribution of low-economic status areas had changed and become more centralized. The communities of Bridgeport, Lower West Side, New City or Back of the Yards, and Fuller Park and Armour Square, all on the Southwest sector, still scored low on economic status. In addition, however, were two other communities bordering the river—South Lawndale and Brighton Park. The centrally located areas of the West Side black ghetto also added to this centralization of low economic status areas in 1960 (the Near West Side, West Town, and East and West Garfield Park). Twelve of the fourteen areas scoring low on economic status in 1960 were situated along this centrally located sector and composed a single pocket.

By 1960 the previously low-status areas of the Southeast Side had raised their economic status except for two areas—Burnside, an old ethnic community, and Riverdale, which by 1960 had become populated by blacks living in the Altgeld-Murray Homes.

In accounting for these shifts one must once again be cautious and recall that these are relative positions for each period and that the decreasing status of the centrally located areas is in part a function of the rising status of the peripheral areas. Nonetheless, the overriding fact is that low economic status areas became centralized during this thirty-year period.

Three isolated pockets of high economic status areas were found in the city in 1930. The communities on the northeastern corner of the city (Rogers Park and West Ridge or West Rogers Park) and on the southwestern corner of the city (Beverly and Morgan Park) suggest the concentric ring model of the city, which depicts high-status communities as a peripheral ring. The third pocket was a sector along the lakefront on the South Side and included Kenwood, Hyde Park, South Shore, and Avalon Park. Although community areas along the lakefront generally have a higher economic status than their bordering inland communities, in 1930 this was more pronounced for the South Side than for the North Side.

By 1960, however, one sees a much stronger sector phenomenon with the addition of the Loop, the Near North Side, and Lincoln Park as high economic status areas. Of the thirteen areas which bordered the lakefront in 1930 five were high economic status areas, whereas in 1960 eight of them were.

The influence of urban renewal upon economic status is clearly demonstrated by Hyde Park's maintenance of high economic status and by the changing status of the Douglas community. In 1930 the Douglas community was a moderately low economic status area with a high percentage black which it has retained throughout the thirty-year period. In 1940 it declined to a low economic status, and in 1950 it regained its moderately low position. In 1960, however, it moved to a moderately high economic position, the highest attained in this thirty-year period, primarily because of the completion in the 1950s of Lake Meadows and Prairie Shores, high-rise middle- and upper-income apartment developments.

On the southwest corner of the city, Beverly and Morgan Park were in 1960 still the only two areas of high economic status. The increase of high economic status areas on the periphery of the North Side was not a generalized concentric phenomenon, for it was not duplicated on the South Side. This may in part be a function of the historical development of these two sections of the city, with the peripheral communities of the North Side in general developing later than those of the South Side.

There was a tendency for centrally located moderately low areas to shift to low economic status (e.g., South Lawndale, West Town), and for centrally located moderately high areas to shift to moderately low positions (e.g., West Garfield Park, Near South Side, Woodlawn, and Greater Grand Crossing—all of these were predominantly black in 1960). Areas more peripherally located, if they shifted position at all, were more likely to move to higher economic positions. For example Jefferson Park, Dunning, and Belmont-Cragin on the Northwest Side, and West Lawn, Ashburn, Mount Greenwood, and West Pullman on the Southwest Side shifted from moderately low economic status in 1930 to moderately high status in 1960. In addition, on the southeastern corner of the city South Deering went from a low economic status in 1930 to a moderately high status in 1960, and Calumet Heights went from a moderately low economic status in 1930 to a high status in 1960.

Family Status of Communities:
Distribution and Changes

The distribution of family status, like the previous two distributions, reflects a combination of both sectoral and concentric phenomena. Looking first at the extremes of the distribution, one sees that in 1930 all eleven of the areas with scores reflecting a low family status were located along the lakefront. Although in later years there was a general decline in the number of low family status areas, the persistence of the low family status sector along the lake is clearly evident. In 1960, for example, seven of the eight low family status communities were still situated along the lakefront.

It is also interesting that these low family status communities along the lake are generally high economic status areas. For example, in 1930 nine out of eleven of these low family status areas were of high or moderately high economic status, and in 1960 six of the eight areas were high or moderately high. In summary, it appears that the low extreme of family status distribution is a sector along the lakefront in communities which are generally of high or moderately high economic status.

At the other extreme of the family distribution, areas of high family status are generally found concentrically in a peripheral ring around the city. For example, of the eleven high family status communities in the city in 1930, all but three were along the city limits. In 1960 eight areas were of high family status, and all but one were along the outer ring of the city.

These high family status communities also are generally of high or moderately high economic status, and this positive relationship becomes stronger over time. For example, in 1930 seven of the eleven high family status areas were of high or moderately high economic status, and in 1960 seven of the eight high family status areas were of high or moderately high economic status. In short, it appears that a disproportionate number of both high and low family status areas are high and moderately high economic status areas, the former found concentrically in a peripheral ring around the city, and the latter situated sectorally along the lakefront.

The two intermediate positions of the family status factor present a rather mixed picture between these very clear distributions of the extremes. But one trend seems particularly clear—the picture becomes more mixed over time. Areas scoring both moderately high and moderately low on the family status dimension are generally found between the lakefront and the peripheral ring, although there is a tendency for the former to be found in the ring, and the latter are more likely to interrupt the continuity of the low family status sector along the lakefront. This tendency for intermediate positions of family status to become more mixed is clearly demonstrated by the fact that in 1930 all sixteen of the most centrally located areas from North Avenue (1600 North) to Pershing Road (3900 South) and from the lake to Cicero Avenue (4800 West) were low or moderately low on family status. By 1960, however, six of these sixteen areas had a moderately high family status.

One reason for this greater mixture of intermediate positions on family status in centrally located areas is the increase of the percentage black in these areas. One has only to recall that in 1960 percentage black in an area and percentage under five were highly correlated. Looking at the map one can see that of the six areas with moderately high family status near the center of the city, four were predominantly black. The invasion of blacks and the consequent rising family status of a community might also explain the decline in the number of areas along the lakefront having a low family status in 1960. Looking more closely at the map for 1960 one can see that the communities from the Loop north to Rogers Park all have a low family status, but on the South Side only one community, Hyde Park, persists as a remnant of the low family status sector from 1930. Of the eight lakefront communities from the Loop south to South Chicago five are predominantly black in 1960 and none of these has a low family status. This suggests not that on the whole black communities have a higher family status than whites, but rather that they have a relatively higher family status than white communities comparably situated in ecological space.

SYSTEMATIC STAGES OF COMMUNITY CHANGE

The previous section described the spatial distribution of

family, economic, and racial-ethnic dimensions among Chicago's local communities and changes in these distributions from 1930 to 1960. This section will more rigorously analyze systematic changes in Chicago's local communities with respect to these dimensions. The analysis is an attempt to test and refine two different perspectives stemming from the Burgess concentric zone model.

The concentric zone model, with its emphasis upon "decentralization" of urban functions and populations, has both a static and a dynamic component. Researchers with a "static" orientation look at spatial distributions and tend to emphasize "uniform" distance gradients. However, researchers having a more explicit concern with dynamic propositions (though often testing them with static data) tend to emphasize "stages" of community change. The static component is exemplified in studies from a number of disciplines which map phenomena at a single point in time in some form of distance gradient outward from the central city. A summary and exemplary statement of findings from this perspective is that by Brian J. L. Berry, which deals with one cluster of variables:

> at the edge of the city are newer, owned, single family homes, in which reside larger families with younger children than nearer the city center, and where the wife stays at home. Conversely, the apartment complexes nearer the city center have smaller, older families, fewer children, and are more likely to be rentals; in addition, larger proportions of the women will be found to work. This "family structure" pattern is consistent with the ideas of Burgess, and has been called by sociologists the "urbanism-familism" scale.[28]

The dynamic component of decentralization, on the other hand, has more often been studied in terms of "stages" of community change. A community or neighborhood at a fixed point in the urban landscape is seen to go through stages of change as decentralization occurs. One of the more frequently cited examples of such stages is the temporal sequence listed by Hoover and Vernon, which focuses on housing and density variables:[29]

1. new single-family subdivisions

2. apartment development
3. downgrading, usually associated with conversion
4. thinning out
5. renewal

Here we will first develop stages of change with respect to economic and family status, then we will see if these are arranged in a concentric zonal pattern and are sequentially ordered over time.

To explore these questions we will first dichotomize each of the two dimensions of family and economic status, thereby creating four possible states (high economic/high family status, high economic/low family status, etc.). We will then explore the probability that an area will move from any one state to the others over time. This is essentially the two-attribute (economic and family status), stochastic (over time) model developed in the work of James Coleman.[30]

In using this model we may make two simplifications of the data which yield essentially similar results. First, one may take time 1 to be 1930 and time 2 to be 1960 and explore the changes of the seventy-five community areas over this entire thirty-year period. Second, one may condense each decade's movements into a single table by summing the changes made during each decade. The universe then consists of 225 (3 × 75) possible moves of communities from one of the four states to another during a decade. I will refer to the second method in the following discussion, since it tends to minimize effects whereas the first maximizes them. Summary results are also presented in table 6 for each decade considered separately—that is, without the simplifications.

The central finding is that each of the four states or positions of communities has a single most probable direction of change. For example, 17 percent of the areas having a high economic/high family status at time 1 change to a high economic/low family status ten years later, and only 6 percent change to all other possible positions (see table 7 and chart 1).

Second, these probabilities of change are nonreciprocal. Although 17 percent move from a high economic/high family position to a high economic/low family position, only 2 percent move in the opposite direction. This nonreciprocal nature of the transitions is true of all four states, and in general

TABLE 6
Period of Change

Effect Parameters[a]	1930–40	1940–50	1950–60	1930–60	t_0–t_{10}
Random Shocks:					
Toward high family status (ϵ_1)	.1000	.1434	.4565	.4196	.2216
Toward low family status (ϵ_2)	.1942	.3243	.0692	.4549	.1893
Toward high economic status (η_1)	.0000	.0478	.1141	.0600	.0512
Toward low economic status (η_2)	.0000	.0811	.1384	.0000	.0710
Interaction effects:					
Of high economic status on family status ($\propto$)	−.1000	−.1434	−.3868	−.4196	−.1958
Of low economic status on family status (β)	−.1052	−.2709	−.0059	−.4010	−.1192
Of high family status on economic status (Θ)	.0445	.2728	.2021	.4251	.1591
Of low family status on economic status (ϕ)	.1670	.1601	.1402	.2913	.1611

SOURCE: Hunter, "Community Change."

[a] The effect parameters were calculated using the approximate method as developed by Coleman, *Mathematical Sociology, pp.* 166–73.

TABLE 7

Summed Positional Changes of Communities over a Decade 1930 to 1940, 1940 to 1950, 1950 to 1960 (Economic Status, Family Status)

		Number				
		Time 2				
		High ES High FS	High ES Low FS	Low ES High FS	Low ES Low FS	Total
Time 1	High ES High FS	37	8	3	0	48
	High ES Low FS	1	34	0	9	44
	Low ES High FS	12	1	49	4	66
	Low ES Low FS	0	3	13	51	67
	Total	50	46	65	64	225

		Proportional Change				
		Time 2				
		High ES High FS	High ES Low FS	Low ES High FS	Low FS Low ES	Total
Time 1	High ES High FS	.77	.17	.06	.00	1.00
	High ES Low FS	.02	.77	.00	.20	0.99
	Low ES High FS	.18	.02	.74	.06	1.00
	Low ES Low FS	.00	.04	.19	.76	0.99

SOURCE: Hunter, "Community Change."

there is three times as great a probability of moving in the predominant direction as in its opposite.

Summary measures of the above findings are seen in the "interaction effects" presented in table 6. The most important and consistent findings are the relative magnitude and signs of the effects. Over all the time periods economic status, both high and low, has an inverse effect upon family status, while family status, both high and low, has a positive effect upon

CHART 1
Summed Positional Changes of Communities
per Decade, 1930–60

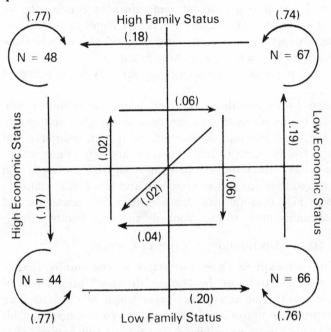

SOURCE: Albert Hunter, "Community Change."

economic status. This means that a community having a high
economic status at time 1 is most likely to change to a low
family status at time 2. Conversely, a community having a
low economic status is most likely to change to a high family
status. On the other hand, the positive effect of family status
means that a community having a high family status at time
1 is most likely to change to a high economic status, while
one having a low family status is most likely to change to a
low economic status. These findings are characteristic of what
Coleman refers to as a system of "mutual negative reenforce-
ment." The example he gives is that hunger leads to eating,
eating leads to nonhunger, nonhunger leads to not eating,
and not eating leads to hunger. This example is more obvious
in its logical causation than are the results of this study, but
it suggests the following: high economic status leads to low

family status, low family status leads to low economic status, and low economic status leads to high family status.

Above all, these results show that by considering the interaction between two different dimensions of community we can empirically derive relatively distinct stages of community change—stages more complex and comprehensive than those based upon divisions of a single continuum.

The four stages of community change may be summarized as:

Stage I — communities changing from *low* economic and high family status to *high* economic and high family status.
Stage II — communities changing from high economic and *high* family status to high economic and *low* family status.
Stage III — communities changing from *high* economic and low family status to *low* economic and low family status.
Stage IV — communities changing from low economic and *low* family status to low economic and *high* family status.

The Spatial Distribution of Types of Change

To further explore these four stages of community change and to relate them to the "decentralization" proposition of urban growth, the community areas which made these four most probable moves are located spatially on a map of Chicago's community areas. Map 5 and table 8 show clearly that these four stages are arranged in a concentric zonal pattern. Communities experiencing stage I changes are most peripherally located, stage II shifts are more centrally located, and stage III and IV changes occur in the most central communities of the city.

Explication of the Stages and Racial Change

The central communities experiencing stage IV changes, from low economic and low family status to low economic and high family status, might be explained as areas of increasing black concentration with a disproportionate number of children. However, only six of the thirteen areas experiencing this stage IV change also had a sizable (> 10 percent) nonwhite population at either the beginning or the end of the decade of transition. A more general explanation accounting for both the nonwhite areas and the remaining seven white areas is

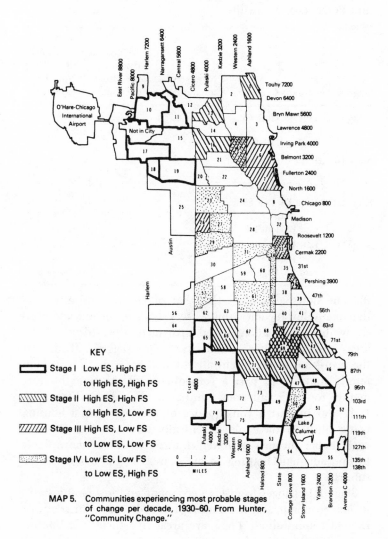

East River 8800
Harlem 7200
Narragansett 6400
Central 5600
Cicero 4800
Pulaski 4000
Kedzie 3200
Western 2400
Ashland 1600

Pacific 8000

O'Hare-Chicago International Airport

Not in City

Touhy 7200
Devon 6400
Bryn Mawr 5600
Lawrence 4800
Irving Park 4000
Belmont 3200
Fullerton 2400
North 1600
Chicago 800
Madison
Roosevelt 1200
Cermak 2200
31st
Pershing 3900
47th
55th
63rd
71st
79th
87th
95th
103rd
111th
119th
127th
135th
138th

Austin

Harlem

Cicero 4800

Lake Calumet

Pulaski 4000
Kedzie 3200
Western 2400
Ashland 1600
Halsted 800
State
Cottage Grove 800
Stony Island 1600
Yates 2400
Brandon 3200
Avenue C 4000

0 1 2 3 4
MILES

KEY

☐ Stage I   Low ES, High FS
            to High ES, High FS

▨ Stage II High ES, High FS
            to High ES, Low FS

▧ Stage III High ES, Low FS
            to Low ES, Low FS

▦ Stage IV Low ES, Low FS
            to Low ES, High FS

MAP 5. Communities experiencing most probable stages of change per decade, 1930–60. From Hunter, "Community Change."

TABLE 8

Stage of Community Change by Distance from Loop
and Percentage Nonwhite

Stage of Community Change		Number of Communities	Average Distance (Miles) from the Loop	Number of Communities with $> 10\%$ Nonwhite Population
Stage I:	Low ES/High FS to High ES/High FS	12	11.1	0
Stage II:	High ES/High FS to High ES/Low FS	8	8.7	2
Stage III:	High ES/Low FS to Low ES/Low FS	9	5.3	4
Stage IV:	Low ES/Low FS to Low ES/High FS	13	5.4	6

the one noted in studies like that of Hoover and Vernon—
that many low-income families seek housing in old and relatively inexpensive homes and apartments located in poorer
areas near the center of the city.[31] This suggests, then, that
the transition of these centrally located areas to areas of high
family status is in part a consequence of the tight housing
market for large but poor families in the metropolitan area.
It is also in part a consequence of the new public housing
being built in these older, centrally located areas. Families
with higher incomes or fewer children would be more likely
to find adequate housing in other areas of the city or in the
suburbs.

Stage III changes from *high* economic and low family status
to *low* economic and low family status also occur in centrally
located communities. These are areas in which a decline occurs in percentage of residents in professional occupations,
median school years completed, median value of homes
owned, or all three. Again, four of these nine communities
have also experienced racial transition, but this is not a factor
in the remaining five. In short, these are communities of low

family status which experience a decline in economic status as poorer, less well-educated residents invade the declining housing market.

The more peripherally located communities experience the stage II change from high economic and high family status to high economic and *low* family status. These are areas experiencing increasing density in multiple-family dwellings, a decline in the proportion of children, a decline in the percentage married, an increased proportion of women in the labor force, or all four. Only two of the eight areas experiencing this transition had also experienced racial invasion, and these are two black middle-class communities on the periphery of Chicago's expanding black ghetto. In short, stage II communities retain a relatively high economic status but change to a lower family status as they become built up and families move to the suburbs.

The outermost ring of transitions (stage I communities maintaining a high family status and raising their economic status) explains the growth of suburbia over this thirty-year period. Middle-class families searching for more space in which to raise their children leave the central city for more sparsely settled newly developing areas of single-family homes on the periphery.[32] We should realize that in 1930 some of these peripheral areas were little more than prairie. For example, Mount Greenwood went from a population of 3,310 in 1930 to 21,941 in 1960, and during the same period Ashburn went from 730 to 38,638. These areas clearly demonstrate that this most peripheral stage I transition is related to the influx of middle-class families into newly developed areas. None of these twelve areas experienced racial invasion during this period.

The location of these stage I transitions on the city's periphery is consistent with the findings of Schnore and others that in newer and smaller metropolitan areas the suburbs have a lower socioeconomic status than the central city, whereas in older and larger metropolitan areas the suburbs have a higher socioeconomic status.[33] In short, I have documented an "evolutionary stage" of peripheral urban communities raising their economic status as the central city grows and these areas come under development.

In addition, these findings show that changes in the family and economic composition of Chicago's local communities cannot be explained solely or even primarily by racial invasion. In short, racial change is related to, though not identical with, family and economic stages of community change. The findings on racial change essentially agree with but further specify the conclusions reached by Taeuber and Taeuber in their study *Negroes in Cities*:

> Traditional accounts of the process of racial residential succession, which stress the low socioeconomic status of the Negro population entering a new neighborhood, the over-crowding and deterioration of housing, the declines in property values, and the flight of whites from the neighborhood are outdated oversimplifications. Expansion of Negro residential areas in recent years has been led by Negroes of high socioeconomic status—not only higher than the rest of the Negro population, but often higher than the white residents of the "invaded" neighborhood. *The invaded areas tend to be occupied by whites of moderately high socioeconomic status, and the housing is predominantly in good rather than substandard condition. . . .* Among both Negroes and whites, the search for better housing is led by those who can best afford it. Patterns of racial transition reflect such general processes of urban change as well as the racial attitudes prevalent in the national society. [Italics added][34]

Sequential Stages of Community Change

These four distinct stages of community change, arranged in a clear concentric pattern, suggest that there is a sequence of transition from stage I on the periphery to stage II, to stage III, and finally to stage IV, most centrally. But, to demonstrate this sequential pattern rather than inferring it from a static spatial distribution, the data must extend far enough in time to capture a community area experiencing at least two transitions. Fortunately, four of the community areas experienced two transitions during the thirty years under study. Of these four, three show changes supporting the above sequence. Both the Near South Side and Oakland made the stage III transition before going through the stage IV transition. Extending the sequence, Greater Grand Crossing made the stage II transition in the forties and the stage III transition in the fifties. Although none of the areas experiencing a stage I transition made another transition during this period, the sequential order is supported for three of the stages.[35]

The stages of change, their zonal pattern, their sequence, and their relationship to racial composition are summarized as follows.

Sparsely settled areas on the fringe of the city with low economic but high family status are most likely to raise their economic status as the central city grows and the area comes under development. This is consistent with and further clarifies the evolutionary sequence of central city–suburban status differentials found in recent studies.

Then areas which have made this transition to a high economic and high family status are most likely to experience a decline in their family status while maintaining a relatively high economic status. In short, for areas in a state of "decline," family status declines before economic status. These are areas having an increased buildup of multiple-family dwelling units, with older but still relatively high economic status residents remaining after younger families have moved. These are also the first areas to experience black invasion. This agrees with recent findings on racial transition by Molotch and others.[36]

Only after experiencing this decline in family status are areas of high economic status likely to experience transition to a lower economic status as lower-class residents invade and the older higher-class residents either move or die. Slightly less than half these communities have a sizable ($>$ 10 percent) nonwhite population. Finally, the most centrally located communities of low economic and low family status are most likely to change to areas of high family status while maintaining their low economic status. This change is apparently due to the movement of poorer families into relatively cheaper housing, both public and private. Again, slightly less than half these communities have a sizable nonwhite population.

Summary

This chapter has shown a general persistence in the ecological structure of Chicago, demonstrated by the consistent emergence of the three factors of residential segregation—economic status, family status, and racial-ethnic status. But within this structural persistence changes are occurring, some systemic, others more episodic.

The episodic changes are indicated in the analysis of the *structure of change*. The analysis asked, "What is changing with what?" The factors of change are varied from one decade to the next, evidently reflecting short-run ecological changes; furthermore, these factors of change are more numerous and complex and are distinct from the relatively persistent factor structures which emerged in the first analysis of *change in structure*.

Nonetheless, the analysis of change in ecological structure, indicated by changes in the factor structures over the four points in time, did demonstrate some consistent and systemic restructuring of Chicago's ecology. First, because of the decreasing communality of the variables, especially the variable of single-family dwelling units, a greater differentiation is apparently occurring in the composition of Chicago's local communities over time. This increased differentiation is also supported by the decreasing percentage of variance explained from 1930 to 1960. These findings lend support to theorists arguing for increased complexity and social differentiation in modern urban societies, and its correlate of increased voluntarism in a citizen's decision of where to live.

In addition, this analysis of change in structure demonstrated that economic status is the dominant factor in residential segregation, especially since 1930. This is coupled to the finding that racial-ethnic status has increased in significance and family status has declined. In short, residential segregation is increasingly a function of prestige and prejudice and less a function of personal life-style and family status. This conclusion is tempered, however, by the finding that racial-ethnic segregation and age segregation are becoming increasingly correlated in central Chicago. Areas with a concentration of foreign born are also likely to be older, and areas having a larger black population are likely to be younger. In short, racial-ethnic segregation is compounded by age segregation.

The spatial distribution of economic, family, and racial-ethnic status among Chicago's community areas shows forces of change that can be interpreted in terms of the concentric zone, the sector, and the multinucleate theories of ecological structure.

For racial-ethnic status there was a general process of dispersion, fitting Burgess's concentric zone decentralization. This dispersion was a function both of black expansion from Chicago's centrally located South Side and West Side ghettos and of more peripheral dispersion of Chicago's older ethnic groups. This finding is consistent with the changes in factor structure noted above. Also, public policy decisions—especially in public housing and urban renewal—have affected Chicago's ecological structure. This may explain discontinuities in the spatial distribution of the three factors considered, discontinuities that assumed a multinucleate pattern similar to that found by Harris and Ullman. For example, large housing projects in the peripheral community of Riverdale sharply raised its black population; the anomaly of increasing black concentration and increasing economic status on the Near North Side was a function of both public housing and urban renewal; and the two isolated pockets of relatively high economic status and mixed racial status within Chicago's South Side black ghetto were caused by the massive private and public urban renewal efforts in the Lake Meadows–Prairie Shores area and in Hyde Park.

For economic status there is an increasing centralization of low economic status areas and a decentralization of high economic status areas, especially on the North Side, over this thirty-year period. This is consistent with the Burgess concentric zone model. Two persistent sectors were also noted that clearly fit the Hoyt sector model—a high economic sector along the prestigious lakefront that shifted from the South Side to the North Side, and a low economic sector near industry stretching along the southwest branch of the Chicago River.

For family status there is a low family status sector along the lakefront and a ring of high family status communities around Chicago's periphery. Both of these extremes of family status have a relatively high economic status. The areas between them are intermediate in family status. Communities lying just inland of the low family status areas generally have a moderately low family status, and the communities farther out, adjacent to the periphery, have a moderately high family status. Furthermore, there is an increase over time in the number of centrally located communities having a moderately high family status. This is due to the movement of poorer families, especially blacks, into relatively cheaper public and private housing.

Above all, the three dimensions of racial-ethnic, economic, and family status exhibit different spatial distributions and also are changing in different ways. This may point to an increasing differentiation among these three dimensions and the forces acting upon them, but spatial distributions can still be adequately described by a combination of the zone, sector, and multinucleate theories—especially if we recognize that the three dimensions are distinct and the spatial patterns exhibited are likely to result from a convergence of vectors or forces.

Finally, I outlined a systemic model of community change patterned in part upon the Burgess concentric zone model. This model simultaneously considers changes in economic and family composition and relates them to racial composition. There is a sequential ordering of stages of community change that are arranged in concentric zones. Neither changes in economic status nor changes in family status considered separately could account for this pattern. The model describes how the economic status of peripheral areas rises as the city expands and fringe areas come under development. Then family status declines, followed by a decline in economic status; and finally the very centrally located low economic/low family status communities raise their family status.

These forces which structure and alter the ecology of Chicago's local communities are leading both to increased differentiation and to fusion. Over time the spatial and factorial ecology is becoming more complex, and is more finely differentiated when its dimensions are considered simultaneously. However, when we focus upon one or another dimension separately, we still see the persistence of general forces of fusion which lead to broad geographical areas having concentrations of high or low economic status, racial or ethnic segregation, and personal life-style or family selectivity. Within each of these broad areas, however, the cross-cutting forces of the other dimensions are producing an ever increasing differentiation.

Part Two   *Symbolic Culture*

Two

*Symbolic Communities
and the Burgess
Natural Areas: A
Historical Comparison*

LANGUAGE, SYMBOLS, AND COMMUNITY

The close associations among the words "common," "communication," and "community" are no accident. The ability to exchange meaning through a shared set of symbols has long been recognized as an integral part of community. From the community of nation-states with their common tongues to the community of deviant subcultures with their argots, language and shared symbols are seen by social analysts and by the participants themselves as a defining criterion of community.[1] Knowing the common symbols and language is often a definition of "membership," for not to know them is not to belong. And the peculiarities of intonation and connotation allow a unique yet common set of meanings and experiences to be expressed and shared, building toward a common perspective and a common culture.

It is significant to this analysis that symbols develop or evolve to represent the community itself. For a nation-state, one might think of a flag or a national anthem. But one set of symbols which is taken for granted at the level of the nation-state is more problematic at the level of the local community—a common name and a set of boundaries.[2] Since the community lacks the omniscience provided by the small group for defining membership through mutual knowledge and direct interaction, and since it lacks the unified structure of a formal organization, a community's name is of central significance for labeling the common whole, and its boundaries are significant for defining its extent and scope. One cannot assert that a name and a set of boundaries guarantee that all other aspects of community are present, but these symbols do represent one reality of community which may have implications for the social, cultural, psychological, and even ecological components of the concept.

To be able to name an area is in no small way to know it. A name distinguishes an area as unique. It is a symbol, a shorthand abstraction, for denoting some mutually perceived and mutually shared communality. When such "naming" takes place one may begin to talk about the existence of symbolic communities. A name is more than a description of an area. "Little Sicily" and "Gold Coast" do connote "Italian" and "wealthy," but they also have explicit territorial referents and are unique. Otherwise "Italian" and "wealthy" may refer to a number of areas, or even to individuals. The name, then, is a symbol of communication that is a shared collective representation about the community itself. In the interaction and communication of individuals both within and without the local community, community names convey properties of both physical and social space.

Names are also significant for identity. The ability to name an area gives an unambiguous status to those living there. It also does this for institutions varying in importance from the Hyde Park Bank and Trust Company to a local bar called the Old Town Ale House. For individuals it means a status comparable to "citizen." "North Sider" and "South Sider" imply distinct loyalties, comparisons, and even competition, whether in talking about leisure institutions such as the White Sox versus the Cubs or the less institutionalized and more invidious status ranking of areas.

Boundaries are another significant component of the symbolic community, especially when it is conceived of spatially. Although the name of an area implies that it can be distinguished from surrounding areas, this distinguishing character becomes heightened as people are able to specify distinct boundaries. To be sure, boundaries may be selected by a variety of criteria, serve a variety of functions, and have a variety of meanings. Perhaps the first question to ask is, "How many residents do define boundaries for their local urban communities?"

Boundaries are significant not only for identification but for social action. In the theory of social action developed by Talcott Parsons, cognition—knowing, or being able to define a situation—is a prerequisite for meaningful social action. Behavior as well as identity may change as one crosses a street and one's status changes from "citizen" to "stranger."[3] Such symbols may themselves constrain, control, and direct behavior. If one is told that people on the other side of the tracks think and act differently, one may believe it and so never cross the tracks to test the "reality" of this shared definition. Furthermore, those across the tracks may think and act differently precisely because they are "expected" to do so. The constraint of symbols is also seen when long-time residents of cities "discover" areas they thought they knew, when in fact they only "knew about" them.

METHODS

The findings in this section are based upon interviews with 801 residents of the city of Chicago during 1967–68, over a period of a year and a half.[4] Approximately ten interviews were taken from each of the seventy-five community areas defined by Burgess and his students in the twenties. The survey instrument was a short, open-ended questionnaire with about twenty questions. I spent approximately one week in each area, traveling around the community, observing it, talking with its residents, shopkeepers, ministers, and community organization members, and completing at least ten resident questionnaires. Respondents were picked from locations which gave broad geographical coverage within each community.

Names and boundaries were ascertained much as in studies by Ross, Foley, and Riemer.[5] Residents were simply asked, "What is the name of this part of Chicago?" and "What are the boundaries of this area?" Essentially no probes were used with respect to names, but with boundaries the most common probe was, "Well, how far does the area go in that direction?" (pointing).

Some researchers have criticized the attempt to define "neighborhoods" or local urban communities by relying upon residents' perceptions, claiming that the results are often only partial, that only a minority have such conceptions, and that there is little consensus either among residents or between their perceptions and other means of delimiting boundaries.[6] Although many researchers take these results as "nonfindings," I consider them problematic and feel they have validity in their own right. The procedures of this survey do not permit an analysis of "consensus" on community boundaries and names, because within a given community area as defined by Burgess a number of different areas might now be defined, and one therefore cannot aggregate responses in this whole area and adequately measure "consensus." However, one can study the characteristics of people who are able to define boundaries as compared with those who cannot, and the characteristics of the areas in which boundaries are often used as compared with those where they are not.

Residents' perceptions and definitions of their local areas are not of course a "holistic" way to define neighborhoods or community areas, but they are an independent reality that should not be ignored or discounted even if they fail to coincide with other methods. To invoke W. I. Thomas, we are asking people to define the situation, to give the reality they perceive and from which they act. If they believe these communities exist, then they exist.[7] The implications of and the relationships between behavior and such symbolic definitions are problematic—they need definition and then explanation. In the following chapters I will define and describe these "realities" and then attempt to explain them.

A NOTE ON "NATURAL AREAS"

Some researchers have suggested that as a result of increasing urban differentiation local urban communities are losing their significance. Some have even argued for dropping the concept of "neighborhood" from our lexicon.[8] Others feel it should be retained in a modified form, whether as Janowitz's conception of a "community of limited liability" or as Riemer's conception of "roving" neighborhoods.[9] These perspectives come closer to explaining the meaning of "community" at the local level than do those that without comparison, or at best with an implicit historical comparison, simply suggest that local communities are insignificant in today's urban context.

This implicit historical comparison, with today's local urban communities, has two sources. The first is the older theoretical discussion, central to the development of sociology, that deals with the major transformations of Western society during the eighteenth and nineteenth centuries. This approach is exemplified in Tönnies's polar shift from Gemeinschaft to Gesellschaft and in Durkheim's movement from mechanical to organic societies. It is echoed by today's mass-society theorists who see large-scale industrial urban society eroding the collective solidarity based upon blood and land. The second source is an offshoot of the first and centers on the discussion of "natural areas," a controversial concept within urban sociology for almost half a century.[10] The natural area was seen by Park and Burgess, its first proponents, as a product of the industrialization and immigration of peasant and rural populations into America's cities at the turn of the century. Even recent studies, such as Gans's *The Urban Villagers*, attest to the strength of this anachronistic model.[11]

The concept of "natural areas" is significant for this study in a number of ways. Most obviously, the natural areas of Chicago defined by Park and Burgess in the twenties formed the basis of the "community areas" used as a sampling frame. This is therefore in a very real sense an explicit comparison with this historical model. It is also significant in another way. Given that we are dealing with the "symbols" of community, names and boundaries, these symbols may be readily communicated and disseminated from authoritative sources and used by residents as the definition of their communities. In short, the work of Burgess and of his colleagues and students, in delimiting natural areas for the city of Chicago may have created the symbols for community that still persist. For example, a recent newspaper series on local communities in Chicago carried a small inset map of each community. The community's name and boundaries were lifted directly from the *Fact Book of Chicago*, the book created by Burgess at the University of Chicago half a century ago.

In short, not only do symbols of community reflect or refer to reality, but, like symbols generally, they may serve to define and create reality. Community organizations and community organizers are becoming increasingly aware that they can create and manipulate such symbols in the hope of heightening a sense of community and community solidarity. Redefining boundaries, borrowing a name from a neighboring high-prestige area, and changing a name that has acquired a bad connotation are all attempts to symbolically manipulate residents' conceptions of their local areas. Such symbolic manipulation has often been used by real estate developers, who, on the basis of a few feet of difference in elevation, label a new development "the Heights" or use a few trees as a reason to call another area "Fair Elms."

This study, then, will explore the "symbolic dimension" of community as having a validity and reality in its own right; but first we should compare the areas under study with the older "natural community areas" of Chicago.

A COMPARISON WITH THE BURGESS COMMUNITY AREAS

In the 1920s Burgess defined seventy-five exhaustive and mutually exclusive community areas for the city of Chicago. A perusal of the recently collected papers of Burgess and his students shows that they were aware of many smaller neighborhoods within these larger community areas, but the latter represented the largest single collective entity for a given part of Chicago at the time of Burgess's research.[12]

First, a visual comparison of the Burgess areas with the areas defined by my respondents shows a greater uniformity in size in the Burgess areas.[13] Mine range from what Burgess might have defined as smaller neighborhoods to an aggregation of several of his areas into a larger single area. This could be the result of two things. First, the Burgess areas may be somewhat "artificial" in that he explicitly tried to define areas of equivalent size and population. A second possibility, even if the first is true, is that there are two forces producing greater variation in size for today's areas. One force leads to increased differentiation, the other toward fusion. This possibility suggests that the unified conception of community as consisting of residential areas (neighborhoods) surrounding some central focal point (usually shopping) just does not define the varied reality of today's urban areas. The unified, functionally integrated community is lost as some functions increase in scale—for example shopping and the labor market —while other functions retain a smaller scale—for example the neighborhood circle of friends and the local school. If we accept these shifting functional bases, the definition of community may be released from its close association with function and people's day-to-day activities and may become a

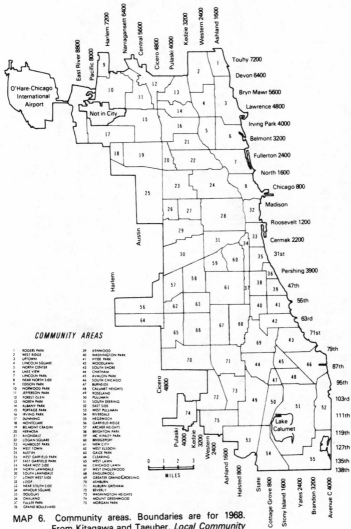

MAP 6. Community areas. Boundaries are for 1968. From Kitagawa and Taeuber, *Local Community Fact Book . . . 1960*, p. ix.

Key to Map 7

1. Rogers Park
2. West Rogers Park
3. North Town
4. Edgewater
5. Andersonville
6. Uptown
7. Ravenswood
8. Ravenswood Manor
9. Lincoln Square
10. Bowmanville
11. Budlong Woods
12. Arcadia Terrace
13. Peterson Woods
14. North Park
15. Hollywood Park
16. Peterson Park
17. Albany Park
18. Mayfair
19. Crazy "K"
20. Sauganash
21. Jefferson Park
22. Wilson Park
23. Forest Glen
24. Gladstone Park
25. Edgebrook
26. South Edgebrook
27. Old Edgebrook
28. North Edgebrook
29. Wildwood
30. Edison Park
31. Oriole Park
32. Norwood Park
33. Old Norwood
34. Big Oaks
35. Irving Wood
36. Belmont Terrace
37. Belmont Heights
38. Schorsch Village
39. Montclare
40. Galewood
41. Portage Park
42. Belmont
43. Cragin
44. Hanson Park
45. Belmont-Central
46. Hermosa
47. Kelvyn Park
48. Belmont Gardens
49. Kilbourn Park
50. Park View
51. Avondale
52. Logan Square
53. Lakeview
54. Belmont Harbor
55. Lincoln Park
56. Park West
57. Wrightwood
58. Sheffield Neighbors
59. Old Town
60. Near North Side
61. Cabrini Homes
62. Gold Coast
63. The Loop
64. Near West Side
65. Wicker Park
66. Buck Town
67. Garfield Park
68. Humboldt Park
69. Austin
70. Lawndale
71. "K" Town
72. Little Village, or South Lawndale

73. Pilsen
74. Chinatown
75. Hicks Homes
76. Dearborn Homes
77. South Commons
78. Prairie Shores
79. Lake Meadows
80. Groveland Park
81. Woodland Park
82. Ida B. Wells Homes
83. Oakland
84. Kenwood-Oakland
85. Hyde Park-Kenwood
86. Hyde Park
87. East Hyde Park
88. South Side
89. Robert Taylor Homes
90. Bridgeport
91. Wentworth Gardens
92. McKinley Park
93. Brighton Park
94. Back of the Yards
95. Canaryville
96. Fuller Park
97. West Kenwood Homes
98. Gage Park
99. West Elsdon
100. Archer Heights
101. Sleepy Hollow
102. LeClaire Courts
103. Garfield Ridge
104. Clearing
105. Lawler Park, or The Village
106. West Lawn
107. Chicago Lawn
108. Marquette Park
109. Lithuanian Plaza
110. South Lynn
111. Englewood
112. Hamilton Park
113. Park Manor
114. Woodlawn
115. South Shore
116. Parkside
117. Jackson Park Highlands
118. O'Keefe Neighborhood
119. Bryn Mawr West
120. Bryn Mawr East
121. South End West
122. South End East
123. Windsor Park
124. Chelten, or Cheltenham
125. Rainbow Beach, or South Shore Drive
126. South Chicago
127. The Bush
128. Millgate
129. South Shore Gardens
130. Veteran's Memorial Park
131. Slag Valley
132. South Deering, or Irondale
133. Jeffery Manor
134. Marionette Manor
135. East Side
136. Fair Elms
137. Pill Hill
138. South Shore Valley
139. Stony Island Park
140. Stony Island Heights

141. Avalon Park
142. Marynook
143. Grand Crossing
144. Burnside
145. Chatham
146. West Chesterfield
147. West Chatham
148. Lillydale
149. Princeton Park
150. Greenview
151. Brainerd
152. Gresham
153. Foster Park
154. Highburn
155. Beverly Terrace
156. Wrightwood
157. Ashburn
158. Scottsdale
159. Ashburn Estates
160. Crestline
161. Beverly
162. North Beverly
163. Beverly Ridge
164. Vanderpoel
165. East Beverly
166. Southwest Beverly
167. Ridge Homes
168. Beverly Manor
169. Ridge Manor
170. Morgan Park Manor
171. Mount Greenwood
172. Morgan Park
173. West Morgan Park
174. Kennedy Park
175. Beverly Woods
176. Ada Park
177. Maple Park
178. Victory Heights
179. Longwood Manor
180. Washington Heights
181. Mount Vernon
182. Euclid Park
183. University Highlands
184. Roseland
185. North Roseland
186. Fernwood
187. Rosemore
188. Rosegrove
189. Sheldon Heights
190. Gano
191. Kensington
192. West Pullman
193. Colonial Village
194. Pullman
195. North Pullman
196. South Pullman
197. London Towne
198. Cottage Grove Heights
199. Altgeld-Murray Homes, or Altgeld Gardens
200. Golden Gate
201. Eden Green
202. Riverdale
203. Hegewisch
204. Avalon Trails
205. Arizona
206. Island Home Trailer Court

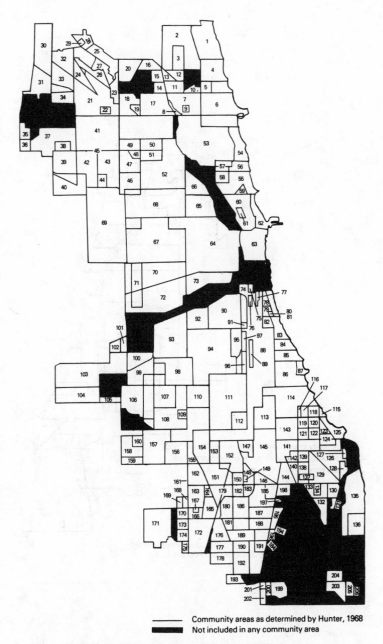

Community areas as determined by Hunter, 1968
Not included in any community area

MAP 7. Community areas as determined by Hunter, 1968.

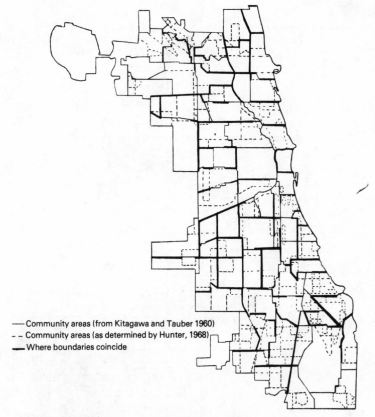

— Community areas (from Kitagawa and Tauber 1960)
- - Community areas (as determined by Hunter, 1968)
— Where boundaries coincide

MAP 8. Comparison of community areas. From Suttles,
Social Construction of Communities, p. 71.

more independent symbolic entity subject only to the ability to define and disseminate a plausible set of symbols.

The definition of community may, in short, be increasingly freed from function. If this is true, we then have remaining what has usually been defined as the basis of "neighborhood," in contrast to "community"—not a functional interdependence, but the mere sharing of a common residential area. From this perspective it is perhaps more accurate to talk about the persistence of "neighborhood" than about the loss of "community."

The persistence of the symbols used to define community is shown by the fact that 42.3 percent of the entire sample gave the same names used by Burgess. An additional 34.9 percent gave a different name to their areas, and the rest either gave no name or simply referred to the names of their streets or housing projects. This 42.3 percent demonstrates that not only is there persistence in the names of such areas, but these names are part of a shared local culture that is fairly widely known.

THE DYNAMICS OF COMMUNITY NAMES

In spite of the general persistence of names since the Burgess era, we can notice several systematic processes of change in the names of Chicago's local communities. These changes in general reflect the differentiation and fusion referred to previously and result in a much more complex definition of local areas.

The process of fusion has eradicated some of the previous distinctions from today's mapping of the city. For example, the differentiations between East and West Garfield Park and between East and West Englewood have been lost, resulting in the fusion of two relatively large community areas. In both areas the fusion is due in part to the black succession and the loss of many ethnic and racial distinctions. The fusion in Englewood was accompanied, however, by a differentiation within this inordinately large community as smaller neighborhoods like Hamilton Park appeared.

Fusion is also taking place in the Rogers Park area in the northeast corner of Chicago. The area just west of Rogers Park was defined as West Ridge by Burgess, but it is now

referred to by most residents as West Rogers Park. Thus to
many people both areas have fused into the much larger area
of Rogers Park. Again, within these fused areas finer neighborhood distinctions are taking place. As in Englewood, we
see fusion accompanied by differentiation.

A different form of fusion occurs when an area's residents
attempt to "borrow" the name and thereby the prestige or
status of a higher-ranking adjacent area. For example, the
neighborhood of Park West has attempted to draw on the
prestige of the very fashionable Lincoln Park community just
to the east. Similar attempts are found in the areas around
Beverly on the   Southwest Side and Norwood Park and Edgebrook on the Northwest Side of the city. In both Edgebrook
and Norwood Park the higher-status neighborhoods are now
referred to as Old Edgebrook and Old Norwood as these
areas attempt to maintain their status in the face of fusion
with lower-status areas.

Differentiation of higher-status areas within larger but generally lower-status communities is one of the more common
forms. Lying along the lake, East Hyde Park has differentiated
itself as a smaller, more prestigious neighborhood within
Hyde Park; Ravenswood Manor, along the North Branch of
the Chicago River, has differentiated out as a one-block-wide
strip of larger, more expensive homes within the Ravenswood
community; and "Fair Elms" is a higher-status small area
within the local community of East Chicago.

We see, then, that the status and prestige of community
names are similar in certain systematic ways to the structure
and functioning of stratification systems generally.[14] On the
one hand lower-status individuals attempt through a "halo"
effect to become identified with a neighboring area of higher
status. On the other hand, those of higher status attempt to
assert the distinctiveness of their area.

Differentiation of small higher-prestige areas may go so far
that the smaller areas no longer consider themselves part of the
larger whole. The Galewood area, for example, was formerly
considered the northern part of Austin, but now it is considered entirely separate. The extreme of this type of differentiation is shown by a small area on the Northwest Side known
as Schorsch Village. Burgess defined this entire community

area as Dunning. However, only the residents of the larger homes in Schorsch Village could give any name for the area. One explanation for the loss of a name is the rapid development and growth of this area, from about 20,000 persons when Burgess was writing to more than 40,000 today. This rapid expansion, especially since World War II, may mean that a local culture has not yet had time to develop and to assimilate the large influx of new residents.

Other areas of the city also lost names, so that the map of Chicago no longer is "exhaustively" covered with community names. This was especially true in the old "Bronzeville" (Chicago's older South Side black ghetto), studied by many earlier researchers.[15] Burgess defined a number of community areas in this ghetto, such as the Near South Side, Washington Park, and Oakland. However, today throughout much of this area one finds no community name except the extremely broad designation "the South Side." The same "loss" of more specific community names was found in Chicago's other major black ghetto, which is now referred to by many of its residents simply as "the West Side."

Another reason for changing community names is the attempt of residents to divest their areas of names which have assumed negative connotations. For example, the white residents of South Lawndale have very consciously attempted to change their area's name to "Little Village." They have even placed large painted signs on many railroad overpasses which read "Welcome to Little Village." In large part this redefinition is an attempt to distinguish the area from the neighboring community of North Lawndale, which over the past decade has become predominantly black.

One such attempt to avoid a bad connotation occurred in the area Burgess defined as New City. Records show that then, as today, the community was known as "the Back of the Yards." The negative connotation previously associated with the stench and squalor of Chicago's stockyards no longer persists, but the name has stuck. The community is now known more positively, in some circles, for its strong ethnic defense against black invasion, for its powerful Alinsky-formed community organization and for its annual "Free Fair." Where the name New City came from only God and Burgess know.

The significance of authoritative sources for naming local areas and changing their names often became apparent during the interviewing. For example, one woman, when asked the name of the local area, immediately retreated to her desk, pulled out a local community newspaper, and proceeded to read the name of the area from the paper's masthead. Other respondents could not recall the name of the area, but when asked about local organizations would give a name and then add that it must be the name of the community as well. Local community organizations are also effective in communicating local names by erecting signs on major thoroughfares leading into the community. Throughout the city one will see signs like the one in Rogers Park, which proudly proclaims, "Welcome to Rogers Park, Community Beautiful." Such boosterism was once more characteristic of small but growing midwest towns on the prairie. An extreme case is seen in the area called "Park West." On light poles at every major intersection of the neighborhood one sees small signs bearing the community's name.

Local organizations, local community newspapers, even the larger metropolitan dailies, and not least the *Local Community Fact Book* of Burgess are all authoritative sources for such community names. The local telephone directories of Chicago, for example, are divided into areas bearing maps and names lifted directly from the *Fact Book*. Such a wide range of potential sources for local names, especially when they might be in conflict, was a source of confusion rather than clarity for residents. When I interviewed neighbors jointly arguments would sometimes develop about the "real" name for the local area. Often one would run for his telephone book or some other source to "prove" his point. This confusion was shown by one pharmacist in West Rogers Park. After naming the area as West Rogers Park he looked at his local telephone book and said quizzically, "Well, I'll be. They call it West Ridge."

For the most part we have been referring to "area" names and their changes. However, another type of name stems from a community focal point. Shopping focal points at major intersections like "Belmont-Central" and "Six Corners" were found at several points throughout the city. Much more numerous were focal-point names radiating from local play-grounds and parks. Such focal points provided names and cognitive references that people used to define their areas even when boundaries were idiosyncratic or indistinct.

In addition, extremely small and parochial names were found in great numbers throughout the city. Such areas, exemplified in Gerald Suttles's study of Chicago's West Side, often consisted of no more than one or two square blocks.[16] The basis of the small area's name might be rooted in a long local history or merely be the result of a housing development less than a year old. It also seemed that such small parochial definitions were more common among the young, especially teen-agers. In one case, the "Crazy K" neighborhood, the name derived from three crooked adjacent streets all beginning with the letter K. These latter fine-scale distinctions point out the need to define, know, and label some local cognitive reality. They show a need for distinguishing an area, on whatever basis, from surrounding areas and give residents a name, a symbol, and a unique status that transform mere space into meaningful place.

BOUNDARIES

Comparing the maps further shows that the boundaries of many of the communities still persist. To be sure, the consensus is perhaps not as great with respect to names, but it does suggest that certain boundaries have remained symbolically significant, perhaps because of their "naturalness." By "natural boundaries" Burgess primarily meant broad avenues or expressways, rivers, large plots of vacant land, and wide swaths of industry or railway yards. These represent barriers to communication, interaction, and functional integration. From another perspective, if boundaries are needed, these perhaps represent the most "convenient" and unambiguous ones available.

It is important to realize that individuals might call something a boundary when in fact some other phenomenon in the perceptual environment is the "real" boundary. Streets provide a relatively explicit and unambiguous boundary and therefore may be the method of articulating boundaries when they are near other perceptual boundaries. Most residents articulated their boundaries as streets (80.1 percent), with the lake (9.0 percent) and railroad or el lines the next most frequently mentioned (7.0 percent). Small numbers also mentioned—in decreasing order—rivers, parks, expressways, and the city limits. To explore the possibility that other elements in the environment may have been the perceptual boundaries for which streets were the most convenient form of articulation, each street response was coded to indicate whether it was within one block of other boundaries such as the lake, rivers, or railroads. Although the respondents did not necessarily have these in mind when they named a street as the boundary, they may have. Furthermore, the frequency with which a street lies near another possible boundary depends on how often these other physical boundaries occur. The accompanying distribution should be interpreted with these qualifications in mind.

Percentage of Streets Given as Boundaries
within One Block of:

park or vacant land 62.6
railroad or el line 54.7
expressway 26.9
city limits 21.6
rivers 13.3
Lake Michigan or Lake Calumet 4.0

(Percentages total more than 100% because respondents gave more than one street boundary.)

What is most obvious from this distribution is the importance of both lines of transportation and large open tracts of land for demarcating areas. These are strikingly similar to the "natural boundaries" and barriers to communication and interaction first proposed by Park and Burgess.[17] A good case for the significance of lines of transportation is demonstrated by the elderly respondent who slowly and pensively began naming the boundaries of her area. After giving three street names she paused and said, "I can't think of the street the bus line runs on over that way."

As was mentioned previously, boundaries may be delimited for a variety of reasons and may be based on any of a number of criteria. I did not explicitly investigate respondents' reasons for naming a specific boundary. But after being asked the name and boundaries of their communities, respondents were asked whether the communities included any distinct neighborhoods. Of the entire sample, 32.5 percent were able to define distinct neighborhoods and 18.0 percent were able to give explicit names to these smaller units. Whether or not neighborhoods were defined is of course largely a function of the size of the initial area defined. If a person first defined a small homogeneous area, it was less likely that he would differentiate smaller neighborhoods within it. For example, looking only at the extremes, of those who defined their area as smaller than 16 square blocks 32.7 percent said there were smaller neighborhoods within it. For those who initially defined their area as greater than 256 square blocks, 43.7 percent said there were smaller neighborhoods within it. The criteria used to differentiate neighborhoods are presented in the accompanying distribution.

Criteria used to Differentiate Neighborhoods

	type of housing	4.6%
Socioeconomic Status	public housing	3.3
	class and wealth	3.1
Racial-ethnic Status	ethnicity	2.6
	race	2.1
Other responses		5.6
Total		21.3%

If the first three criteria are grouped as representing socioeconomic status, as they apparently do, and the last two are grouped under racial-ethnic status, one sees that 11.0 percent used class criteria, and 4.7 percent used racial-ethnic criteria. The importance given these criteria is similar to the ordering found in the ecological data in chapter 2 regarding the three factors of residential segregation. The socioeconomic factor was most significant, followed by the racial-ethnic factor.

THE DYNAMICS OF COMMUNITY BOUNDARIES

Even though the nature of local community boundaries shows a persistent similarity to the "natural boundaries" of Burgess, nonetheless numerous boundary changes have occurred ove this fifty-year period. Like changes in area names they exemplify systematic changes occurring throughout a number of different social systems.

A central problem in theories of stratification is how to establish clear divisions or boundaries between classes. If status ranking is a continuum, how does one distinguish clearly between the middle class and the working class? Do we ask for people's perceptions and definitions of the classes as Warner did? This is closely related to the number of classes that can be distinguished. Are there six as Warner found in Yankee City, or four as Centers found in his survey of the social psychology of class?[18] In large part, the answers depend on how the distinctions or boundaries between classes are drawn.

The importance of area of residence as a dimension of status or class ranking is found in a number of studies from a wide range of perspectives. Warner's Index of Status Characteristics (ISC) included an evaluation of the home and its surrounding neighborhood.[19] From a different perspective the Duncans showed in their now-classic article "Residential Distribution and Occupational Stratification" that there is a very distinct segregation of occupations by local residential area. Clearly, then, area boundaries are a mechanism for delimiting class and status boundaries, and we should fully expect to see stratification processes occurring with spatial boundaries and their definition as symbols of class distinctions.

The clarity or ambiguity of spatial boundaries shows similarities to the clarity and ambiguity of class boundaries. To preserve or maintain status, people are likely to draw distinct boundaries between themselves and those lower in status. In turn, those lower in status are likely to blur the boundaries between themselves and those higher in status. My data and observations appear to support this for spatial boundaries as well. In a later section we will see, for example, that the higher the class the more likely people are to delimit distinct boundaries for their local area. One reason may be the exclusion versus inclusion this may imply.

The dynamics of social mobility are also clearly demonstrated in local areas and in the crossing of "boundaries" such mobility implies. A distinction should be made between individual and structural mobility.[20] Individual social mobility, translated into spatial areas and boundaries, simply means that a person is likely to move to an area of higher social status to make his social and spatial positions consistent.[21] But

structural mobility of an area, like structural mobility generally, is an attempt to increase the status ranking of the collectivity or the area as a whole. Individuals will, of course, reap
the rewards of such upward mobility while avoiding the costs
of breaking ties with their local area, its citizens, and its institutions.

Numerous examples of these processes were found throughout the city. For example, on the Northwest Side is a neighborhood on the southern edge of a large forest preserve and
golf course. Rather than viewing this parkland as a barrier,
residents of the neighborhood view it as a focal point linking
them to Edgebrook, the higher prestige community north of
the park. However, the residents of "South Edgebrook," as
they call it, are in reality more similar in class and housing
to their neighbors across the street than to the residents of the
wealthier and larger homes in Edgebrook. The residents of
Edgebrook do not acknowledge this claim for higher status;
they do not consider the neighborhood south of the park to
be part of Edgebrook. A similar neighborhood on the Southwest Side is defined by its residents as "Northeast Beverly."
But the residents of the higher-status Beverly community,
separated from this neighborhood by railroads and a major
thoroughfare, do not consider it part of their community.

There are of course other social factors which lead to the
extension and contraction of community boundaries and
thereby produce the general fusion and differentiation of communities. One set of fairly distinct boundaries are those separating white and black communities. As blacks invade a
previously all-white community, the boundary will often be
redefined to exclude blacks from the cognitive community defined by whites. As a man in Austin said when asked about
the eastern boundary of his community, "Well, it used to be
the tracks, but blacks have moved this side of them, so I guess
now you would have to say it's Cicero Avenue." This cognitive
redefinition of boundaries becomes less feasible, however, when
clear and distinct boundaries have been established and are
maintained within a strong local culture. Black movement
across such boundaries does not lead to cognitive redefinition,
but brings a sense of "invasion." Such boundaries, therefore,
assume characteristics of international boundaries, even to

the point of being defended by violence. The bombing of black homes in Cicero made national headlines several decades ago, and more recently black families moving into the Roseland area, across a distinct boundary of a major expressway, were subjected to such violence.

One of the strongest of such racial boundaries stretches along a two-mile strip of Ashland Avenue. This boundary was the line drawn by a federation of small local organizations known as "Father Lawlor's Block Clubs," after the Catholic priest who led the fight in these predominantly white ethnic neighborhoods. One can see this broad avenue as a boundary both on the current maps and on those Burgess drew more than fifty years ago. The boundary has remained in the local culture, although undoubtedly its meaning and significance have recently been heightened.

The points above exemplify one possible function of ambiguity of boundaries as opposed to strong cognitive clarity. Where less consensus exists, the greater ambiguity may permit residents to redefine cognitive boundaries to suit their psychic and social needs. But where such boundaries are distinct and are part of a strong local culture, there may be heightened antagonisms across these boundaries and even a thwarting of what some consider the "natural" ecological processes of invasion and succession. In short, heightened symbolic definition of local areas may directly affect the ecological processes and structure of the city.

By and large the community boundaries we are concerned with do not involve any formal legal definition. The only notable exception is in communities bordering the city limits, where an unambiguous legal boundary is well known and is often cited by residents. Somewhat surprisingly, respondents only occasionally used ward boundaries and names to define the local area. Another group of authoritative sources, however, are generally more successful in establishing a formal set of local boundaries—local community organizations. We will analyze these in greater detail later, but it should be noted here that such organizations have clear spatial boundaries that define both scope of activity and base for potential membership. They do not exist in a vacuum, for there invariably are neighboring organizations with their own set of community boundaries. As the organizations grow or the local area changes their spatial boundaries are likely to grow and change as well. This results in a series of overlapping boundaries, with neighboring organizations often competing for residents' identification and commitment. Overlapping of community boundaries not only produces confusion and ambiguity but means that residents do not necessarily see the city as divided into mutually exclusive local areas. One resident who lived in such an overlapped area laughingly bemoaned the situation: "I don't know which community I belong to. I can take my choice!" This statement highlights both the ambiguity arising from overlapping boundaries and the voluntarism that allows residents to symbolically "join" the community of their own definition and choosing.[22]

When ambiguity exists for symbols of local communities, and especially their boundaries, one result is what Albert Reiss has called the "ego community."[23] In this situation people tend to define boundaries which place them in the center of the community. Only when there exists a clear and powerful "natural boundary" or when a boundary is part of a strong and persistent local culture do we find residents placing themselves at the very edge of a community. However, a number of respondents who lived next to a large railway embankment or an expressway skipped over these natural boundaries and gave a more egocentric definition to their local area, often because social boundaries were more operative, such as school or parish borders. This egocentric definition of community also leads to finer differentiation within today's local communities.

Further ambiguity and lack of consensus about boundaries are caused by "focal point communities." These are communities defined from a central focal point, usually a shopping area, whose strength for local identification decreases with distance from the node. Such communities have very indistinct boundaries, if any, and generally overlap the more common area boundaries surrounding them. Examples are Lincoln Square, Belmont-Central, and Six Corners. Residents immediately adjacent to such centers usually gave this as the area name, and had difficulty giving distinct boundaries. Farther from the center, this name was less frequently mentioned.

To summarize, there is close affinity between social and physical space and social and physical boundaries. The distinctions and divisions of community boundaries are often only the symbolic representation of significant social divisions and distinctions. Furthermore, the dynamic processes associated with these systems of social differentiation can be recorded and analyzed in the structure and dynamics of local areas and their boundaries.

Second, local boundaries are often ambiguous. Rather than considering this a totally negative aspect of current urban life, we should see some of the positive consequences it may bring both to individual residents and to the social systems of the communities. The nonrigid and informal character of these boundaries allows greater change and freewheeling in the system than might be permitted by a more rigidly fixed and widely shared set of administrative boundaries. Of course there are potential costs to such ambiguity, such as confusion about collective identity and loss of commitment and responsibility at the local level.

Third, we should not lose sight of the symbolic character of community boundaries. As symbols, they are on the one hand subject to manipulation and conscious redefinition, and on the other hand are subject to reality testing and thereby provide a relatively quick psychic and collective readjustment to the rapid changes occurring in today's urban milieu. Although they may provide more facile readjustments than would rigid administrative boundaries, they are also a conservative constraint. To the degree that they are contained within a strong local culture they preserve and maintain the historical continuity of an area, thereby shielding residents from the consequences of social and ecological change. In short, the names and boundaries of local areas may be subject to a "symbolic lag" which adjusts more quickly than formal lags and yet provides a cushion and a barrier to rapid urban change.[24]

Finally, like all social boundaries, boundaries of local communities are mechanisms that both exclude and include. These two processes produce the dynamic outcome I have been describing, the dialectic of community fusion and community differentiation.

FORMS OF COMMUNITY

The most common way to conceptualize a local community is to view it as an "area"—that is, a two-dimensional bounded surface. However, two other types of communities emerged from my observations and interviews—the "focal point" and the "strip." I will refer to these three—areas, focal points, and strips—as "forms" of community, meaning that the typology combines a physical dimension and a functional dimension.[25]

The Area

The first form of community, the area, is the most frequently found. The area consists of a two-dimensional space with some basis of commonality which distinctly separates it from surrounding areas. This is essentially the same as the earlier concept of "natural areas" except that no assumption is made about the "naturalness" of an area's formation and structure. It would be fruitless to list all the bases for defining the commonality of areas, for these range from obvious characteristics of the residents such as race, ethnicity, and social class to more subtle physical characteristics such as housing style or the presence of curved or crooked streets.

But the significance of the area as a form of community is that, regardless of the criteria used, residents do have some sense of a collective commonality, a shared physical space, and are capable of distinguishing their area from others by clear and symbolically meaningful boundaries.

The Focal Point

The second form of symbolic community, the focal point, emphasizes a convergence of physical form and social function. Like the cathedrals in the walled cities of the Middle Ages, or like skyscrapers in the commercial city of today, some symbolic element may serve as a focal point in many local urban communities, conveying not only a dominating physical presence but a convergence of significant functions in the life-space of local residents.

A central location, especially a retail center, was often a component of the natural areas conceived by Burgess and earlier writers.[26] The community was seen to extend from the intersection of two major streets, with retail stores located at this point and with distinct neighborhoods found in the four quadrants of the grid. Communities therefore were thought of as functionally integrated trade areas, with homogeneous residential neighborhoods surrounding the trade center. With the increasing mobility of the population by automobile and with the creation of fewer and larger-scale shopping centers, this functional retail definition of community has been redefined. But since it is still important to know the significance of focal points as an element of the symbolic community, I asked respondents, "Are there any central locations in your area?"

More than three-fourths (78.4 percent) said their community had at least one central location, and 19.9 percent were able to name two or more. The central locations most commonly mentioned were shopping areas (48.2 percent), followed by parks (18.3 percent), schools (3.4 percent), and community centers (3.1 percent), and in some places factories or industries. It is clear, then, that a large percentage of the population does have an image of their community centering on a focal point. However, even though many residents are able to specify focal points, not all such potential focal points actually operate as the key element in community identification. They are especially unlikely to do so when they are surrounded by very strong "area" forms of community. But when competing bases of identification are not present, one finds a varying identification with the focal point, strongest for residents living closest and decreasing in intensity for residents living farther from it.

Local shopping centers, parks, schools, and community centers are obvious referents for functional integration of local areas that would plainly provide a basis for local identification. But the significance of industries and factories is an anachronism from a period when home and work were less differentiated than today. In Millgate and Irondale, two neighborhoods on the Southeast Side of the city, the iron- and steelworks have great importance in residents' conceptions of their local areas. Perhaps the two most historically significant industrial focal point communities are the Back of the Yards and Pullman. The stockyards, which constitute a large and now vacant area in the center of the former community, were for decades the primary place of employment for surrounding residents and an integral part of the definition of the local community and of the city of Chicago itself. Pullman was the utopian planned company town founded by George Pullman in 1880 on what was then the outskirts of Chicago. Its distinctive row houses, the community center and the hotel, the surrounding railroad yards, and above all the Pullman factories which "put a nation on wheels" still provide a powerful set of symbols for distinguishing Pullman as a unique local community. Most of the factories, which stretch along the entire eastern edge of the community, are now vacant and boarded up, but their dark and paneless windows and their brooding presence are a reminder of their historical significance to both the community and the nation. It is a history which has entered the local culture and is familiar to today's residents, and a history which some older respondents proudly said that they helped make.

The Strip

The strip is a "form" of community that emphasizes some *linear* element in the environment which provides the basis for a symbolic identification of the area.

Strip shopping is perhaps the most frequently found linear element in the urban environment, but it is rarely the basis of community identification. More often it appears to separate perceptual communities and neighborhoods. This was true, for example, of shopping strips separating Old Norwood from Norwood Park and Gladstone Park from Jefferson Park on the Northwest Side, and Hollywood Park from North Park on the North Side.

The strongest single linear element in the city is of course the lakefront. At several points along the lake residents' strong association with this linear element produces symbolic representations of the strip form of community. This was perhaps strongest on the Near North Side in the area which was the basis of Zorbaugh's classic *The Gold Coast and the Slum.*

Of course the linear element of the lake is reinforced by the marked status and housing differences found only two blocks in from the lake, west of State Street. With the redevelopment of the Old Town area and the building of Sandburg Village these differences are diminishing, but the symbolic representation of the Gold Coast as a separate area persists.

The Robert Taylor Homes on the South Side of Chicago are another example of a linear form of community. These high-rise public apartments stretch for approximately two miles along the Dan Ryan Expressway, from 39th Street to 55th Street. The high-rise quality distinguishes them from the surrounding area, and the strong linear element is reinforced by the expressway. Both the Taylor Homes (which are almost all black) and the expressway operate as a defining boundary separating white ethnic populations to the west and the black community to the east. TRU (Taylor Residents United) provides a structural support for this symbolic community. This local organization's stated goal is "to unite the residents of Taylor Homes into a community."

Few linear elements in the environment do function as the basis of a symbolic community. Other neighborhoods and communities lying along the lakefront, the rivers, or the expressways have not taken these linear elements as a unifying basis of identification. In fact, such elements were considered by the "old Chicago school" as the more obvious natural boundaries, separating areas rather than bringing them into a common social unity. Of course the mere physical presence of these linear elements is perhaps least significant. For, as Park says, "geographical barriers and physical distances are significant for sociology only when and where they define the conditions under which communication and social life are actually maintained."[27] The strip form of community shows that these "geographical barriers" may themselves be the basis for providing a common identity, fostering communication and social life, and creating a symbolic community.

SUMMARY

There is a widespread ability of residents to identify symbols of their local communities, and a high degree of persistence between the names and boundaries given by my respondents and those Burgess found half a century ago. This means that these names and boundaries have entered the local culture and, like symbolic culture generally, are widely communicated and serve to define the local reality of residents.

But there are dynamic forces which alter the symbolic definition of many communities; forces which lead sometimes to increased differentiation and sometimes to fusion. This is shown by the much greater variation in the size of the areas defined by my respondents compared with the more "uniform" areas defined by Burgess. These dynamic changes in local symbolic communities reflect the interplay of both social and ecological forces. For example, ecological changes in the spatial distribution of such social dimensions as class and race produced changes in the symbolic definition of local areas: fusion and differentiation in names, and expansion and contraction of boundaries. However, for some communities these local symbols may persist in spite of such ecological and social changes. Again, this attests to the strength of local cultures and to the independence of such symbolic definitions from ecological and social definitions. Finally, the strength of these local symbols of community may even alter, or at least retard, the ecological and social forces of change pressing upon them.

Three forms of community are the area, the focal point, and the strip. The area, the form most frequently found, is a two-dimensional bounded space of "commonality," however this may be defined by local residents. The focal point community often lacks clear boundaries but instead radiates out from some focal point significant in both form and function, such as a shopping center or a park. The strip, the form of community least frequently found, is defined by an extremely strong linear element in the environment and is usually reinforced by ecological and social factors.

We have focused on the "natural areas" defined by Burgess fifty years ago and have analyzed factors of persistence and change that have produced both fusion and differentiation in the symbolic mapping of Chicago's local communities. The focus has been upon these local areas as objects of analysis and, more specifically, as *"social* objects" perceived and defined by residents. Although at times these symbolic definitions reflect the persistence of local cultures, at other times they appear ambiguous, contradictory, and egocentric. But they are nonetheless the "definitions" of the local "situation" upon which many residents base their actions. How these symbolic definitions of local communities vary from individual to individual and from community to community will be explored in the following chapter.

Three

Symbolic Communities:
Cognitive Definition

VARIATIONS IN COGNITIVE CLARITY

So far we have looked at a general summary of elements of
the symbolic community as perceived by respondents in the
city of Chicago. But not all residents see their communities in
the same way, and not all communities give residents a similar
reality to confront. Therefore it is important to describe and
then to explain variations in the cognitive image.

To explore these variations we will focus on two elements
of the symbolic community, its name and its boundaries. Residents' ability to name and bound their local areas is considered an operational measurement of the clarity of their
cognitive image of the local area. Those knowing no name and
unable to give boundaries are considered to have a less clear
definition of their situation than those who both know a name
for their area (whether it is shared or not) and are able to
completely bound it (whether or not their boundaries coincide with their neighbors'). Furthermore, a person's identification *of* his community may be expected to tap his identification *with* the community.

It is expected that the ability to define a community will
vary in terms of a person's social position—that is, a person's
position in social space will influence his ability to locate
himself in physical space. Following a long tradition that
stems in part from Merton's dichotomy of "locals" and "cosmopolitans," we will look at two general sets of social statuses.[1]
First are those social statuses that both define and reflect a
person's position within his local area. Second are the social
statuses of more general significance; which not only influence
a person's local social position but also define him in terms
of a national or more general social structure. The local
social statuses would include length of residence and involvement in local community organizations, and more general

social statuses would include race and various measures of class such as income, education, or occupation. We will also look at how a person's "feelings" about his community—how he evaluates it and how attached to it he feels—may be related to the clarity of his cognitive image. Finally, we will look at how certain characteristics of the community itself may produce variations in the clarity of this symbolic definition.

LOCAL SOCIAL STATUSES

One of the more obvious and unambiguous local social statuses is the number of years lived in a community. Some may consider this a questionable "status," but the local distinctions between "newcomers" and "old-timers" are very real. It is a social typology that legitimates and qualifies a person's behavior within a community, signifying investment and commitments to a local area and its citizens. Studies have shown length of residence to be important for variables ranging from "alienation" to "zone" of residence.[2] It can be expected, if only because time increases familiarity, that the longer a person has lived in a community, the greater will be his awareness of symbols used to name and bound it.

Indeed, my data show that this is one of the strongest relationships found throughout the study (see tables 9 and 10). For example, 27.5 percent of those living in an area less than a year do not know its name, but this drops to 9.7 percent for those living in an area for more than twenty years. Also, only 40.0 percent of those living in an area less than a year are able to give four boundaries, but of those living in an area for more than twenty years, 79.2 percent know four boundaries. However it appears that this cognitive knowledge is acquired rather quickly, since the biggest jump occurs between those living in an area for less than a year and those there for a year or more. Also, the name of an area apparently is acquired more readily than the finer distinction of boundaries. A person's residential history also affects cognitive familiarity. Those living in an area all their lives are most likely, of course, to know a name and boundaries. And those who have previously lived in another area of Chicago are more familiar with names and boundaries than those who have lived only

TABLE 9

Percentage Not Knowing a Name for Local Community

Age:	Under 20	20–29	30–39	40–49	50–59	60–69	70+
	10.3	18.5	13.6	11.8	16.2	12.1	19.2
N = 755	(29)	(108)	(154)	(187)	(105)	(99)	(73)

Sex:		Male		Female	
		15.3		13.8	
N = 785		(307)		(478)	

Family Status:	No Children	Children Grown	Children Home
	11.9	22.7	13.5
N = 349	(59)	(75)	(215)

Class:	Upper	Middle	Working	Service
	2.8	8.9	20.2	16.0
N = 671	(36)	(282)	(297)	(56)

Race:		White		Black	
		11.4		22.1	
N = 770		(571)		(199)	

Length of Residence:	Less than 1 Year	1–4 Years	5–9 Years	10–19 Years	20+ Years
	27.5	16.9	17.0	13.6	9.7
N = 733	(40)	(130)	(135)	(191)	(237)

Residential History:	First Area of City Lived In	Previously Lived in Another Area of City	Lived All of Life in This Area
	27.3	15.5	5.8
N = 583	(66)	(431)	(86)

Location of Friends:	Inside Area	Outside Area	Both Inside and Outside
	14.1	14.9	12.3
N = 777	(177)	(396)	(204)

Organization Membership:	None	Church Only	One	Two or More
	18.0	15.4	7.1	0.0
N = 789	(494)	(65)	(183)	(47)

Organization Membership and Awareness:	None	Knows Only	Belongs	Both Belongs and Knows of Others
	25.6	9.5	6.5	5.1
N = 767	(273)	(283)	(93)	(118)

Location of Work:	Inside Area	Outside Area	Both Inside and Outside
	7.6	12.8	16.2
N = 521	(79)	(29)	(413)

TABLE 9—Continued

Location of Food Shopping:	Inside Area	Outside Area	Both inside and outside
N = 789	14.2 (578)	13.5 (155)	16.1 (56)

Location of Church Attended:		Inside Area	Outside Area
N = 724		12.9 (511)	15.5 (213)

Location of Recreation:	None	Inside Area	Outside Area	Both Inside and Outside
N = 785	14.7 (102)	14.1 (135)	15.3 (439)	9.2 (109)

Place of Attachment:	This Area Only	This Area and Another	Another Area	None
N = 748	12.5 (329)	13.3 (83)	16.4 (171)	17.6 (165)

Evaluation of Area:	Positive	Negative	Ambivalent	Noncommital	None
N = 779	11.5 (340)	18.2 (99)	14.6 (82)	12.3 (203)	27.3 (55)

Economic Status of Area:	High	Moderately High	Moderately Low	Low
N = 801	6.8 (132)	11.4 (228)	15.3 (288)	23.5 (153)

Family Status of Area:	High	Moderately High	Moderately Low	Low
N = 801	5.9 (85)	12.4 (346)	17.1 (293)	22.1 (77)

Racial-Ethnic Status of Area:	High Black– Low Foreign- Born	"Mixed," Mostly White	"Mixed," Some Foreign- Born	High Foreign- Born–Low Black
N = 800	22.1 (181)	3.4 (116)	13.1 (406)	18.6 (97)

in one area. In short, people moving to Chicago from out of town may not have known where they were moving as clearly as those already from Chicago, who knew what they were getting into.

Studies have repeatedly shown that local orientations of residents tend to be heightened by another set of variables

TABLE 10

Percentage Knowing Four Boundaries of Local Community

Age:	Under 20	20–29	30–39	40–49	50–59	60–69	70+
	71.4	68.5	69.9	68.6	70.5	75.8	52.8
N=750	(28)	(108)	(153)	(185)	(105)	(99)	(72)

Sex:		Male		Female	
		73.8		65.3	
N=780		(305)		(475)	

Family Status:	No Children	Children Grown	Children Home
	69.5	62.7	62.7
N=347	(59)	(75)	(213)

Class:	Upper	Middle	Working	Service
	86.1	76.9	64.6	60.0
N=666	(36)	(281)	(294)	(55)

Race:		White		Black	
		75.8		49.7	
N=766		(567)		(199)	

Length of Residence:	Less than 1 Year	1-4 Years	5-9 Years	10-19 Years	20+ Years
		40.0	59.7	70.1	64.0	79.2
N=728		(40)	(129)	(134)	(189)	(236)

Residential History:	First Area of City Lived in	Previously Lived in Another Area of City	Lived All Life in This Area
	60.6	65.9	82.6
N=580	(66)	(428)	(86)

Location of Friends:	Inside Area	Outside Area	Both Inside and Outside
	62.7	69.6	72.5
N=772	(177)	(391)	(204)

Organization Membership and Awareness:	None	Knows Only	Belongs	Both Belongs and Knows of Others
	50.6	76.1	77.4	83.1
N=762	(271)	(280)	(93)	(118)

Location of Work:	Inside Area	Outside Area	Both In and Out
	69.6	73.9	35.2
N=517	(79)	(409)	(29)

Location of Food Shopping:	Inside Area	Outside Area	Both Inside and Outside
	68.2	73.2	69.0
N=784	(573)	(56)	(155)

TABLE 10—Continued

Location of Church Attendance:	Inside Area	Outside Area
	71.8	65.1
N = 719	(507)	(212)

Location of Recreation:	None	Inside Area	Outside Area	Both Inside and Outside
	56.4	72.4	71.3	67.0
N = 780	(101)	(134)	(436)	(109)

Place of Attachment:	This Area Only	This Area and Another	Another Area	None
	75.0	78.0	63.9	58.5
N = 743	(328)	(82)	(169)	(164)

Evaluation of Area:	Positive	Negative	Ambivalent	Non-commital	None
	71.6	52.6	67.9	72.3	61.8
N = 744	(339)	(97)	(81)	(202)	(55)

Economic Status of Area:	High	Moderately High	Moderately Low	Low
	79.5	76.8	64.1	55.3
N = 796	(132)	(228)	(284)	(152)

Family Status of Area:	High	Moderately High	Moderately Low	Low
	81.2	69.3	64.7	66.2
N = 796	(85)	(345)	(289)	(77)

Racial-Ethnic Status of Area:	High Black– Low Foreign-Born	"Mixed," Mostly White	"Mixed," Some Foreign-Born	Low Black– High Foreign-Born
	48.6	85.3	69.6	82.8
N = 795	(181)	(116)	(405)	(93)

centering on the life cycle and the family. Local neighborhoods, as William H. Whyte has suggested, are the province
of children.[3] Even Charles Horton Cooley's early discussion
of "primary groups" emphasized the significance of the neighborhood peer group in the socialization process.[4] Children,
and people having children, are therefore more likely to be
drawn into the social and symbolic life of the local community. My data show only a slight relationship between age
and the ability to define the symbols of the local area. Respondents in their teens were the most likely to know a name for

their area and the second most likely to know all four boundaries. On the other hand, those in their twenties, who are
likely to be mobile and single, are most likely not to know
a name for the area and are second least likely to know all
four boundaries.

There is little relationship between sex and cognitive clarity, however, in contrast to the expectation that females,
being more rooted in the local area through children and the
home, would have a clearer symbolic definition of the local
area than would males. In fact, males are slightly more likely
to know four boundaries for their area (74.0 percent vs. 65.0
percent). Similarly, having children has little effect on an
individual's symbolic definition of the area. There is even a
slight tendency for those without children to have a clearer
cognitive image than those having children (70 percent know
four boundaries versus 63 percent).

In contrast to these slight or negative relationships, the
family status of the area does show a strong positive relationship to cognitive clarity. People from higher family status
areas (as defined by the factor scores of communities on this
dimension) have a clearer cognitive image of their area (only
5.9 percent do not know a name, and 81.2 percent know four
boundaries) compared with those from low family status areas
(22.1 percent do not know a name and only 66.2 percent know
four boundaries). This finding, in contrast to the individual
correlates, indicates that the presence of children and family-
centered life may perpetuate the symbolic image of the community in a local culture to all individuals living there independent of their own family status.

From previous studies, one would expect that participating
in local organizations and having friends in the local area
would heighten orientation to the local area and increase
familiarity with the symbols defining the community.[5] My
findings clearly show that involvement in local organizations
heightens the clarity of the image of the local area. For example, of those not belonging to any organization, 18 percent
do not know a name for the area, but of those in two or
more local organizations none do not know a name. Only
64.8 percent of those not belonging to any organization know
all four boundaries, compared with 91.5 percent of those

belonging to two or more organizations. Moreover, merely knowing of such organizations, even without belonging to them, markedly increases the probability of knowing a name and boundaries for the local area. This implies that local community organizations have an effect beyond their membership in perpetuating and disseminating the defining symbols and local culture of an area.

Whether one's friends live mostly within or outside one's local area does not produce the expected relationship. Those with friends both inside and outside the local area are slightly more likely to know a name and boundaries than those with friends solely inside. This suggests that spatial boundaries may be more evident to those who cross these boundaries in their social interaction and activities. Membership in social structures (here, friendship patterns) that are both internal and external to the local area may result in a heightened awareness of the limits of the community, both socially and spatially. The need for "external" inputs and comparative referents to heighten local awareness and cognition was noted by Gans in his study of Boston's West End: he observed, "there was relatively little interest in the West End as a physical or social unit. . . . Indeed, only when the outside world discovered the West End and made plans to tear it down did its inhabitants begin to talk about the West End as a neighborhood, although of course, they never used this term."[6] This might also explain why males, who are likely to work outside the local area, were slightly more likely to know boundaries for their local area than were females (73.8 percent vs. 65.3 percent), and also why individuals without children were slightly more likely to know local boundaries than were those with children (70 percent vs. 63 percent).

These findings lead us to the conclusion that length of residence and participation in local social structures do affect awareness of the symbols of a name and boundaries used to define local areas. Furthermore, local organizations appear to perpetuate and communicate these symbols of local culture even to nonmembers. An individual's family and life-cycle statuses do not appear to affect awareness of these local symbols. However *areas* including more families apparently are more likely to maintain a local culture that perpetuates such symbols, regardless of individual family statuses. In addition, there is some evidence that participating in social structures that transcend the confines of the local community produces a heightened awareness of the social and spatial limits of the community and the symbols used to define it.

GENERAL SOCIAL STATUSES

The literature dealing with the impact of class and race upon people's orientations to their local communities presents an ambiguous, if not contradictory, picture. On the one hand, some studies of life in lower-class and black communities depict the provincial, limited horizons of residents, with an emphasis upon dense personal networks, often including kin.[7] In a similar vein, some studies of middle- and higher-class communities (mostly suburbs) stress the relative social and geographical mobility of their residents.[8] With wider horizons and an increased desire to participate in more "cosmopolitan" social systems, they have less investment and involvement in the local area. These studies agree that lower-class individuals and blacks have a clearer cognitive definition of their local communities than higher-class individuals and whites. Similarly, the development of black pride and a heightened positive consciousness of "the black community" might be expected to increase black residents' symbolic awareness of names and boundaries in the local areas.

On the other hand, there are studies which stress the social isolation and alienation of residents in poorer and black communities compared with those from wealthier and white areas. The greater involvement of whites and higher-class people in organizations, compared with that of blacks and those from the lower class, would result in increased interaction at the local level and a greater awareness of the symbols used to define the local community. In addition, my findings suggested that individuals who move beyond the local area both spatially and socially are more likely, through juxtaposition, to be able to name and bound their local areas than are those whose daily life space is disproportionately rooted in the local area. In short, because of their greater involvement beyond the local area, those who are higher-class or white should have a clearer cognitive image of their communities than those who are lower-class or black.

With respect to both class and race, my findings support the second of these general propositions. Whites are clearly more likely than blacks to know a name for an area and to give four boundaries. Similarly, individuals from higher occupational categories (occupation being measured for head of household) are more likely to do so.

These results are also borne out when one looks not at individual racial and class characteristics but at the socioeconomic and racial characteristics of the areas. Residents of higher socioeconomic status and white areas are more likely to know a name and boundaries than residents of lower socioeconomic status and black areas. It seems clear that the limited horizons and local orientation of blacks and lower-class individuals do not result in greater cognitive clarity about their local areas.

However there are some additional findings which indicate a need for caution in interpreting these results, especially when one compares white and black respondents. Comparing the *types* of communities defined by black and white respondents suggests a different interpretation. In the lower-class, and especially the black, communities, the local area is defined as a much smaller social and spatial organization—the street, the block, or the housing project—whereas the social organization and symbolic definition in white and higher-class areas pertain to a larger, well-defined community area. For example, 14.6 percent of blacks gave a "street name" as the name of their area, and another 9.5 percent gave the name of their housing project. Only 1.7 percent of white respondents gave these. The data also show that blacks are slightly more likely to define smaller areas even when they do give all four boundaries. For example, 13 percent of whites defined an area smaller than sixteen square blocks, while 33 percent of blacks did so. This suggests that in black communities the level of community is likely to be a social block rather than a larger community area. If we assume that in such areas primary relationships and personal knowledge define individuals in terms of relatively tight social circles, then there it is less significant to define oneself and one's community in terms of a unique named area with distinct boundaries.

COGNITIVE CLARITY AND FUNCTIONAL ACTIVITY

I have suggested previously that there is an increasing independence of the symbolic definition of community from its functional bases. As different functions display a variety of scales, a given symbolic definition of community is not constrained to match a set of coinciding functional areas. From this perspective one might expect the symbolic elements of community to be little related to functional utilization of the local community.

On the other hand, my findings on social integration suggest that as people go about the routine activities of the daily life-space, these activities should lead to an increased awareness and clearer cognitive definition of their local areas. The findings with respect to length of residence suggest that this might be so for the longer one lives in a community the greater is one's familiarity with symbols used to define the community.

To explore these questions I asked people about the location of four functional activities—work, shopping, worship, and recreation—and asked whether they performed them mostly inside or outside the community. Although there are slight variations, in general the findings show that whether a person works, shops, worships, or finds recreation inside or outside the local community has no consistent relationship to his ability to name the area and define its boundaries. In short, it appears that knowing the symbols used to define the community is not related to functional utilization of the community.[9]

COMMUNITY SIZE

When we compared the maps made by Burgess with my own symbolic communities we noticed that my communities showed a much greater variation in size than his. At that point I talked about the forces of differentiation and fusion and the increasing independence of symbolic definitions from functional utilization. To understand these forces more fully we will now look at some of the meanings different-sized areas have for their residents, and at some of the reasons why one person defines a small social block as "his" community while his next-door neighbor may define a large "region" covering as much as a quarter of the city as "his" community.[10]

For residents who gave completely encapsulated boundaries, I have computed the number of square blocks contained in their areas. These were then broken into four groups: 16 square blocks or less, from 17 to 64 square blocks, from 65 to 256, and 257 square blocks or greater. The number of respondents falling into each group was 92, 191, 208, and 64, for a total of 555 (see table 11).

Two points should be noted. First, I did not include people who were unable to give complete boundaries. Many of these gave a very small symbolic definition of their community, such as their street, their block, or their housing project. These might have been included in the group defining the smallest areas, but the size of their areas simply could not be clearly determined. Second, "size" is used here to refer to spatial area, which surely does not mean equivalent population since there is a wide range of density in Chicago's community areas. I did not have the resources to calculate or estimate the population of each of the 554 communities the respondents delimited, and so spatial area rather than population is the measure used for community size.

For the most part the findings with respect to size are as expected and further strengthen some of the propositions suggested in the previous sections. In comparing my findings with the Burgess research on "natural areas" we should note that the smaller the area defined, the less likely people are to have a name for it. And when a name is given, the smaller the area, the less likely it is that the name is the one used by Burgess. This supports the idea that Burgess was attempting to establish equivalent community areas throughout the city and that this level of identification does not conform to the variety of levels defined by many of today's residents. It also suggests that residents defining smaller areas are not as dependent upon "a name" as a distinguishing symbol as are those defining larger areas. Perhaps residents operating at this smaller level of "the social block" rely much more on personal

TABLE 11

Percentage of Responses to Selected Variables, by Size of Area Defind

Response	Size of Area (in square blocks)			
	>17 (N=92)	17–64 (N=191)	65–256 (N=208)	>256 (N=64)
Named area by:				
Burgess name	25.0	40.3	58.2	62.5
Other name	40.2	45.5	35.6	29.7
No name	19.6	10.5	4.8	4.7
Performed inside the area:				
Work	4.4	8.3	13.0	15.6
Shopping	50.5	70.5	81.2	78.1
Worship	50.5	64.4	75.0	67.2
Recreation	14.3	16.1	20.7	17.2
Gave one or more central locations	68.5	79.8	86.3	80.9
Named as a central location:				
Shopping	35.9	46.3	58.2	54.7
Community center building	14.1	2.7	5.3	7.8
Park or school	13.1	26.9	20.2	17.2
Lived in area where family status was:				
High	50.0	58.4	58.6	51.5
Low	50.0	41.6	41.4	48.5
Had lived in area:				
0–9 years	40.0	36.4	31.7	30.2
10–19 years	30.0	22.1	22.4	15.9
20+ years	23.3	30.5	39.5	46.0
Belonged to one or more local organizations	33.0	29.9	35.1	39.1
Knew of and/or belonged to one or more local organization	67.1	64.4	71.6	82.8
Race was:				
Black	36.3	12.5	14.9	17.2
White	60.4	82.8	82.7	81.2

Table 11—Continued

Individual class status was:				
High	39.6	42.7	52.9	37.5
Low	44.0	47.4	33.2	46.0
Lived in area where economic status was:				
High	40.2	54.7	54.3	42.2
Low	59.8	45.3	45.7	57.8

knowledge and face-to-face contact. In any case, if the city were so finely and distinctly differentiated at this level it might produce a "cognitive overload," too fine and too distinct a differentiation to be generally known, remembered, and widely used throughout the city.[11] Therefore at this level one is likely to get no name, simply a street identification or an extremely parochial nickname.

Furthermore, in agreement with the Burgess distinction between residentially homogeneous "neighborhoods" and functionally integrated "communities," we find that the smaller the area defined the less likely people are to define a central location. Also, as one might expect, the smaller the area defined, the more likely it is that the functional activities of work, shopping, worship, and recreation will be performed outside the local area.

When we look at the "types" of central locations defined by residents, we find variations by size of area that support the proposition that the different scales of different functions lead residents to define a multiplicity of symbolic communities. For example, shopping is the most frequently mentioned central location for areas of all sizes, but the smaller the area defined, the less likely it is that shopping will be mentioned as a central location.

Community centers or single buildings are most likely to be mentioned as focal points by people who define the smallest areas, and parks and schools are more likely to be mentioned by people who define an intermediate-sized community. This shows not that symbolic communities are completely independent from function, but rather that they may exist at a number of different levels. These different levels correspond to the different scales of different functions. Therefore, depending upon the salience of different functions in people's life-spaces, they may hold different-sized cognitive maps and give different symbolic definitions of their communities.

This is also supported by the findings relating size of area to family and life-cycle characteristics of residents. Somewhat contrary to expectations, those without children were likely to define smaller areas than those with children. However, when we look at family status characteristics of the areas, those from low family status communities are more likely to define the extreme sizes (either smallest or largest) and those from high family status areas are most likely to define an intermediate-sized community. These two findings taken jointly suggest that those without children know and define an area very close to home, or a large-scale area encompassing more of the totality of their daily life-space. In contrast, having children or living in areas where families abound tends to pull people out of the home into the surrounding area, but restricts them to a level which encompasses the functions associated with the family and child-rearing. And perhaps within the high family status communities, it is the strong persistent local culture maintained in local institutions like school and church that leads to a symbolic definition of community oriented to this immediate level of families and children.

Increasing length of residence also seems to pull people out of a narrowly circumscribed home environment. The longer the length of residence, the larger the area defined. And those belonging to or at least knowing about local organizations are slightly more likely to define a larger area. Again, increased social involvement within the community apparently widens one's horizons beyond one's immediate social and spatial setting. Furthermore, it is likely that these organizations perpetuate a fairly distinct set of community boundaries that are likely to reflect a broader base and a larger area.

We previously noted that blacks generally define smaller community areas than do whites. And we see that as the size of the area increases the proportion of higher-class individuals defining that size of area also increases (except for the largest areas). These findings tend to support the idea of more limited spatial horizons and a stronger local orientation on the part of blacks and lower-class individuals. When we look at socioeconomic characteristics of areas, however, we find a phenomenon similar to that found for family status. A majority of residents defining the smallest and the largest areas come from low economic status communities, but a majority of those defining the intermediate-sized areas come from communities of high economic status. This would also explain the anomaly that the proportion of higher-class individuals who define the largest areas decreases compared with other sized areas, while the proportion of lower-class individuals defining this size increases. The metaphor of a tumbleweed comes to mind. Where roots at the point of residence are narrow and shallow, one is likely to be blown over a greater expanse of territory. The cactus, however, spreads its roots wider and deeper and is not moved from its immediate locale by buffeting winds.

Besides cognition, there are two other orientations toward local communities that will be explored more fully in the next chapter. These are attachment and evaluation or, more generally, "sentiments" toward the local community. These two orientations are again taken from Parsons's "theory of social action." For meaningful social action to occur, besides "knowing" or defining a situation a person must also be able to evaluate the situation and its components as either "good" or "bad" for the realization of his goals. Finally, he must cathect with the situation, like or dislike it, and generally react emotionally to it.

I tapped these two orientations by asking respondents two open-ended questions about their "feelings" and "attachments" to their local areas. Generally these three orientations of cognition, evaluation, and attachment are seen either as somewhat independent orientations or simply as positively related to one another. The data show that in fact the more positive the evaluation and the greater the attachment to the local community, the greater is the cognitive clarity of the symbolic definition. That is, the more likely people were to evaluate their community as a good place, and the more likely they were to say they felt attachment to it, the more likely they were to know its name and boundaries. I am not arguing for any causal direction with these findings; I am merely pointing out the positive direction of the relationship.

When we look at the relationships between size of area and evaluation and attachment, the picture becomes more complex. First, there is no variation by size of area in evaluating the area simply as a good or a bad place to live. However, we do find that the larger the area, the greater the likelihood of people's expressing ambivalent evaluations—that is, mentioning both good and bad aspects of the community. It seems that people defining a larger area are including a greater diversity and heterogeneity, some of which they like, some of which they don't. This is also supported by the relation between residents' evaluations of *people* in their area and size of area. The larger the area, the more ambivalent the evaluation of its people. In addition, we see that those defining the smallest area are most likely to have an unqualified positive evaluation of the people. This has implications for a number of previous findings. It strengthens the conclusion that smaller areas are more dependent upon a relatively close circle of primary relations than are larger areas. And it implies that by cognitively defining a smaller community area, a person is able to exclude people and elements he does not like.

I feel, therefore, that I must qualify Greer's contention that neighborhoods operate as "inclusive" membership groups in contrast to nonterritorial associations, which are "exclusive" membership groups.[12] Instead I suggest that the definition of neighborhood boundaries may also serve this "exclusive" function. Perhaps nowhere is this so significant as in whites' exclusion of blacks from the cognitive definition of their area. As blacks move into a previously white area, the cognitive boundary of the community is likely to shift for whites so as to exclude blacks from "their" community. This shifting cognitive definition is probably less likely to take place when clear and unambiguous boundaries define the community, boundaries that have perhaps been a part of the local culture for generations. Therefore, as we observed in the last chapter, throughout the city we find certain black-white boundaries approaching the character of international boundaries; and if the boundaries are not cognitively redefined, movement across the boundary becomes "invasion."

Those who define the smallest areas are most likely to say their community is either all black or all white. In contrast, those who define a larger symbolic community are more likely to say their area is racially mixed. In addition, we found that more than 80 percent of white respondents who said blacks lived "near" their areas knew all four boundaries, compared with only 65 percent of whites who mentioned "no problems" in their communities. In short, the implicit threat of "invasion" tends to heighten the awareness of symbolic boundaries.

Answers to the question about attachment were coded by whether respondents felt *no attachment* to any area of Chicago, or attachment only to their *own area*, only to *another area*, or possibly to *both* their area and others. Relating attachment to community size, we find, somewhat surprisingly, a slight relationship indicating that the smaller the area defined, the smaller the proportion of residents expressing attachment only to their own area. However, this does not mean that people defining a small area necessarily feel less attachment to it, for we also see that those who define the smallest areas are most likely to express attachment to *both* their area and some other in the city. Again, this finding fits with those noted above for family status and class. There we found that those having an extreme parochial orientation were also most likely to have an extreme cosmopolitan orientation. People who define an extremely small area as "their" community are more likely to have a diversity of attachments which include other areas throughout the city as well as their own limited one. Defining an extremely small local community therefore should not be prematurely defined as a local or extremely parochial orientation. In fact, it may be the definition held by precisely those who are least parochial and most "cosmopolitan" in their travels, interests, interaction, and general orientation.[13]

LEVELS OF COMMUNITY

Both this study and the studies of Burgess and his students found that residents define a variety of sizes of local communities. For any given piece of territory within the city there are likely to be a number of communities which include it as part of their domain. Since these different communities are arranged in a hierarchical or concentric fashion, I will refer to this phenomenon as "levels of community." The highest level includes large "regions" within the city, such as "the Roseland area" and "the Englewood area," and also the large compass sectors of "the South Side," "the West Side," and "the Northwest Side." The next level is approximately the size of the "community area" as initially delimited by Burgess. Within these communities one finds smaller residential units—"neighborhoods"—and within these are smaller distinguishable "social blocks."

There are a complex series of functions and types of social organization characteristic of each of the levels of community. The variety of scales different functions exhibit, and the varying types of social organization, are closely related to the perception of different "levels of symbolic community." The social block appears to have the most primary interaction but the least spatial distinctiveness. There are not likely to be any institutions so finely differentiated as to serve the collective needs of such a small unit. Furthermore, such a fine differentiation results in so many social blocks that they would cause a "cognitive overload" if they were used for symbolic identifications throughout the city.

The other extreme of symbolic communities, "the region," has the clearest spatial distinctiveness, for it is likely to be widely known and easily communicated as a symbolic identification to all residents of the city. However, such a level is so broad and includes such heterogeneity that it cannot convey social distinctions with which residents may symbolically identify. It is the least likely to involve primary relationships among its members, and except through federation of smaller units is unlikely to be a basis of collective social action. There are institutions which operate at this broad level, such as major outlying shopping centers and general regions of employment. But though they can define residents in physical space and provide a general social classification, such areas are too broad to capture finer social distinctions and too inclusive to provide any but the most minimal local identifications, sentiments, and attachments.

At the levels of the neighborhood and community *both* primary interaction and spatial distinctiveness are maximized,

making these the "symbolic communities" most often identified and communicated by local residents. In addition, a variety of institutions are specifically geared to operating at these
levels and scales: churches, schools, minor retail stores, and
even political parties. Neighborhoods are distinguished from
communities in that they are less related to functional utilization and depend more upon the simple fact of sharing a
commonly defined residential area. The community level also
provides such an identification, but it is likely to include a
local shopping center, churches, and other institutions and
to exhibit greater heterogeneity among residents than do
neighborhoods.

In conclusion, several general observations should be made
about these "levels of symbolic communities." First, some of
these communities and neighborhoods may be seen to divide
the city in a horizontal two-dimensional or "segmented" manner. In this sense they serve an "exclusive" function, differentiating or dividing the territory into "my area" and "your
area." However, given that there are levels of community, a
third or vertical dimension serves an inclusive or fusion function by combining "my area" and "your area" into "our
area." Both the horizontal differentiation and the vertical
fusion are significant in establishing a shifting though meaningful symbolic social and spatial order for residents throughout the city.

Second, we should note that the level of community a
person defines is likely to vary with his location in the social
structure of both the local area and the city. An individual
is likely to define a level of symbolic identification consonant
with his functional, psychic, and social needs. This also means
that he is likely to alter his symbolic level of identification—
his "reference" community—as he changes status.[14] Depending
upon which status is salient and what the role demands of
the status are, a person may define different levels of community as he comes to occupy different statuses throughout his
lifetime, and even as he changes statuses in the day-to-day
routine of satisfying his "life-needs."

SUMMARY

This chapter has explored variations in residents' cognitive
definitions of the symbols of their local communities. Not

only do different communities confront their residents with different realities, thereby producing such variation, but individuals may confront the same community from different perspectives and different social positions. The needs and demands of the various roles associated with different statuses produce systematic variation in the symbolic definition residents give to their local areas. For example, whites and higher-class individuals are more likely to know the symbols (names and boundaries) for their local areas than are blacks and lower-class individuals. However, a higher proportion of blacks than whites define a smaller-scale community at the level of the immediate social block, a level which less often has a distinctive name and boundaries. Furthermore, lower-class individuals who did define boundaries for their communities were more likely to define very small or very large areas, whereas higher-class individuals defined intermediate-sized areas. Lower class life perhaps may produce an extremely parochial orientation immediately surrounding the home (in partial support of the "limited horizons" thesis of the "culture of poverty"). However, it might also produce a very large and vague cognitive definition of community covering large regions within the city.

There is a similar curvilinear relationship between size of area and family status characteristics. For example, people without children or from areas of low family status defined the extremely small or extremely large areas, whereas those with children or from high family status areas tended to define an intermediate size of community. In general, those with statuses implying more social integration in the community (membership in local organizations, greater length of residence) were more likely to know the symbols of their communities. Integration into the local social structure tends to pull one out of the narrow confines of the immediate social block surrounding the home, where some less well integrated residents remain, but such local social integration tends to constrain one to a level of community less extensive than that defined by others who are less well integrated into the local social structure.

There is also some evidence that individuals whose statuses would be expected to demand greater movement outside the confines of the local community (males versus females, and

those in their twenties versus other ages) are more aware of
the symbols used to define the local area. This suggests that
interaction with others outside the community may heighten
the social and spatial limits of community "identity" for local
residents.[15]

Finally, these variations in symbolic communities suggest
a reconception of local urban communities involving "levels
of community" or "community hierarchies." Such levels run
from the smallest "social blocks" to larger homogeneous residential "neighborhoods," to still larger, more functionally
integrated "communities," and finally to broad extensive "regions" covering wide sections of the city. Furthermore, there
is evidence that this cognitive differentiation and fusion of
different levels of symbolic communities is intimately linked
to various levels or "scales" of social and ecological differentiation found within the city. The level of community identified is likely to vary from resident to resident and for the
same resident over time depending upon the particular statuses or social positions he occupies. This reconception of
community suggests varying commitment or "limited liability" on the part of local residents, both because of the varying
needs and demands of various statuses and because of the
differential ability of different levels of community to satisfy
them.

Having looked in this chapter at symbolic identification *of*
communities, we will turn next to symbolic identification *with*
communities as we explore the *sentiments* of community expressed by local residents.

Four

Symbolic Communities: Sentiment

INTRODUCTION

In the last chapter we explored variations in residents' cognitive definitions of their local communities. This chapter will explore a second general dimension of orientation to local communities—the expression of sentiment.

Defining a situation, as elaborated in Talcott Parsons's "theory of social action," involves more than merely knowing the situation in a cognitive way.[1] For meaningful action to occur a person must be able to *evaluate* the situation and its elements as "good or bad," "positive or negative" for the realization of his goals. Now communities are not merely situations *within* which social action occurs, for symbolic communities especially are collectivities and social entities and are themselves the objects of such evaluations. For example, if a person who is about to move is very concerned about upward social mobility for himself and his children, his "evaluation" of different communities as aiding or hindering this may be critical in his decision about where to locate.

In addition to "knowing" and "evaluating" a situation and its elements, it is also necessary, according to Parsons, to cathect or be emotionally involved with the situation and its elements. Only out of such "emotion" comes motion or, in more sociological terms, "action." Again, symbolic communities are socially defined entities or objects which individuals will either "like" or "dislike" and to which they will be differentially attached.

To be sure, we expect that evaluation and attachment to the local area will be related to and dependent upon evaluations of and attachments to people, institutions, and various other elements of the local community, and we will study and examine these relationships in this chapter. However, I am emphasizing that the communities themselves are the objects

117

of such sentiments. Just as they are cognitively defined by residents as collective representations of some common whole, so too do these symbolic communities call forth different evaluations and different degrees of attachment.

This theoretical perspective is not new, though a new emphasis is the distinction between the two local sentiments of evaluation and attachment.[2] Much of the traditional theoretical discussion of community does stress the moral sentiment of community, the "we feeling" of identification with and attachment to the community as a social collectivity. These sentiments were at the root of Tönnies's and Durkheim's polar types of societies, and it was these sentiments which Weber saw falling before the efficient juggernaut of rational society.[3] The express purpose of this chapter is to assess the variations in this sentiment toward local urban communities, and in correlates of it. The general proposition being considered is that individuals who occupy social statuses which are more oriented to the social structure of the local community will have a greater proportion of their life-space involved in the local context, and that this in turn will produce greater attachment to and more positive evaluation of the local community.

The dependent variables for this section are taken from two items of the interview instrument. The first asked, "When you think of this area, what feelings come to mind?" Responses to this item were coded in several ways, but of interest here is the *evaluative* dimension (good versus bad, positive versus negative), and the categories were:

Positive—if the respondent mentioned only positive aspects of the local community (42.6 percent)

Negative—if the respondent mentioned only negative aspects of the local community (12.4 percent)

Ambivalent—if the respondent mentioned both positive and negative aspects of the local community (10.3 percent)

Noncommital—if the respondent replied but mentioned neither positive nor negative aspects of the area (25.5 percent)

"None"—if the respondent said that no feelings came to mind or he never thought about it (6.8 percent)

(The remaining 2.4 percent gave noncodable responses.)

The second item used to measure attachment to the local community asked, "What areas of Chicago do you personally feel any attachment to?" Responses to this item were coded as follows:

Here—if respondent said only his local area (41.4 percent)
Here and other—if the respondent mentioned his own area plus one or more others in the city (10.4 percent)
Other area in city—if respondent mentioned another area in the city and not his area of residence (21.3 percent)
None—if a respondent said he felt no attachment to any area (20.6 percent)
Other—if a respondent mentioned the city as a whole, some area out of the city or gave no answer (6.3 percent)

Specific derivative hypotheses will be advanced later in this chapter. First we will explore variations in evaluation and attachment by general social statuses such as race and class and will also relate them to differences in the characteristics of the communities—namely, their economic, family, and racial-ethnic status. We will then relate sentiment to local social statuses such as length of residence and participation in local voluntary associations. Finally, there will be a brief analysis of the relationship between the cognitive definition of the symbolic community and expressions of sentiment toward it.

GENERAL SOCIAL STATUSES
AND LOCAL SENTIMENT

As was suggested above, certain statuses which are normatively defined throughout the society involve varying values and perspectives which may be expected to produce different orientations toward one's community of residence. The norms, rights, and duties composing a status may prescribe varying degrees of social and psychological involvement in the local area. One of these social-psychological investments involves attachment and evaluation of the local community.

CLASS AND RACE

Class, as measured here by occupation, may be hypothesized to be related to local sentiments in two opposite ways. One might be called the "mass society" theory of the local commu-

nity and the other the achievement of a "valued community."
The former suggests an inverse relationship between class and
local sentiment and the latter a positive relationship.

On two accounts one might expect there to be more positive expressions of sentiment toward the local community by
lower-class individuals and less by those in the upper class.
First, studies such as Gans's *The Urban Villagers* suggest that
community orientation is stronger for lower-class slum communities in urban areas; but the hypothesis is only implicit,
for there is no direct comparison between upper- and lower-
class communities. This chapter explicitly explores variations
in local attachment and evaluations between different classes
and in different economic status areas. The implicit comparison in Gans's study is also supported by writers espousing
"mass society" theories about transformations in orientation
toward local communities. Stein's *The Eclipse of Community*,
Warner's study *Yankee City*, and studies by Schulze and by
Fried and Gleicher all point to the withdrawal of middle- and
upper-class individuals from social and psychological involvement in their local communities.[4] They would expect this to
be reflected in a less positive evaluation of an area and fewer
expressions of attachment to the local community by upper-
class people than by lower-class.

The theory of the achievement of a "valued community"
posits a positive relationship between social and spatial distance. It considers, along with individual status characteristics,
the various status characteristics of the communities within
which the classes are segregated. It is expected that lower-
class individuals will reside in areas having fewer of the
amenities which would lead to a positive evaluation of the
local area, and that such areas will therefore be less likely to
be the objects of strong personal attachment.[5]

In general the findings support the second hypothesis, for
they show a positive relationship between social class and
positive expressions of sentiment toward the local community.
This is especially true with respect to evaluation of the area.
Specifically, almost fifty percent of those in the highest occupational category volunteered an unqualified positive evaluation of their local area, but less than a third of those in the
lowest occupational category did so. Furthermore, residents

TABLE 12
Percentage Evaluating Local Area Positively, by Class, Race,
and Economic and Racial-Ethnic Status of the Area

Class:	Upper	Middle	Working	Service
	47.2	44.0	42.1	30.4
N = 671	(36)	(282)	(297)	(56)
Race:		White		Black
		47.5		28.8
N = 768		(570)		(198)
Economic Status of Area:	High	Moderately High	Moderately Low	Low
	43.9	50.2	40.9	33.6
N = 797	(132)	(227)	(286)	(152)
Racial-Ethnic Status of Area:	High Black	Mixed	Mixed	High Foreign-Born
	27.9	46.6	46.5	49.5
N = 796	(179)	(116)	(404)	(97)

TABLE 13
Percentage Expressing Attachment to Only the Local Area, by
Class, Race, and Economic and Racial-Ethnic Status of the
Area

Class:	Upper	Middle	Working	Service
	33.3	44.9	40.1	35.7
N = 672	(36)	(283)	(297)	(56)
Race:		White		Black
		43.6		35.7
N = 770		(571)		(199)
Economic Status of Area:	High	Moderately High	Moderately Low	Low
	40.9	39.5	43.2	40.8
N = 797	(132)	(226)	(287)	(152)
Racial-Ethnic Status of Area:	High Black	Mixed	Mixed	High Foreign-Born
	33.9	41.4	44.7	41.2
N = 798	(180)	(116)	(405)	(97)

of high economic status areas were more likely to evaluate
their areas positively than were people from low economic
status areas.

There is some evidence that upper-class individuals lose attachment to local communities. For example, professionals and managers are the group with the smallest proportion expressing attachment only to the local area (33 percent): even in the lowest occupational group a slightly larger percentage express attachment to their local area (36 percent). For the remaining occupational categories, the lower the class the lower the proportion expressing local attachment. However, the highest occupational category also has an inordinately large proportion expressing attachment to *both* their local area *and* another within the city (31 percent compared with approximately 10 percent for the other occupational categories). This suggests that the upper-class individuals have not lost their attachment to the local community but that it has become more diffuse, and that they are also attached to other areas of the city.[6]

There is no relationship between the economic status of the area and the proportion expressing attachment to the local community. This, in conjunction with the findings about individual class, suggests that *evaluation* of the local area is more dependent upon both individual and community class status than is attachment to the area, and it adds additional support to the "valued community" proposition.

From the valued community hypothesis one would expect that blacks would show much less positive sentiment toward their local communities than would whites. Not only are the amenities of local urban communities inequitably distributed through ecological segregation of classes, but the further restrictions of race suggest that even fewer amenities are available to blacks than to whites in the nation's urban areas, since blacks operate in a much more restricted housing market. Therefore, one would expect that a much smaller proportion of blacks would express positive attachment to the area and have a positive evaluation of it.

The findings support this hypothesis, and again the relationship is stronger for evaluation of the area than it is for attachment (see tables 14–17). Only slightly more than one-fourth of the blacks gave a positive evaluation of their areas, but almost one-half of the whites did, and 44 percent of the whites expressed attachment to the local community compared with 36 percent of the blacks. Similarly, residents of high black status areas are less likely to express a positive evaluation of the community (28 percent) than are those from other areas (approximately 47 percent). Again the difference is not quite as great in attachment to the local areas, for 34 percent of those from high black areas expressed attachment, and approximately 42 percent of those from other areas did so.

When one controls for length of residence the relationship between *evaluation* and race persists, with a smaller proportion of blacks than whites expressing a positive evaluation of the area for every length of residence category. But the relationship between *attachment* and race disappears when one controls for length of residence.

TABLE 14

Percentage Evaluating Local Area Positively, by Length of Residence and Race

| Race | Length of Residence | | | | |
	Less than 1 Year	1–4 Years	5–9 Years	10–19 Years	20+ Years
White	53.3	45.2	48.1	50.8	47.8
N=515	(15)	(84)	(79)	(128)	(209)
Black	32.0	26.8	28.3	35.7	18.2
N=190	(25)	(41)	(46)	(56)	(22)

TABLE 15

Percentage Expressing Attachment to Only the Local Area, by Length of Residence and by Race

| Race | Length of Residence | | | | |
	Less than 1 Year	1–4 Years	5–9 Years	10–19 Years	20+ Years
White	13.3	25.0	36.7	41.4	60.8
N=515	(15)	(84)	(79)	(128)	(209)
Black	12.0	26.8	32.6	41.4	72.7
N=190	(25)	(41)	(46)	(56)	(22)

TABLE 16

Percentage Evaluating Local Area Positively, by Race
and by Economic Status of the Area

Race	Economic Status of Area			
	High	Moderately High	Moderately Low	Low
White	44.5	53.6	47.6	38.9
N=570	(110)	(181)	(189)	(90)
Black	44.4	34.2	25.6	25.0
N=198	(18)	(38)	(90)	(52)

TABLE 17

Percentage Expressing Attachment to Only the Local Area,
by Race and by Economic Status of the Area

Race	Economic Status of Area			
	High	Moderately High	Moderately Low	Low
White	41.8	39.6	45.3	51.1
N=527	(110)	(182)	(190)	(90)
Black	38.9	39.5	40.7	23.1
N=199	(18)	(38)	(91)	(52)

When one controls for the economic status of the area the
relationship between *evaluation* and race persists for all economic status categories except the highest. In short, blacks
living in high economic status areas are just as likely to
evaluate the area positively as whites in those areas, but in
lower economic status areas whites are more likely to evaluate
the area positively. The relationship between *attachment* and
race disappears when we control for economic status of the
area, except for the lowest economic status areas. Blacks from
low economic status areas are much less likely than whites
from similar areas to express attachment to the local community, but for the three higher economic status categories
blacks are just as likely as whites to express attachment to
the local area.

In short, then, my findings support the "valued community" hypothesis for the relationships between class and race
and *evaluation* of the local area. But the expression of attach-

ment to the area does not appear to depend so much upon class and race, except in the extremely poor areas.

In line with the earlier finding that evaluation of the local community may be distinct from evaluation of one's fellow residents, it is interesting to note the racial difference in evaluations of *people* living in the local area. Whereas a greater proportion of whites than blacks had a positive evaluation of the *area* in which they lived, the data show that a larger proportion of blacks (32 percent) than whites (12 percent) gave an unqualified positive evaluation of the *people* living in the community. This suggests again that evaluation of the local area includes more than just the evaluation of the people within it. But this also lends additional support to previous findings that blacks and whites have decidedly different conceptions of local communities. If blacks are more likely than whites to operate at the smaller "social block" level of symbolic identification and social organization, one would expect them to have a more positive evaluation of residents within the area, for the social organization at this level emphasizes primary interaction rather than the secondary and more formal interaction characteristic of larger levels of community identification.

LOCAL SOCIAL STATUSES
AND LOCAL SENTIMENT

Age, Sex, and Family Status

The previous chapter demonstrated that certain ascriptive statuses centering on the family and the life-cycle do produce varying orientations to the local community and to residents' cognitive images of it. This section will relate these same statuses to sentiments toward the local community. It seems likely that those whose statuses require disproportionate activity in the context of the local community will have more positive sentiments toward it. Specifically, the youngest and the oldest, those with children compared with those without, and females compared with males should express more attachment to the local community and should be more likely to evaluate it positively (see tables 18 and 19).

In general, the data relating age to local *evaluation* show little variation; but in support of the curvilinear hypothesis,

TABLE 18

Percentage Evaluating Local Area Positively, by Age, Sex, Individual Family Status, and Family Status of the Area

Age:	Under 20	20–29	30–39	40–49	50–59	60–69	70+
	46.4	34.3	39.6	44.4	38.1	50.5	48.6
N = 753	(28)	(108)	(154)	(187)	(105)	(99)	(72)

Sex:	Male		Female	
	42.5		42.6	
N = 783	(306)		(477)	

Family Status	No Children	Children Grown	Children Home
	37.9	60.0	33.5
N = 348	(58)	(75)	(215)

Family Status: of Area:	High	Moderately High	Moderately Low	Low
	48.2	45.1	40.2	35.1
N = 797	(85)	(344)	(291)	(77)

TABLE 19

Percentage Expressing Attachment to Only the Local Area, by Age, Sex, Individual Family Status, and Family Status of the Area

Age:	Under 20	20–29	30–39	40–49	50–59	60–69	70+
	58.6	26.9	39.6	43.9	43.4	44.4	45.2
N = 756	(29)	(108)	(154)	(187)	(106)	(99)	(73)

Sex:	Male		Female	
	42.0		40.9	
N = 786	(307)		(479)	

Family Status:	No Children	Children Grown	Children Home
	37.3	44.0	44.2
N = 349	(59)	(75)	(215)

Family Status of Area:	High	Moderately High	Moderately Low	Low
	35.3	42.5	43.3	35.1
N = 799	(85)	(346)	(291)	(77)

those under twenty and those over sixty are slightly more likely to evaluate the area positively, and those in their twenties are slightly less likely to do so. The data on *attachment* show much stronger support for the curvilinear hypothesis. For example, 59 percent of those under twenty and 45 percent of those in their seventies expressed local attachment, while only 27 percent of those in their twenties did so.

Sex appears to be unrelated to variations in local orientation, since roughly equal proportions of males and females expressed positive evaluations of the local area and attachment to it.[7]

The relationship between family status, measured here by the presence or absence of children in the home, and local attachment supports the hypothesis only weakly. Of both those with children at home and those whose children had left home, 44 percent said they felt attachment to the local community. However, slightly fewer of those without children (37 percent) expressed local attachment. This suggests that rearing children in an area, either currently or in the past, is likely to produce attachments to the area itself. During the interviews, such attachments were often expressed not only for the current area but for areas previously lived in. For example, when several older female respondents were asked why they expressed attachment to some area previously lived in, they said that it was where their children played, grew up, and went to school and church, and was in general where they had raised their families. The positive sentiments involved in family relationships are generalized, it seems, to the setting—the community—in which these relationships take place.[8]

The relationship between family status and *evaluation* of the area is just the opposite of that expected. People without children are slightly *more* likely to give a positive evaluation of the area (38 percent) than those with children (34 percent). However, a majority (60 percent) of those whose children have left home evaluate the local area positively. These findings suggest that the difficulties of rearing children in the urban environment are likely to lead to a negative evaluation of the local community, and that those without children, or whose children have left home, view the urban environment less negatively. However, when one controls for family status *of the area* (see table 20), those *with* children at home in *high* family status areas are more likely to express a positive evaluation of the community than those without children, while

TABLE 20
Percentage Evaluating Local Area Positively, by Individual
Family Status and by Family Status of the Area

Individual Family Status	Family Status of the Area			
	Low	Moderately Low	Moderately High	High
No children	37.5	55.0	23.5	20.0
N = 58	(16)	(20)	(17)	(5)
Children home	14.3	29.3	37.9	60.0
N = 215	(21)	(92)	(87)	(15)

those *without* children in *low* family status communities are
more likely to express a positive evaluation of the area than
those with children. In short, the relationship between family
status and evaluation of the area depends upon a correspondence between family status of the *individual* and family
status characteristics of the *community*.[9]

Length of Residence and Residential History

The previous chapter showed that clarity of the cognitive
image of the local community increased with length of residence. Similarly, one would expect those living in an area
longer to evaluate it more positively and to be more likely
to express attachment to it. However, the data show that
evaluation of the area varies little by length of residence (see
table 21). However, when we look at attachment to the area,
a marked variation occurs: only 12 percent of those living in
the area less than a year expressed attachment to it, compared with 62 percent of those living there twenty years or
more (see table 22).

It is not surprising that more than two-thirds of those who
had lived in an area all their lives expressed attachment to
only the local community, while only about one-third of those
who had lived in another area or outside the city expressed
local attachment.

However, those who had previously lived in another area of
the city were most likely to evaluate their current area of
residence positively (43 percent), whereas the other two categories had roughly equal proportions (35 percent) evaluating

TABLE 21

Percentage Evaluating Local Area Positively, by Length of Residence and Residential History

Length of Residence:	Less than	1 Year	1–4 Years	5–9 Years	10–19 Years	20+ Years
		40.0	40.0	38.5	46.1	45.6
N = 733		(40)	(130)	135)	(191)	(237)

Residential History:	First Area of City Lived In		Previously Lived in Another Area of City		Lived All of Life in This Area	
	34.8		43.0		36.0	
N = 582	(66)		(430)		(86)	

TABLE 22

Percentage Expressing Attachment to Only the Local Area, by Length of Residence and Residential History

Length of Residence:	Less than	1 Year	1–4 Years	5–9 Years	10–19 Years	20+ Years
		12.5	25.4	34.8	40.3	62.0
N = 733		(40)	(130)	135)	(191)	(237)

Residential History:	First Area of City Lived In		Previously Lived in Another Area		Lived All of Life in This Area	
	36.4		32.3		68.6	
N = 583	(66)		(431)		(86)	

it positively. These "intracity migrants," we previously found, are also likely to have a clear cognitive image of the local community. If individuals choose to move to a new part of the city after having lived in another area, they can pick the area which will best suit their needs and interests, and they will therefore be more likely to have a positive evaluation of the community.[10] This might also help explain the lack of a relationship between length of residence and evaluation of the community.

Local Participation: Informal and Formal

The findings noted above suggest that the sentiments of evaluation of the local community and attachment to it are separate expressive orientations. Furthermore, it appears that evaluation is more dependent upon general social statuses which reflect differential access to amenities within the local community, whereas attachment reflects the integration of a resident into the local social structure and the number and types of interpersonal relationships he has established. If this is true, one would expect those with friends within the local area to express more attachment to it than those who have most of their friends outside of the local community. Furthermore, there should be little or no relationship between location of friends and evaluation of the area.

The same hypothesis also suggests that those who participate in local voluntary associations should be more attached to the local area than those who do not. Furthermore, this participation should not so strongly affect evaluation of the local area (see tables 23 and 24).

TABLE 23

Percentage Evaluating Local Area Positively, by Location or Friends and by Organization Membership and Awareness

Location of Friends:	Inside Area	Outside Area	Both Inside and Outside
	42.9	41.7	46.6
N = 777	(177)	(396)	(204)

Organization Membership:	None	Church Only	One	Two or More
	38.4	49.2	49.2	48.9
N = 787	(492)	(65)	(183)	(47)

Organization Membership and Awareness:	None	Knows Only	Belongs	Both Belongs and Knows of Others
	40.8	39.6	49.5	45.8
N = 766	(272)	(283)	(93)	(118)

The findings support these hypotheses. For example, there is no relationship between evaluation of the area and location of friends, since an equal proportion of those with most friends in the area and those with most friends outside the area evaluate it positively. However, more than half of those with most friends living inside the area expressed attachment to the local community, but only about one-third of those whose friends lived outside the area did the same.

The data also confirm the positive relationship between local positive sentiments and participation. For example, more than half of those belonging to two or more organizations expressed attachment to the local area, compared with only slightly more than a third of those belonging to no local

TABLE 24

Percentage Expressing Attachment to Only the Local Area, by Location of Friends and by Organization Membership and Awareness

Location of Friends:	Inside Area	Outside Area	Both Inside and Outside	
	52.5	34.1	47.5	
N = 777	(177)	(396)	(204)	
Organization Membership:	None	Church Only	One	Two or More
	36.4	43.1	49.7	51.1
N = 799	(494)	(65)	(183)	(47)
Organization Membership and Awareness:	None	Knows Only	Belongs	Both Belongs and Knows of Others
	37.7	38.9	47.3	50.8
N = 767	(273)	(283)	(93)	(118)

voluntary associations. The same is true for evaluation of the local area, and as expected the relationship is slightly weaker.

In short, then, both formal and informal participation and interaction in the local area are associated with more attachment to the local area. Formal participation is also associated with a more positive evaluation, but informal participation (friendship patterns) is not.[11]

The previous chapter showed that awareness of local voluntary associations, in addition to membership in them, was associated with a clear cognitive image of the local community. This chapter's findings suggest that the amount and type of social interaction in the local community are critical for establishing affectual ties to the local community. Knowledge or awareness of such "organized local activities" is decidedly different from actual participation. Therefore one would not expect significant variation in local attachment and evaluation for those who are aware of local organizations but do not belong compared with those who neither are aware nor belong. The critical differences should appear only for those who belong to such organizations.

The data support this hypothesis. Those who are aware but are nonparticipants and those who are both unaware and nonparticipants have essentially the same proportion expressing a positive local evaluation and a similar proportion expressing attachment to the local area. Only for those belonging to such organizations are the proportions expressing local attachment and positive evaluations increased.

Location of Work, Shopping, Worship, and Recreation

The expectation is that those who utilize the local community and its facilities for work, shopping, worship, and recreation will be more likely to express positive evaluations of the local area and will feel more attachment to it than those who perform these functions outside the local area. Using the area in these ways should help integrate individuals into the social structure of the local community and therefore increase their positive sentiments toward it.

The findings suggest that performing these functions inside the local area leads to a greater attachment to it. But there is no consistent relationship with evaluation of the local area and functional usage of it (see tables 25 and 26). There is one exception. Those finding recreation inside of the local area are more likely to evaluate the area positively than those finding most of their recreation outside of the community.

In short, all of these functions, if performed within the local area, serve to integrate people into the local social structure and increase their attachment to the local community.

TABLE 25
Percentage Evaluating Area Positively, by Location of Work, Shopping, Worship, and Recreation

Activity	Done Inside Area	Done Outside Area	Done Both Inside and Outside
Work	41.8	42.1	31.0
N=521	(78)	(413)	(29)
Food shopping	32.0	42.9	41.1
N=787	(577)	(154)	(56)
Church attendance	42.9	42.3	——
N=723	(510)	(213)	——
Recreation	52.6	39.1	41.3
N=681	(135)	(437)	(109)

TABLE 26

Percentage Expressing Attachment to Only the Local Area, by Location of Work, Shopping, Worship, and Recreation

Activity	Done Inside Area	Done Outside Area	Done Both Inside and Outside
Work	54.4	40.1	34.5
N = 522	(79)	(414)	(29)
Food shopping	43.5	32.9	41.1
N = 790	(579)	(155)	(56)
Church attendance	45.4	31.0	—
N = 724	(511)	(213)	—
Recreation	51.9	37.1	42.4
N = 683	(135)	(439)	(109)

COGNITIVE IMAGE OF THE AREA
AND LOCAL SENTIMENT

The previous chapter showed a relationship between the two dimensions of symbolic communities being explored, cognition and sentiment. This section will analyze this relationship by treating local sentiments as dependent variables and the clarity of the cognitive image as the "explanatory" variable.

The data show that those knowing all four boundaries of the local area are somewhat more likely to evaluate the area positively, but the relationship is relatively weak. However, those knowing all four boundaries are much more likely to express attachment to the local area than those knowing no boundaries (see tables 27 and 28).

Differences in evaluation and attachment are also found by whether a person knows a name for his area, and by the *type* of name given. Those giving an "areal" name to the community are most likely to express local attachment, whereas those giving a "street name" are the least likely to express attachment. This suggests that these individuals do not conceptualize the area either cognitively or affectively. Those living in public housing are even less likely to express local attachment than those knowing no name for the area. The public housing projects appear to operate as very distinct

TABLE 27
Percentage Evaluating Local Area Positively, by Ability to
Name the Area and Its Boundaries

Ability to Name Area:	No Name Given	Same Name as Fact Book	Another Name for Area	Street Name	Project Name
	34.5	42.6	48.2	30.6	36.8
N = 786	(113)	(340)	(278)	(36)	(19)
Ability to Name Boundaries:		Know None		Know Four	
N = 693		38.3		45.2	
		(149)		(544)	

TABLE 28
Percentage Expressing Attachment to Only the Local Area,
by Ability to Name the Area and Its Boundaries

Ability to Name Area:	No Name Given	Same Name as Fact Book	Another Name for Area	Street Name	Project Name
	36.3	45.3	42.8	18.9	26.3
N = 787	(113)	(340)	(278)	(37)	(19)
Ability to Name Boundaries:		Know None		Know Four	
N = 694		30.9		45.1	
		(149)		(545)	

symbolic communities cognitively, but little positive sentiment
is directed toward them. Evaluations are again less variable
than attachments, but those giving an areal name are slightly
more likely to evaluate the community positively than those
giving a street name, a project name, or no name at all.

In short, those who have a clear cognitive image of the
local community are slightly more likely to evaluate the area
positively than are those who do not, but they are much more
likely to express attachment.

SIZE OF AREA AND SENTIMENT

We also see that sentiments toward the local community vary
with the size of the area defined. Table 29 shows that positive
or negative evaluations do not vary by size, for equal proportions see their community positively or negatively regardless

TABLE 29

Evaluation of Area, Evaluation of Local Residents, and Attachment to Area, by Size of Area Defined

Response	Size of Area (in square blocks)			
	<17 (N=91)	17–64 (N=191)	65–256 (N=208	>256 (N=64)
Evaluation of area:				
Positive	45.1	47.4	44.2	37.5
Negative	12.1	8.4	9.6	14.1
Ambivalent	8.8	8.4	9.1	20.3
Noncodable	34.1	35.8	37.0	28.1
Total	100.1	100.0	99.9	100.0
Evaluation of local residents:				
Positive	18.7	9.9	15.9	9.4
Negative	3.3	3.1	2.9	1.6
Mixed	41.8	53.9	52.9	53.1
Other	36.3	33.0	28.3	35.9
Total	100.1	99.9	100.0	100.0
Attachment to Area:				
Here	39.6	43.7	44.2	57.8
Here and another	15.4	9.4	14.4	4.7
Another	19.8	21.4	21.2	14.1
None	25.3	25.5	20.2	23.5
Total	100.1	100.0	100.0	100.1

NOTE: Totals may not sum to 100% because of rounding.

of the size of the area. But it is clear that the largest areas defined had the largest proportion expressing *ambivalent* evaluations. In short, defining a smaller area reduces the complexity of the environment and permits a more clear-cut evaluation of the area as a good or a bad place. But a larger area includes greater heterogeneity, and this more complex environment confronts a resident with a mixture of good and bad elements, so that he gives a more ambivalent evaluation.[12]

Once again we see that evaluating a community is different from evaluating people living in the community. Those defining the smallest area gave the most positive evaluation of its residents. Again, the exclusion function of symbolic communities is apparent.[13] By defining a smaller area one can narrow one's social boundaries to include predominantly people one evaluates more positively and exclude those one sees more negatively. This is also borne out by the finding that people who define larger areas are more likely to have an ambivalent evaluation of the area's residents than those who define the smallest areas.

When we turn to the sentiment of attachment we find a somewhat different relationship to size of area. Here, the larger the area defined, the greater is the attachment to the area. People who define the smallest areas are most likely to express attachment to other areas, or to both other areas and their own. Once again we see the curvilinear relationship that we previously noted for class and family status. Those defining the smallest areas are not necessarily lacking in local orientation, but have more diffuse sentiments that include not only their own area of residence but other areas as well.[14]

SUMMARY

In general, this chapter has shown that expressions of local sentiment (attachment and evaluation) are highly variable. The findings collectively suggest that general social statuses, especially race and class, are very important in accounting for variations in residents' *evaluations* of local communities, probably because evaluations of areas are based upon amenities within the community, which are highly variable owing to the ecological segregation of race and class.

Local *attachment*, however, appears to depend less upon such general social statuses and much more upon a resident's status or social position within the local community. In short, these findings suggest that attachment to an area is dependent upon an individual's social integration and primary interaction within the local area. The positive sentiments and attachments generated in such interaction seem to be generalized to the setting in which they occur.

These findings taken together suggest a model interrelating the major variables, which is shown in the accompanying diagram.

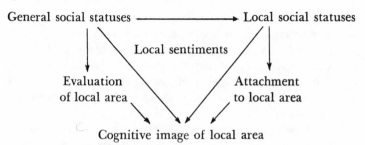

General social statuses ⟶ Local social statuses

Local sentiments

Evaluation
of local area

Attachment
to local area

Cognitive image of local area

Specifically, the findings of this chapter support a "valued community" theory relating race and class to local sentiments. The higher the class the more positive the evaluation of the area, and whites generally have a more positive evaluation than blacks. This latter finding persists when one controls for length of residence and for economic status of the area. Also, those from low economic status areas and those from high black status areas generally have a less positive evaluation of their local community than those from high economic areas and those from generally white areas. Class and race are less strongly related to attachment than to evaluation; and the lower the class generally the less the attachment. However, those in the highest class express less *exclusive* attachment to their local area than other classes, but they express more *diffuse* attachment which includes other areas as well as their own. In short, these individuals have not lost their attachment to their local communities, as some "mass society" theorists suggest; their attachments have merely become more diffuse. Blacks show less attachment than whites, but if one controls for length of residence the relationship disappears. When one controls for economic status of the area the relationship also disappears for all areas except those of the lowest economic status. In these communities blacks are less likely than whites to express attachment to the local area. The data also suggest that blacks have a more positive evaluation of their fellow residents than do whites. It is suggested that this is because blacks operate more at the social and symbolic level of the "social block" and that the primary interaction characteristic of this level leads to more positive sentiments toward one's neighbors.

The findings show a curvilinear relationship between age and attachment (highest for those under twenty and over sixty and lowest for those in their productive years, especially their twenties). A similar but much weaker relationship is found between age and evaluation of the local area. There is no relationship between sex and evaluation of or attachment to the local area.

Families with children generally have greater attachment to the local area, but a more negative evaluation of it, than those without children. However, when we control for family status of the area, in high family status areas those with children have a more positive evaluation of the area than those without, while in low family status areas those without children have a more positive evaluation. This "structural effect" suggests that the relationship between family status and evaluation of an area depends upon a correspondence between *individual* family status and family status characteristics *of the area*.

One sees that the longer the length of residence the greater the attachment, but there is no relationship between evaluation and length of residence. Those participating within the local area both *informally* (most friends in the area) and *formally* (membership in local voluntary associations) are more likely to express attachment than those not participating locally. The location of friends does not affect evaluation of the area, but formal participation does. Those who belong to local organizations evaluate the area more positively than those who are not members. Knowledge of local organizations unaccompanied by direct social participation does not affect local evaluation and attachment.

In general, if one shops, works, worships, and finds recreation inside the community he is more likely to express attachment to it than if he performs these functions elsewhere. There is no relationship between where one performs these functions and evaluation of the area except for recreation. Those finding recreation inside the area are more likely to evaluate the area positively than those finding recreation outside, which suggests that recreational facilities are an amenity that is taken into consideration in residents' evaluation of their local communities.

Cognition and sentiment of the symbolic community are also related: those with a clear cognitive image of the area are much more likely to express attachment to the local area and slightly more likely to evaluate the area positively.

Finally, the size of area defined is associated with local sentiment. Those defining the largest areas give more ambivalent evaluations of the local area, have move mixed feelings about their fellow residents and give somewhat less positive evaluations of them, and express greater attachment to the local area than those defining the smallest areas. However, those defining the smallest areas are more likely to express attachment to both their area and other areas throughout the city, which suggests a more differentiated and spatially diffuse set of local attachments.

In conclusion, residents do express sentiments toward their local symbolic communities as objects of orientation. However, these orientations of evaluation and attachment are highly variable between residents and between communities. Overall, class and race, the most significant factors of ecological segregation, are also the most significant variables in determining evaluation of local communities. Attachment, on the other hand, depends less on these general social statuses and more upon the degree to which the day-to-day routine of an individual's life-space integrates him into the social structure of the local community. In short, evaluation and attachment are distinct symbolic sentiments, each affected by a different set of social and ecological variables. The overall result is high variation and fine differentiation in the expression of sentiment toward local urban communities.

An elderly woman exemplified this variation and differentiation, and echoed the sentiments of a number of respondents, when she spoke almost tearfully about the neighborhood where she had raised her family: "It makes me sad; it's a slum now, but I still love it!"

Part Three   *Social Structure*

Five   *Community Organizations: Participation and Structure*

Community organizations are often considered to be the formal structural embodiment of local community solidarity. Large or active organizations are taken by some writers as the operational definition of a viable community, and much of the literature on "community organization" is explicitly concerned with establishing such formal social structures.[1] From the writings of de Tocqueville, emphasizing the importance of voluntary associations in preserving democratic societies, to current national surveys of local participation and its correlates, the significance and meaning of such voluntary, organized groups has been a central concern in American sociology. Some writers have seen them as an essential mechanism for integrating the individual into both local and national social structures;[2] others, however, feel they are examples of segmental and secondary interaction displacing the more meaningful and integrating primary ties of "community."[3]

However, a more differentiated conception of "community" social structure, such as this research is based on, necessarily involves considering not only these locally based formal organizations, but also informal social structures (such as visiting and neighboring), use of local facilities (such as shopping, recreation, and work), and the shared cultural representations and symbolic definitions of local areas. The purpose of this chapter is twofold: to relate some of the other dimensions of community social structure to membership in local voluntary associations, and to present a brief analysis and give some examples of the varying goals and structures of those local community groups.

LOCAL PARTICIPATION

First we will explore variations in membership in and awareness of local voluntary associations and their relationship to residents' varying social status, both local and general, and to characteristics of the communities in which they are situated. It is especially necessary to emphasize that membership in such organizations is itself an important local social status. Therefore, when discussing the relationship of membership to other "local" social statuses, the question of causal direction is problematic, and it is probably best to view the relationships as joint interaction between the variables, or simply as concomitant variations.

The first part of this chapter will explore local organization membership and awareness in relationship to the general social statuses of race and class. We will then focus upon more local social statuses such as age, sex, family status, friendship patterns, and length of residence; and finally, we will examine the relationship between participation and two dimensions of the symbolic community—clarity of the cognitive image and evaluation-attachment.

LOCAL PARTICIPATION AND
GENERAL SOCIAL STATUS

Because local voluntary association membership has been of such central concern in American sociology, there are a great number of studies exploring the correlates of organizational participation. Therefore the findings presented here will perhaps shed little new light and might be considered simply a statement of "sample characteristics."[4]

But there are two characteristics of the data which generate some new findings and suggest additional lines of inquiry. First, there has been much rhetoric about an awakened, organized populace in the nation's large cities. Since this sample was taken in 1967–68, it may offer some new findings simply because of the concerns with local community control stemming out of the late sixties. Second, in this research local community associations are defined more broadly than in other studies, so as to include local block clubs. These are often very diffuse structures without names or formal mem-

bership and goals, but nonetheless I have included membership in them as participation in "local voluntary associations."
My experience and some data from this research indicate that
these block clubs are more prevalent in the black communities of Chicago than in white areas. Therefore this study may
depict more participation than previous research, or at
least participation of a different kind and by different individuals.

RACE AND CLASS

From previous studies one would expect that the higher the
class the greater the participation in community organizations, and that whites are more likely to be members of local
community organizations than blacks.

The findings do show that those of the highest occupational
group are more likely to participate (42 percent) than those
of the lowest occupational group (14 percent). Furthermore,
as table 30 shows, those from high economic status areas are
more likely to participate (39 percent) than those from low
economic status areas (25 percent).

TABLE 30

Percentage Belonging to Local Voluntary Organizations, by
Class, Race, and Economic and Racial-Ethnic Status of the
Area

Race:		White		Black	
		28.9		28.6	
N = 770		(571)		(199)	
Class:	Upper	Middle		Working	Service
	41.7	35.1		26.9	14.3
N = 671	(36)	(282)		(297)	(56)
Racial-Ethnic Status of Area:	High Black	Mixed	Mixed		High Foreign-Born
	26.7	33.6	29.0		26.8
N = 797	(180)	(116)	(404)		(97)
Economic Status of Area:	High	Moderately High	Moderately Low		Low
	39.3	24.6	29.3		25.0
N = 798	(132)	(227)	(287)		(152)

However, the data show that blacks are just as likely as whites to be members of local community organizations (29 percent for each). This suggests that either the black communities of Chicago are just as highly organized as the white communities or that the inclusion of block clubs (which are found mostly in black areas) has equalized the proportions, or both. And blacks are just as likely as whites to be aware of such organizations (see table 31).[5]

TABLE 31
Percentage Aware of or Belonging to Local Voluntary Organizations, by Class, Race, and Economic and Racial-Ethnic Status of the Area

Race:	White		Black	
	62.4		60.4	
N = 770	(571)		(199)	
Class:	Upper	Middle	Working	Service
	86.0	68.5	61.2	46.4
N = 671	(36)	(282)	(297)	(56)
Racial-Ethnic Status of Area:	High Black	Mixed	Mixed	High Foreign-Born
	57.2	66.3	62.6	62.9
N = 797	(180)	(116)	(404)	(97)
Economic Status of Area:	High	Moderately High	Moderately Low	Low
	64.4	63.9	63.7	53.3
N = 798	(132)	(227)	(287)	(152)

When we consider the "racial-ethnic status" of the communities, people from black areas and those from areas with a high percentage of foreign-born are the least likely to participate (27 percent in each), while those from white, non–foreign-born areas are slightly more likely to participate (34 percent). One should recall that this is an ecological correlation of "community characteristics" with individual participation and does not represent individual correlates of participation.

When we control for economic status of the area in general the relationship holds: blacks are just as likely as whites to participate except in the highest economic status areas, where blacks are more likely to participate than whites (see table

32). One reason for this may be that the opportunity for participation outside the local area characteristic of upper-class individuals is not as readily available to blacks as it is to

TABLE 32

Percentage Belonging to Local Voluntary Organizations, by Race and by Economic Status of the Area

Race:	Economic Status of Area			
	Low	Moderately Low	Moderately High	High
White	26.6	29.0	24.9	37.3
N=571	(90)	(190)	(181)	(110)
Black	25.0	28.6	23.7	50.0
N=199	(52)	(91)	(38)	(18)

whites of comparable status. Therefore blacks in these higher economic status areas participate to a greater extent within their ghetto communities.[6]

In short, it appears that upper-class individuals are more likely to participate in local community organizations than are lower-class individuals; blacks are just as likely as whites to participate, and there is a suggestion (given the small case size) that blacks from higher economic status areas are more likely to participate than whites from these areas.

LOCAL PARTICIPATION AND
LOCAL SOCIAL STATUS

Age, Sex, and Family Status

The previous chapters have explored the relationship between the ascribed statuses centering on the life-cycle and kinship and have generally found important differences in local orientations. Here also it is expected that individuals whose ascribed statuses require that a disproportionate amount of their daily activities be performed within the local area will be most oriented to it in terms of psychic and social investment and therefore will be most likely to participate in local organizations. Specifically, females should participate more than males because of their home- and local-centered activities; the oldest and the youngest should participate more than those in their productive years, and especially those in their twenties; and those with children at home should participate more than those without children. One would expect awareness of organizations to have the same relationship to these ascribed statuses as actual participation (see tables 33 and 34).

TABLE 33

Percentage Belonging to Local Voluntary Organizations, by Age, Sex, Individual Family Status, and Family Status of the Area

Age:	Under 20	20–29	30–39	40–49	50–59	60–69	70+
	34.3	17.6	33.1	34.7	30.3	29.3	19.2
N=755	(29)	(108)	(154)	(187)	(105)	(99)	(73)

Sex:				Male		Female	
				27.7		29.5	
N=785				(307)		(478)	

Family Status:	No Children		Children Grown		Children Home	
	25.4		30.6		39.0	
N=349	(59)		(75)		(215)	

Family Status: of Area:	High	Moderately High	Moderately Low	Low
	35.3	30.7	27.1	19.5
N=798	(85)	(345)	(291)	(77)

The data on age suggest little variation in association membership, with two exceptions. Those in their twenties and those over seventy are the least likely to participate (only 18 percent and 19 percent respectively, compared with about one-third of the other age groups). Although the findings in general do not support the curvilinear hypothesis, nonetheless those in their twenties were the least likely to join such groups. In terms of awareness, those in their thirties and forties are the most likely to *either* belong to or know of such groups, and even 40 percent of those in their twenties were aware of them, although they did not belong. This suggests that such organizations have an impact beyond mere membership; furthermore, it underscores the *voluntary* aspects of such associations, for the data suggest that approximately one-third of the sample "knew" of local organizations but "chose" not to join.

TABLE 34

Percentage Aware of or belonging to Local Voluntary Organizations, by Age, Sex, Individual Family Status, and Family Status of the Area

Age:	Under 20	20–29	30–39	40–49	50–59	60–69	70+
	55.2	57.3	67.6	67.3	60.0	55.5	52.1
N=755	(29)	(108)	(154)	(187)	(105)	(99)	(73)

Sex:		Male		Female	
		60.4		63.2	
N=785		(307)		(478)	

Family Status:	No Children	Children Grown	Children Home
	50.9	56.0	74.0
N=349	(59)	(75)	(215)

Family Status of Area:	High	Moderately High	Moderately Low	Low
	72.9	62.0	61.5	50.7
N=798	(85)	(345)	(291)	(77)

The data again suggest little variation in participation between males and females. Although the latter were slightly more likely to both know of and belong to local organizations, the difference is only three percentage points.

With respect to family status the findings demonstrate the expected role of children in integrating their parents into the organized life of the local community. For example, only one-fourth of those with no children belong to one or more local organizations, compared with almost 40 percent of those with children at home. Furthermore, those whose children have grown and left home are intermediate in the proportion participating.

The data on awareness of local organizations suggests even more strongly that children integrate their parents into the social structure of the local community, symbolically if not interactionally. Almost three-fourths of those with children at home either belonged to or knew of local voluntary associations, in contrast to only one-half of those with no children and a slightly larger percentage (56 percent) of those whose children were grown. Children, then, appear to operate as significant communication links transmitting cognitive information about the local community to their parents, and this in turn may lead to increased local participation.

With respect to family status of the area, the data show quite clearly that the higher the family status of the area the more likely an individual is to participate in a local community organization.

Length of Residence

Previous studies have suggested that length of residence has little relationship to the likelihood of belonging to local community groups. The findings from this study suggest, however, that this may have been due to the gross categories utilized in the analysis (see table 35). The results here are

TABLE 35
Percentage Belonging to Local Voluntary Organizations, by Length of Residence and Location of Friends

Length of Residence:	Less than 1 Year	1–4 Years	5–9 Years	10–19 Years	20+ Years
	10.0	25.4	30.4	29.9	30.4
N = 733	(40)	(130)	(135)	(191)	(237)

Location of Friends:	Inside Area	Outside Area	Both Inside and Outside
	33.9	23.2	34.8
N = 777	(177)	(396)	(204)

similar to those of Zimmer,[7] which showed an increasing participation with increasing length of residence up to five years and a leveling off after this. For example, there is little variation in the proportion participating after five years of residence (approximately 30 percent). But for those living in an area from one to four years a smaller percentage is likely to participate (23 percent), and for those living in an area for less than a year only 10 percent participate. Like the findings in previous chapters, these results suggest that if an individual is oriented to participation in the local community, this orientation is rather quickly translated into actual involvement.

There is little variation beyond the first year of residence in the proportion knowing of or belonging to local organizations (see table 36). A smaller proportion of those living in

TABLE 36
Percentage Aware of or Belonging to Local Voluntary Organizations, by Length of Residence and Location of Friends

Length of Residence:	Less than 1 Year	1–4 Years	5–9 Years	10–19 Years	20+ Years
	45.0	62.3	65.9	61.8	65.4
N = 733	(40)	(130)	(135)	(191)	(237)

Location of Friends:	Inside Area	Outside Area	Both Inside and Outside
	59.9	61.1	66.7
N = 777	(177)	(396)	(204)

an area less than a year belongs to local organizations, but roughly the same proportion is aware of such groups. This suggests that if an individual is going to be aware of organizations he has already learned of them during his first year of residency.

Friendship Patterns

In a seminal study referred to earlier Morris Axelrod concluded that "formal and informal group participation were found to vary positively together."[8] This finding called for a reinterpretation of the relationship between primary and secondary relations in an urban environment, suggesting that these two modes of participation may be supportive rather than contradictory. The findings here show this same relationship between participation in the local area and whether most of a resident's friends lived outside or inside the area. More than one-third of those who said most of their friends live within the area belong to one or more local associations, but less than one-fourth of those with most friends living outside of the local area belong.

However, those having friends outside of the area are no less knowledgeable about organizations operating within their community than those with most friends within the area. Although they are just as likely to know of such groups, they are less likely to join, probably because most of their friends are not likely to be members.

UTILIZATION OF LOCAL FACILITIES

Let us now consider the broader definition of local social status—the utilization of local community facilities—to see if the location of these functional activities inside or outside of the community is related to membership in local voluntary associations. One would expect that people who use the facilities of the local community would be more concerned about the local area and have a greater degree of interaction within it, and would therefore be more likely to be members of such organizations, than those who carry on these activities outside the community (see table 37).

Contrary to these expectations, those who work inside the community are no more likely than those working outside to be members of local community organizations. The same holds true with food shopping: those shopping outside are just as likely to belong as those who do most of their shopping inside the local community. Again, those who find most of their recreation within the community are no more likely to belong than those who go outside of the area. However, those who find recreation *both* inside and outside of the local area are slightly more likely to belong to local voluntary associations than those staying mostly inside *or* those going mostly outside. This relationship did not appear for shopping and work (see tables 37 and 38).

THE SYMBOLIC IMAGE AND
LOCAL PARTICIPATION

Previous chapters have shown that those participating in local organizations are likely to have a clearer cognitive image of the local area, to express more attachment to the local area, and to evaluate it more positively than those who do not participate. In this section the same relationships are explored by reversing the direction of analysis to see if variations in cognition and sentiment are related to local organization membership.

TABLE 37
Percentage Belonging to Local Voluntary Organizations, by
Location of Work, Shopping, and Recreation

Activity	Done Inside Area	Done Outside Area	Done Both Inside and Outside
Work	31.6	32.7	24.1
N=521	(79)	(413)	(29)
Food Shopping	28.4	28.4	34.0
N=789	(578)	(155)	(56)
Recreation	31.1	28.9	40.4
N=683	(135)	(439)	(109)

TABLE 38
Percentage Aware of or Belonging to Local Voluntary Organizations, by Location of Work, Shopping, and Recreation

Activity	Done Inside Area	Done Outside Area	Done Both Inside and Outside
Work	68.3	64.5	72.4
N=521	(79)	(413)	(29)
Food Shopping	62.5	60.6	62.5
N=789	(578)	(155)	(56)
Recreation	63.0	64.0	67.0
N=683	(135)	(439)	(109)

The findings are rather consistent, and in general those who have a clearer or more complete cognitive image of the local area are more likely to belong to local organizations (see table 39). For example, those who named the area, compared with those who were unable to, and those who knew all four boundaries, compared with those who knew none, are more likely to be members of one or more organizations (32 percent versus 12 percent and 34 percent versus 14 percent). The same applies to awareness of local organizations: those knowing a local name and boundaries are also more aware of local organizations than those not knowing these elements of the cognitive image (see table 40). These elements of cognition, then, are closely related.

TABLE 39

Percentage Belonging to Local Voluntary Organizations, by Ability to Name Area and Its Boundaries

Ability to Name Area:	No Name Given	Same Name as Fact Book	Another Name
	11.5	31.7	33.8
N = 731	(113)	(340)	(278)

Ability to Name Boundaries:		Know None	Know Four
		14.1	33.6
N = 694		(149)	(545)

TABLE 40

Percentage Aware of or Belonging to Local Voluntary Organizations, by Ability to Name Area and Its Boundaries

Ability to Name Area:	No Name Given	Same Name as Fact Book	Another Name for Area
	34.5	64.8	61.2
N = 731	(113)	(340)	(278)

Ability to Name Boundaries:		Know None	Know Four
		37.6	70.3
N = 694		(149)	(545)

The same results are found with respect to local sentiments. For example, one-third of those with an unqualified positive evaluation belong to one or more local organizations, whereas those expressing an unqualified negative evaluation or no evaluation are less likely to belong (24 percent compared with 18 percent). Similarly, those expressing attachment to only the local area are most likely to belong (35 percent), and this proportion declines in order for those whose attachments are local *and* elsewhere (31 percent), elsewhere only (27 percent), and none at all (17 percent) (see table 41).

Awareness of local organizations, however, appears to be unrelated to local sentiments. Those giving negative evaluations are as likely to be aware of such organizations as those giving positive evaluations, and those expressing attachment elsewhere are just as aware as those expressing attachment to the local area (see table 42). The only exceptions are those who gave no evaluation and those who said they felt no

TABLE 41
Percentage Belonging to Local Voluntary Organizations, by Attachment to and Evaluation of the Local Area

Evaluation of Area:	Positive	Negative	Ambivalent	Noncommittal	None
	33.3	24.3	28.1	28.1	18.1
N = 778	(339)	(99)	(82)	(203)	(55)

Attachment to Area:	Here	Here and Other	Other in City	None
	35.0	31.3	26.9	16.9
N = 748	(329)	(83)	(171)	(165)

TABLE 42
Percentage Aware of or Belonging to Local Voluntary Organizations, by Attachment to and Evaluation of the Local Area

Evaluation of Area:	Positive	Negative	Ambivalent	Noncommittal	None
	62.5	63.6	67.1	61.6	43.7
N = 778	(339)	(99)	(82)	(203)	(55)

Attachment to Area:	Here	Here and Other	Other in City	None
	65.0	67.5	63.2	52.8
N = 748	(329)	(83)	(171)	(165)

attachment anywhere. Both of these are less likely to be aware of local groups.

SUMMARY

In general, the findings have shown that awareness of local organizations is higher than actual participation in them, and that awareness varies less in relationship to the independent variables explored here than does participation.

The results are generally consistent with previous studies exploring correlates of organizational participation for some of the independent variables: The higher the class the more the participation. Those with children are more likely to participate in local organizations and much more likely to be aware of them. Those in their twenties are less likely to participate than those who are older or younger, and those living

in an area for more than five years are more likely to participate than those living there less than five years and much
more likely than those living there for less than a year. Again,
awareness does not vary with length of residence. Furthermore, those with friends living in the local area are more
likely to participate than those with most friends living outside, which suggests a positive relationship between primary
and secondary or informal and formal modes of interaction
within the local community.

However, no relationships were found between organizational participation and sex, or between participation and
utilization of the local area versus other areas for work, shopping, and recreation. Positive relationships were found between cognition and evaluation of and attachment to the local
community and organizational participation.

Perhaps the most surprising finding was the lack of a relationship between race and participation. Blacks are just as
likely as whites to participate in local community organizations. This may be due to the increased organizational activity of black urban residents, to my extension of the operational definition to include block clubs, or to both. When
economic status of the area is controlled blacks from the
highest economic status areas are more likely to participate
than whites, but this is offered only as a suggestion because
of the small case size.

We have seen that variations in individual social statuses
are related to variations in involvement in local organizations.
However, to more fully explore the nature of this involvement
and the nature and significance of these organizations we
now focus upon the organizations themselves.

COMMUNITY ORGANIZATION STRUCTURE

This section will explore the role of local voluntary associations in local community structure and assess the varying
structures and goals of more than 250 local community organizations studied in 1967–68. Information on these voluntary organizations was gathered through personal interviews,
telephone interviews, and questionnaires mailed to officers or
staff members. The data, though incomplete or lacking en-

tirely on many organizations, include such items as community areas of operation and boundaries, structure, affiliations, general goals, and specific projects and activities. For a small number there is also information about membership size and funding. The following analysis is a comparative case study of fifteen of the larger organizations (see Appendix 2).

FUNCTIONS OF COMMUNITY
ORGANIZATIONS FOR LOCAL
COMMUNITY STRUCTURE

A Framework for Interaction

We have seen that approximately one-third of the sampled residents claim membership in local voluntary associations. Although such membership is often interpreted as less integrative "secondary interaction," the findings also show that this is often related positively to greater "primary interaction" within the local community. It appears that the demands of the "external" structure for organized and formal interaction give rise to more informal interaction, increasing primary ties and positive sentiments toward the local community and its residents. Furthermore, some of the larger federated organizations, which we will explore in more detail shortly, have an explicit goal of creating one type of primary group, the block club. These smaller primary units of "neighbors" give the individual a source of primary interaction and "friendship," and these more diffuse affectual ties are beneficial to the organization itself for sustaining involvement and motivating the voluntary activities of members to achieve organizational goals.[9]

One might also reverse the causal relationship between informal and formal participation. For example, the former is often a basis of recruitment to the latter. Furthermore, the mere existence of an organization tends to legitimate specific actions by informal groups and also guarantees voluntary coparticipation of individuals.[10]

To fully understand the importance of local community groups one should see them in their political context. The presence of a formal structure for achieving organized interests through increased efficiency and specifically stated goals implies political concerns and the search for power. More recently formed local organizations state this explicitly in such phrases as "people power," "community power," and "community control." Such power leads not only to the satisfaction of individual interests and organizational goals, but to a generalized sense of efficacy for local residents. The "quest for power" and its consequences for organizational structure and goals will be analyzed later, but here the important point is that this increased sense of efficacy should be considered a motivating force leading to a circular spiral of increased activity, interaction, and local attachment.

A Local System of Communication

The close association between the concept of community and the process of communication was stressed heavily by Robert Park in many of his writings.[11] The local community organization may be viewed as a significant system of communication serving to integrate the individual into the local social structure as do more specific media of local communication such as the local community press.[12] Through its organizational meetings this is a two-way process, aggregating the upward flow of demands and dissatisfactions of individual residents, organizing them into more general "issues," and disseminating them as community goals both to the residents of the area and to agents outside the community.

Many of the organizations have of course learned the public relations approach of a well-planned press release to both the citywide and the local press; but many also have monthly or even semimonthly "newsletters" ranging in format from a single-page mimeographed flyer to a full press layout complete with pictures and advertisements which rivals the independent community press. An interesting example of the evolution of an organization's newspaper is the dual-language (Spanish and English) *Lincoln Park Press* (*La Prensa de Lincoln Park*), which in its first volume went from a simple typed format with hand drawings, saying on its masthead "Donations Appreciated," to a professionally printed "newspaper" on newsprint, complete with pictures and advertisements of local businesses and selling for ten cents. The paper is published by the Concerned Citizens of Lincoln Park.

An example of cooperation between the local voluntary organization and the independent community press is found in Little Village. The Little Village Community Council has its own column in the *Lawndale News*. A full analysis of the content of these local community newspapers is beyond the scope of this study, but they were useful in assessing specific activities of the various organizations.

Through its meetings and newspapers the local community organization provides, in part, a needed lower-level interpretation of events and has a communicative function which helps to integrate the community. As was shown before, awareness of these local organizations was generally greater than actual participation, which indicates the extensiveness of this communication function for the local community..

An Embodiment of Local Symbolic Culture

Through its communication system, explicit and informal, the local community organization also serves to heighten the "symbolic identification" of the local area. The fact that most of the organizations have names, many of them including the name of the local area, and that they have well-defined boundaries of operation, means that the symbolic image of the local area in which such an organization operates is likely to be clearer than those in which it does not. During the interviewing I noticed that residents frequently relied upon their knowledge of the local organization to give a local name and boundaries. And often the name of the local organization would supersede some other name for the area. This was found in South Lawndale, now frequently referred to as "Little Village," and also on the South Side, where the community area of Kenwood had been split in two—Kenwood-Oakland and Hyde Park–Kenwood—the two sections having organizations with those specific names. That this type of identification of an area occurs helps explain the changing and often conflicting names given to an area, for often an organization seeking expansion need only expand its boundaries of operation and the area becomes redefined. The same is of course true for retrenchment of boundaries when that may be to the organization's benefit, as it may have been for the South Shore Commission when it redefined its western boundary as Stony Island. This new boundary has become the established borderline for the community, excluding a large number of blacks living west of it.[13]

The community organization also operates as the structural embodiment of local culture through the participation of long-time residents and through the organization's "files." The former situation is exemplified by the executive secretary of the Beverly Area Planning Association—its only full-time paid staff member. He has lived in Beverly since 1910 and recalls when the community was still separated from the city by a wide expanse of prairie. The best example of the preservation of local history and culture by a local community organization is the three-volume history of the Northwest Federation of Improvement Clubs, compiled by its officers and covering the years from 1914 to 1964.

As was noted in chapter 2, I also found explicit attempts by local community groups to define the names and boundaries of local areas by erecting street signs. Such signs heighten the symbolic image of a local community not only for local residents but also for "strangers" simply passing through.

In short, the local community organization operates as a significant structural embodiment of the symbolic culture of the community, preserving it and at times altering it as the need arises.

A Planner of Ecological Structure and Change

In a general way the purpose of many of the local community organizations in the city, if not all of them, can be seen as an attempt to control ecological structure by aiding or altering the processes of invasion, succession, and competition. Many of the small homeowners' organizations are explicitly oriented to maintaining property values through beautifying the area, improving municipal services, and reporting zoning violations. Similarly, the many organizations concerned about urban renewal and rehabilitation—the Hyde Park–Kenwood Community Conference and the Lincoln Park Conservation Commission, for example—are specifically oriented to *planning* a reversal of what until a few years ago were *natural* processes of invasion, movement, and decay. These planning orientations imply an increased social awareness of the ecological forces shaping the city—to the extent that the natural processes are countered by planned processes of change and maintenance of a specific ecological structure for the local community.

Although many plans may center on the *maintenance* of a particular ecological structure of the community—as in pressing for specific zoning regulations and surveillance against violations—the genesis of such organized activity is often the threat of real or anticipated invasion. The most noteworthy invasion involving organized community response is of course black invasion, and on the perimeter of the expanding black ghetto one can find a variety of organizations attempting to thwart this process.[14] This is of course no new phenomenon and is adequately explored by Mikva in her analysis of organizational response to the Supreme Court's ban on restrictive covenants in 1948.[15] Groups like the South Shore Commission, the organization of block clubs by Father Lawlor along Ashland Avenue, and the recent activities of the Back of the Yards Council are all oriented to at least maintaining the presence of whites in their communities, if they are not directly concerned about keeping blacks out.[16]

Of course the organized response is not directed solely at black invasion or even invasion of differing population types, but may be a response to institutional invasion, as in the formation of The Woodlawn Organization, which opposed the expansion of the University of Chicago's south campus. One of the more frequent responses to invasion, however, is brought on by government planning. Citizens' organizations which form to oppose public housing, new expressways, or even bussing are often objecting directly to the threat of some ecological transformation of their local area.

It is apparent from this brief overview that local community organizations operate in a variety of ways to either maintain or alter the several dimensions of local urban communities explored here. We will now consider the variations in the specific goals and structures of some of the larger organizations found throughout the city.

ORGANIZATIONAL GOALS AND STRUCTURES

This analysis is based upon data about fifteen of the larger community organizations found in Chicago in 1967–68 (see Appendix 2 for a list of these organizations). There are two general approaches one might take in analyzing local community organizations. The first derives from social work and community welfare literature and emphasizes considering both community and individual needs in organizing local citizens for ameliorative action.[17] The second approach is more central within sociological literature and emphasizes the study of the structural characteristics of "formal organizations" and the relationships among these characteristics in the achievement of organizational goals.[18]

More recent developments have brought these two approaches into closer contact. The "natural systems" approach[19] to the study of formal organizations emphasizes the necessity of studying the context of these organizations in order to better understand their structure and functioning. This should prove more advantageous in the study of community organizations than previous models which focused solely upon internal structure. It is also more fitting to the focus of this research—the significance of the interplay between local voluntary organizations and their local urban communities. Furthermore, the recent emphasis in the community organization literature upon *organizational goals* and their relationship to community needs ties this approach to a central element in more general sociological analyses of "formal organizations." Out of this combined approach has also come a realization of the importance of studying *inter*organizational relationships, especially in studies of health and welfare councils and studies of urban renewal.[20]

THE CENTRAL FINDING:
HIERARCHICAL FEDERATIONS

It was expected that the data on local organizations would reveal a large number of small independent local organizations, consisting primarily of home- or property-owner organizations in the white areas and small welfare or service organizations in the black communities. Each of these, it was expected, would be oriented to rather limited or specific concerns of the local community. This was, of course, in addition to the highly publicized but less numerous organizations such as The Woodlawn Organization (TWO), the Hyde Park–Kenwood Community Conference, and the Back of the Yards

Council. However, the data reveal that these small independent local organizations are organized into a large number
of federated organizations covering a much more extensive
spatial area of the city. More than half the small organizations (which total over 250) are known to be affiliated with
one or more community organizations. Since the data are
incomplete on some of these organizations, the proportion
may even be greater. Therefore not only is the city covered
in quilt-like fashion by the small independent community
organizations, but most of it is also covered by these higher-
level and more extensive federations.

Not only are most of the organizations members of some
federation, but this process of federation extends through
several hierarchical levels, with federated community organizations themselves being members of even more extensive
"regional" federations within the city. A good example of
this federated structure is the Greater Lawndale Conservation
Commission (see chart 2). Extending from the executive committee and the board of directors of the commission are four
levels of community organization. The *association of block
club councils* includes three *districts*, each district has two to
four *block club councils*, and each block club council includes
three to twenty-three *block clubs*. Each of these levels has a
well-defined geographical area of operation, dividing up the
North Lawndale community, and many have clearly identifi-
able names—for example, the Triangle Neighbors Community
Organization, which is a block club, and the West Lawndale
Community Council, which is a block club council.

Although most of the federated organizations consist of
only two hierarchical levels (neighborhood groups and the
federated community organization) and cover only one community area, some extend through as many as four levels (the
Greater Lawndale Conservation Commission, noted above)
and cover large "regions" of the city which include several
community areas (e.g., the Roseland Area Planning Association, which encompasses Roseland, Pullman, West Pullman,
and Riverdale).

This hierarchical federated structure of local community
organizations is not completely new. In Mikva's study of
homeowners' organizations in Chicago after the Supreme

CHART 2
Organizational Structure of the Greater Lawndale
Conservation Commission

Executive committee
Board of directors
  —Lawndale Businessman's Association (118 members)
  —Association of Block Club Councils (an executive director)
    ———District 1 (a staff aide)
                          A. Block club council: Little Community Council—11
                             block clubs
                          B. Block club council—17 block clubs
                          C. Block club council: West Lawndale Community
                             Council—11 block clubs
                          D. Block club council—23 block clubs
    ———District 2 (a staff aide)
                          A. Block club council—15 block clubs
                          B. Block club council—14 block clubs
    ———District 3 (a staff aide)
                          A. Block club council—20 block clubs
                          B. Block club council—10 block clubs
                          C. Block club council— 3 block clubs

---

Most of the block clubs have only street names, but the following are
some of those having more specific names:

Spic and Span	Youth Progressive Club
The Homan Community	Ogden Courts Parents Club
The Better Community	The Triangle Neighbors Community
Progressive Block Club	Organization

Court decision of 1948 banning restrictive covenants a number of these federated organizations are discussed.[21] However,
it does appear that the number of federated organizations
has increased dramatically since that time. Mikva lists five
active federated "regional" organizations in the city, but at
least three times that many are active today. Of the five she
discusses three are still active—Northwest Federation of Improvement Clubs, Southtown Planning Association, and the
Beverly Area Planning Association. One of the organizations,
the Taxpayers Action Committee, has apparently been replaced by the federated Roseland Area Planning Association,
which operates in the same general area. The other organization appears to have disbanded.

To understand why this federated structure should be so
prevalent and to find the reasons for its emergence, the fol-

lowing analysis will focus upon several characteristics of both the small local organizations and the federated organizations they form. Specifically, we will look at the genesis of both the local organizations and their federations, at their different goals, activities, and functions, their relative bureaucratization, and their differing resources.

A COMPARATIVE ANALYSIS OF LOCAL
AND FEDERATED COMMUNITY
ORGANIZATIONS

Genesis

In almost all cases the smaller local community groups appear to have been organized first. But once a federation is formed it may actively seek to organize new local groups in neighboring areas. For example, of the ten or so neighborhood groups making up the Beverly Area Planning Association, three have been organized by the Planning Association itself, and the other seven constituted the original organizational base of the federation. Similarly, the Lincoln Park Conservation Commission (LPCC) was formed in 1954 through the efforts of two smaller organizations, the Old Town Triangle Association and the Mid-North Association. Since that time LPCC has been active in establishing other organizations, such as the Sheffield Neighbors Association, started in 1955. These attempts at local organization by federations are especially made by organizations based upon the small unit of the block club. Larger federations usually delegate this activity to the intermediate neighborhood groups, for it requires a rather close and constant contact with "block captains" to insure involvement and participation.

The specific "causes" leading to community organization are too numerous and complex to pursue in this brief analysis, but many may be attributable to the various forms of "invasion" mentioned in the previous section. Mikva's research, for example, is explicitly concerned with the formation of local community organizations in an attempt to thwart black invasion in the wake of the ban on restrictive covenants. The closely related issue of locating public housing in white communities was also raised at this time and spawned new organizations as well as providing new issues for existent

organizations. It may be expected that the recent federal judi-
cial decision requiring the Chicago Housing Authority to
erect "dispersed site" public housing will lead to similar organizational response. Responses to racial change are also seen
in Father Lawlor's formation of block clubs in the Southwest
Community area to keep blacks from moving west of Ashland
and in the South Shore Commission's slightly different emphasis on getting whites to move into its area. The bussing
issue also led to some extremely large organizations—all composed of previously existing local groups—such as the Greater
Northwest Civic Association and the extremely large but
apparently short-lived Operation Crescent, which covered the
white areas of the Northwest, West, and Southwest sides of
the city.

Within the black communities of the city a great deal of
indigenous community organization is taking place, in addition to the professional organization of these areas by full-
time community organizers. Several large religious and ecu-
menical bodies provide a great deal of financial assistance
(e.g., the Interreligious Council on Urban Affairs, the Meth-
odist Rock River Conference, the Roman Catholic Archdio-
cese of Chicago, and the Chicago Presbytery of the United
Presbyterian Church).

One "type" of organization genesis that was found for
several local community groups is the threat that some major
institution like a university or a hospital will move out of the
area. The importance of Illinois Institute of Technology and
Michael Reese Hospital in the redevelopment of the Douglas
community, and of the University of Chicago in Hyde Park
and in the formation of the Hyde Park–Kenwood Community
Conference and the more closely affiliated Southeast Community Organization, has been well documented.[22] In the
Lincoln Park area the Sheffield Neighbors Association was in
part created because McCormick Seminary was considering
moving to Indiana in the early fifties because of the deterioration of the neighborhood. Instead of moving the seminary
joined with De Paul University and Alexian Brothers Hospital to help upgrade the area. All provide resources as well
as their facilities to the local organization and to residents of
the local area. Similarly, on the Far North Side, North Park

College was considering moving because of neighborhood deterioration, but instead it joined with neighboring Swedish Covenant Hospital and formed the North River Commission. The result has been a close cooperation between the local institutions and the community organization in attempting to upgrade the area.

In short, the genesis of local community organizations has a variety of "causes," many but not all being some form of "invasion"—impending or real. Federated organizations are formed on the already well-established organizational base of local community associations, and the federation may in turn generate more of them.[23]

GOALS AND ACTIVITIES

To understand more fully the relationship between the local organizations and their larger federated structures, let us now consider the specific goals, activities, and functions of these two levels of community organization. This analysis relies upon three dimensions of community organization goals outlined by Mayer Zald—a group's orientation may be internal or external, to individuals or to groups, and to maintenance or to change.[24] In general, my data suggest that the larger federated organization is more likely to be pursuing goals through specific activities which are oriented to *groups external* to the community in the hope of bringing about community *change*. On the other hand, the local organization is more likely to be oriented to *individuals within* the community in hopes of *maintaining* some valued characteristic of the area. Furthermore, somewhat tautologically, the goals of the larger federated organization are wider in that they apply to the entire area in which it operates, whereas the specific goals of the local community group are restricted to its own small area of operation.

By and large, the external groups to which the larger federation is often oriented are the various governmental bureaucracies performing services on the level of the local community. These range from the Police Department to the Board of Education and the Department of Urban Renewal. It appears, in short, that the federated structure is a community organizational response to the more extensive and broader impact generated by the decisions and policies of those various governmental bureaucracies. Just as Robert Dahl documented the changing power structure of New Haven as governmental decisions shifted from concern over *individual* benefits to *collective* benefits,[25] it appears that the growth of federated community organizations is a response designed to match on an equal level the power of these various departments of city government. Although the response often is in conflict with the city bureaucracy, close cooperation is also found. Examples of conflict are the previously mentioned Greater Northwest Civic Association and Operation Crescent, which formed in opposition to the Chicago Board of Education's bussing policy and were successful in bringing about a revision of the plan. Another example is the Northwest Community Organization, which opposed the planned "crosstown expressway" that would run through its area. At one of its own meetings the organization was denounced by several of the aldermen in the area it serves, and its director was called an "alien" and an "outside agitator."[26] The possibility that these larger community organizations might represent an independent political force within their communities is undoubtedly of some concern to the established Democratic party organization. The often outright opposition of established political institutions to local community organizations as independent bases of power was one of the major reasons given by Daniel Patrick Moynihan for the government's rapid retreat from the War on Poverty's Community Action Program.[27]

Examples of close cooperation between these larger federated organizations and city bureaucracies are most common in relationships with the Department of Urban Renewal. Many of the organizations are actively engaged in drawing up planning proposals for rehabilitation and renewal of their areas and in soliciting local, state, and federal funds. This cooperative orientation of the North River Commission was shown in its 1968 annual report, which self-contradictingly read:

> Liaison with City Agencies—For any neighborhood
> program of *self*-improvement to be successful the help of
> governmental agencies is essential. Therefore, the commis-

sion will act as a liaison between the community and official public agencies [italics added].

However, this statement points out the general fact that these larger organizations are explicitly designed to deal with governmental bureaucracies in the interest of local residents. In short, they provide an integrative link between the local community and its citizens and the higher levels of urban government. In an interview the president of a local community group, the Sheffield Neighbors Association, gave a specific example of the relationship between the federated organization and the local group when he said, "We donate money to LPCC and they in turn represent us to the City and in court for such things as housing violations."

Given that the larger federated organizations are explicitly oriented to representing their communities on an equal level with larger external bureaucracies, what does this imply for the activities and goals of the smaller local community organizations? In general, it appears that these local organizations have unique functions because they are "primary groups" of neighbors.[28] As such, these local groups can provide more adequate social control and public surveillance than the larger and more formally structured federated organizations. For example, the president of one of the oldest local community organizations in the city, Ravenswood Manor Improvement Association, founded in 1914, described his group as primarily "a zoning watchdog." This division of labor between the two levels of organization is also clearly demonstrated by the Allied North Side Community Organization (ANSCO). ANSCO itself was concerned with trying to persuade the city to purchase the land of the old Edgewater Golf Course for a park and school site, in competition with several developers who wanted to build high-rise apartment buildings on it. While the federated organization was engaged in this, its constituent neighborhood groups were concerned about flooding of basements, adequate plowing of snow, zoning violations, and awarding prizes for the best maintained lawns and gardens in the area.

There is also evidence that once the local organizations have joined into a larger federation they develop new goals and activities which are closely related to the more general goals of the federated organization. For example, during the 1950s both the Old Town Triangle Association and the Mid-North Association were principally property owners' groups concerned with the "beautification" of their areas. However, after the formation of the Lincoln Park Conservation Commission, and especially since 1962, they have been actively engaged in the planning and implementation of the 18.5 million dollar Phase I renewal and rehabilitation project for their local area. Similarly, after the formation in 1961 of the federated North River Commission, one of the previously existing local community groups, the Albany Park Community Council, went through a complete reorganization, shifted its goals and activities, and changed its name to the Albany Park Action Conference.

One of the principal functions of the local community organization is to serve as a "framework" providing primary interaction for residents of the area. Since they are voluntary groups, the rewards or motivation for increased or even continued involvement are less specific than remuneration or coercion.[29] Instead, it is in part the primary interaction itself which motivates individuals to continued involvement. Findings from previous studies and in the first part of this chapter have shown that primary ties in the local area are closely related to participation in local voluntary organizations.[30] Therefore the local community organizations provide a reward structure which benefits both the local organization and the larger federated organization and which the latter could provide only partially, if at all.

BUREAUCRATIZATION AND RESOURCES

A further explanation of why these two levels operate in functionally distinct but complementary ways has to do with basic structural differences—their degree of "bureaucratization" (meaning here the presence or absence of a full-time paid staff or of a part-time voluntary staff) and their resources in money and personnel. In general the federated organizations, because of their more extensive area of operation and larger membership, have enough money to maintain at least one full-time staff member. The much smaller local community organization, however, relies almost exclusively on part-time volunteer work from its members and officers. All the larger organizations under review have at least one full-time paid staff member, and the Greater Lawndale Conservation Commission has a paid staff of nine—six part-time and three full-time. Only one of the member organizations has a paid staff member, and this is because the Rogers Park Community Council shares the offices and facilities of the federated Allied North Side Community Organization. Furthermore, the divergence in expenditures is quite marked between the two levels. For example, the smaller groups usually operate on a budget of several hundred dollars, although a few may have several thousand dollars. But the large federated organizations have budgets ranging from $30,000 to more than $100,000. Also, a full-time staff increases the likelihood of obtaining outside funding.

Consequently, the larger organizations generally have greater financial resources and are therefore able to hire professional staff members, but no single local community organization is extensive enough in membership to provide these financial resources and paid personnel. As was stated before, the unique contribution of the local community organization appears to be its "primary group" structure, which permits it to reward continued involvement and to function as the local agent of social control and surveillance for the larger but more bureaucratized federated organization.

SUMMARY

This section has briefly explored the goals and structures of fifteen of the larger community organizations operating in Chicago during 1967–68. The principal finding is that a federated hierarchy of community organizations throughout the city adds a social organizational dimension to the two- dimensional ecological structure of the city which was explored previously and was expected here.

This federated structure appears to be a community organizational response to the collective benefits, increased scope, and increasingly extensive impact of decisions by citywide bureaucracies. These federated organizations, then, are to be understood in relation to the political context in which they operate. They serve as an integrating mechanism between the citizens of the local community and the governmental bureaucratic structures of the city as a whole.

The component local organizations generally provide decidedly distinct but complementary functions for the federated organization. Their basic structural property—the primary group—explains their unique functions of providing local social control and surveillance as well as continuing motivation or reward for involvement.

Local community organizations, especially the larger federations, emerge through interaction between the local community and agents and structures external to the community. These external agents may include neighboring communities, which often have their own organizations, but of increasing importance are governmental agencies—even federal agencies and programs. I was unable to explore fully the essentially political relationships and roles of these local organizations, relationships which vary in form from conflict to cooperation and roles which range in content from assertions of local autonomy and "community control" to dependency and the legitimate local representation of larger powers. Regardless of the form of the relationship and the content of the role played, however, these external linkages are significant not only in sustaining and heightening local community awareness but also in defining the local community for its residents. A perspective which overemphasizes the "grass roots," spontaneous, and indigenous growth of local community organizations overlooks the degree to which such organizations—and the local communities generally—are dependent upon these external relationships and their often planned and purposeful inputs.[31]

Six

Local Urban Communities and the Symbolic Order: A Summary and Synthesis of Findings

INTRODUCTION

The central purpose of this study has been to explore transformations in the ecology, symbolic culture, and social structure of local urban communities brought about by the increasing scale of modern urban society. I have focused on the local communities of the city of Chicago in large part because almost fifty years of research has accumulated since they were initially studied in the twenties by Robert Park, Ernest Burgess, and others of the old Chicago school.[1] I have used a "triangulation"[2] of data and research strategies, in hope of more accurately depicting the historical changes and current structure of these local communities and in hope of gaining a more comprehensive and integrated understanding of the important theoretical dimensions of "community."

Some writers have hypothesized that an increase in scale in society would result in both fusion of previously segmented units into new collective wholes and an increased structural differentiation within these new units. Ecologically, this increase in scale would mean that as urban growth continued, relatively isolated and autonomous local communities would be pulled into a functionally interdependent urban community, and each local community would come to occupy a specialized "functional niche" or position within this overall ecological structure. The older ascriptive community ties based upon kinship and ethnicity would decline in significance, and population would become more mobile and would come to be distributed among local communities on the basis of achieved statuses such as occupation and class.[3] Second, it has been hypothesized that this fusion and this differentiation would produce a cultural-symbolic "loss of community" as urban residents recognize their areas less clearly, evaluate them less highly, and become less attached to them.[4] Finally, some sociologists have hypothesized that this fusion and differentiation would disrupt the social structure of local communities which are based primarily upon inclusive spatial groups and supporting local institutions, and that these would be superseded by more expansive, aspatial, and exclusive membership groups based primarily upon interest.[5]

In the following pages I will summarize my findings about these hypothesized consequences of the urban increase in scale and suggest some reconceptualizations needed to understand community in today's complex urban setting.

ECOLOGICAL STRUCTURE AND CHANGE

The factor analyses for 1930, 1940, 1950, and 1960 show that economic status, family status, and racial-ethnic status consistently emerge as the three principal factors of population segregation in Chicago's seventy-five community areas. However, we also notice that important changes in the ecological structure of the city occurred over this thirty-year period. In support of the hypothesis that increasing scale leads to greater variation or differentiation in the spatial distribution of Chicago's population, the proportion of variance explained decreases from 1930 to 1960. This is apparently partly due to the increasing similarity in housing stock among Chicago's community areas, which makes it less indicative of, or decreasingly correlated with, the distribution of other variables in the analysis. This homogeneity in housing is probably due to the continuing buildup of the city and to the inclusion of multiple-family dwelling units in areas which previously comprised almost entirely single-family homes.

Although economic status, family status, and racial-ethnic status consistently emerge as distinct dimensions of ecological structure, they vary in their significance or relative explanatory power over the thirty-year period. Family status decreases in importance, racial-ethnic status increases and economic status remains relatively constant as the most powerful dimension of population segregation. In short, the effects of increasing scale are not uniform, but have different consequences and lead to different ecological distributions for each of the three dimensions. However, these shifts in relative importance are somewhat interrelated. For example, the decreasing importance of family segregation and the increasing importance of racial-ethnic segregation are both in large measure attributable to the shifting, over time, of the variable "percent under five years of age" from the former dimension to the latter. This means that in 1960 the segregation of the city's foreign-born and black populations into separate areas was overlaid, or correlated with, a segregation of ages. The foreign-born areas generally have an older population and the black areas generally have a younger population.

To further explicate Chicago's ecological structure and change I then "mapped" the distribution of economic, family, and racial-ethnic status among the seventy-five local communities for each of the four points in time. By relating these dimensions of "social area analysis" directly to Chicago's "natural areas" I was able to analyze the zonal, sectoral, and multiple nuclei spatial distributions of these dimensions and to see changes in them over this thirty-year period.

In general, over time the economic status of Chicago's community areas shows a tendency to become more systematic in a concentric manner. The lower economic status areas of the city become more centralized, whereas the higher economic status areas are increasingly distributed around the periphery of the city. This also shows that the economic factor of population segregation retains a relatively high explanatory power over these thirty years. In spite of this general trend, however, a low economic sector still stretches outward near industry along the Chicago River, and a high economic sector persists along Lake Michigan—especially on the North Side of the city.

In contrast to the spatial distribution of economic status, the decreasing explanatory power of family status as a factor of segregation is shown in its decrease in systematic spatial distribution. For example, the eleven community areas making up the lakefront sector between Uptown and Woodlawn all had a low family status in 1930. By 1960 five of the eleven had shifted to a higher family status. Similarly, in 1930 the sixteen most central community areas of the city were all of low or moderately low family status, but by 1960 six had shifted to a moderately high family status.

The spatial distribution of racial-ethnic status among the communities shows a third pattern of spatial structure and change. The increasing importance of this factor over time is mainly due to the increasing number of black residents in the city and to their concentration in a central but rapidly expanding ghetto. Similarly, by 1960 a greater number of areas had a high *ethnic* concentration, relative to the city as a whole, but this is a function of the *decreasing* proportion of foreign-born residents in the city and of their gradual dispersion into more community areas. The loss of systematic segregation of the ethnic or foreign-born population is offset by the increasing importance of racial segregation. This, in conjunction with the previously noted age segregation of older and foreign-born areas from younger and black areas, accounts for the overall increasing importance (explanatory power) of the racial-ethnic factor of population segregation.

In analyzing these changes in spatial distribution we also noted the marked effect which large-scale public policy decisions on land usage (e.g., location of expressways and public housing) may have in rapidly altering the economic, family, and racial-ethnic status of Chicago's local communities. Such decisions sometimes produce ecological anomalies in the spatial configuration of the city, since an area may come to have an economic, family, or racial-ethnic status which is in sharp contrast to that of adjacent communities. To understand the ecological structure and change of Chicago's local communities, therefore, it is necessary to look not only at the "natural" ecological and economic forces of land usage but at the increasing effects of conscious governmental planning and of the response of local organized groups.[6]

In a further attempt to explicate the forces of ecological change, I performed a series of factor analyses based upon correlations between *changes* in variables over each of the three decades, 1930–40, 1940–50, and 1950–60. This analysis of "the structure of change" (as opposed to the previous analysis of "change in structure") highlights historically specific factors of change which vary from decade to decade. These factors reflect the impact of societywide social forces occurring in each decade—the Depression of the thirties, the war of the forties, and the relative "Peace and Prosperity" of the fifties. They are related to and help explain the more general changes in ecological structure previously observed.

Finally, our exploration of ecological structure and change pointed out an evolutionary sequence of stages which communities are likely to experience when changes in economic, family, and racial-etchnic status are considered jointly. These most probable stages of community change were found to be systematically distributed in concentric zones and to follow an ordered sequence. The most centrally located community areas of low economic and low family status were most likely to shift to low economic and high family status. This change is in part the result of blacks' moving into previously all-white areas—six of the thirteen central communities experiencing this "most probable" change also had a significant (more than 10 percent) black population. However, seven of the thirteen areas remained white, which suggests that this transition was also partly due to an influx of poorer white families. Poor families, operating in an extremely tight housing market, have generally located in old but cheap buildings or in new public housing, both of which are found near the central core of the city. The second centrally located set of transitions is in communities which first were of high economic and low family status, but changed to a lower economic status while retaining their low family status. These are areas simultaneously experiencing a flight of middle-class residents to more peripheral areas and an invasion of lower-class residents from more central areas. Also, four of these nine communities had a significant black population during their period of transition. In the third, more peripheral, ring the transitions involved changes in family status and not in economic status. Here, areas of high economic and high family status shifted to low family status while retaining their high economic status, because of the aging of residents and the movement of families to more peripheral areas while the economic status of the area remained relatively constant. This shows that for communities in a state of "transition" a decline in family status is likely to precede a decline in economic status. This stage of change is also associated with the first invasion of middle-class blacks into white communities at the edge of the ghetto, since two of these areas had a significant black population. Finally, the communities farthest out, but still within the city limits, experienced changes which reflect the continued movement of population to the suburbs during this period. As they come under development, sparsely settled areas of high family and low economic status are raised to a higher economic status while retaining their high family status. These findings agree with those who posit an evolutionary sequence of city-suburban status differences as cities grow and mature. The suburbs of smaller and younger metropolitan areas have a lower socioeconomic status than the central city; but in older and larger urban areas the suburbs have a higher socioeconomic status. None of these areas had a significant black population. Overall, these findings have documented four "most probable" stages of community change, which show a clear concentric distribution, and a sequential order of community succession that is related to the increasing scale and growth of the city over the past thirty years.

Cultural-Symbolic Structure and Change

Many writers have hypothesized that the increasing scale and complexity of urban life would cause an "eclipse" or "loss" of community. Increasing scale, with its spatial and organizational reliance upon ever larger units of association, was supposed to undermine the local social structure and its related identification as a meaningful symbolic community. The increasing complexity of the division of labor, the reliance upon segmented secondary relationships, as opposed to primary relationships, the emphasis upon achieved occupational and "economic" dimensions of stratification, and the increased geographical and social mobility of the population would generate at worst personal and social disorganization and at best nonspatial "communities of interest." Such "communities of interest" were thought to be qualitatively distinct from and antithetical to older, more stable ascriptive ties, such as those based upon ethnicity and kinship, which are more intimately linked to a spatial residential community. However, the findings of subsequent empirical research have qualified these hypothesized consequences and refined the much-too-simplistic theory.

More recent writers have advanced the theory of a "community of limited liability" in which ascriptive ties and local community orientations still exist but commitment is partial and varied, depending upon an individual's needs and interests and the ability of the local community to satisfy these demands. The implication for a local resident is that "when the community fails to serve his needs, he will withdraw through either departure . . . or merely lack of involvement."[7]

In short, the calculus of "the community of limited liability" suggests that an individual's local orientation, his "sense of community," is likely to vary with particular statuses he occupies, within both the local social structure and the wider society, and by demographic and social characteristics of the community itself. Furthermore, as our research has shown, communities must also be considered as symbolic variables which range in scale from small social blocks to larger neighborhoods and communities to large regions of the city. These "hierarchies of community" imply that an individual may select a level of symbolic community that best satisfies the needs and interests associated with his particular social statuses, and that what is defined as *the* community may vary between individuals and for the same individual in different settings and at different times.

This study of the symbolic culture of Chicago's local communities has drawn on W. I. Thomas's concept of "the definition of the situation,"[8] Park's perspective of the symbolic order of "the city as a state of mind," Burgess's formulation of "natural areas," and Parsons's elaboration of the cognitive, evaluative, and affective orientations of "social actors" toward their situation. I have therefore viewed local communities as "collective representations" or symbolic "objects" of orientatation, and as "situations" of action requiring definition by local residents. Specifically, I have explored changes in the symbolic order of Chicago by comparing today's local communities with the "natural areas" delimited by Burgess almost fifty years ago. I then explored variations in residents' cognitive, evaluative, and affective orientations toward their local communities and related these to three sets of independent variables—first, "general" social statuses of residents such as race and class; second, "local" social statuses such as membership in local organizations; and third, demographic characteristics of the communities themselves.

The findings on cognition about the local area show a widespread ability of residents to define and delimit their local community areas. More than three-fourths of the respondents gave a name to their local area, and more than two-thirds were able to give completely encapsulating boundaries. The symbolic definition of local areas must have a certain persistence over time, since more than 40 percent used the same community names Burgess found in the twenties. This points out the degree to which such symbols are maintained and transmitted by local community cultures, and also suggests that Burgess's work in delimiting these community areas itself may have became an "authoritative source" for defining Chicago's local communities, contributing to their persistence if not their creation. The ninety areas discussed here represent the largest distinctly defined communities for any given geographical part of the city. That the number of areas is greater today implies, naturally, a finer cognitive and symbolic differentiation, corresponding to a more complex ecological differentiation and a concomitant loss of community identification based solely upon ecological and functional criteria. I also found, although less frequently, *fusion* of several older areas into single larger cognitively defined communities. However, when this fusion took place it was usually accompanied by differentiation within the larger area. The overall result was that several different levels of spatial identification were found, from the small "social block" to larger homogeneous residential "neighborhoods" to larger more functionally complete "communities" to the largest "regions" of the city such as the "Roseland Area" or "the West Side" and "the South Side." There is some evidence, from the Burgess collection in Regenstein Library at the University of Chicago, that Burgess and his students themselves found a variety of levels of identification in the twenties, and Burgess drew a distinction between larger, functionally defined "communities" and the smaller homogeneous residential "neighborhoods" which they comprise. The seventy-five community areas defined therefore represent a reification or abstraction, for he was obviously attempting to operate on or define a single level of community. However, from my interviews it was apparent that for any geographical part of the city residents may define a number of different levels, and the level defined as "the community" varies between individuals and for the same individual at different times.

When I analyzed the dynamics of name and boundary changes for the commmunities over this fifty-year period I observed close parallels between forces of social and spatial differentiation. The connotations of a name and the stability and clarity of boundaries symbolize significant social distinctions, and changes in them are indicators of important social and ecological forces operating within the city. Also, the communities themselves are collective representations or "social facts" that may independently affect these social and ecological processes.

For example, as black in-migration occurred within an area, white residents would often simply redraw the boundaries of their community to exclude the black population.[9] In short, they redefined the situation by manipulating their symbols of community. But if the local culture perpetuated a distinctive "natural boundary" that was widely shared among residents, such idiosyncratic redrawing of boundaries was less likely to occur. Black in-migration then became defined as "invasion" and was met by resistance and at times by force.

Similar parallel social and spatial processes were observed with respect to class or status rankings of local communities. Residents of an area adjacent to a higher-status community would sometimes attempt to "borrow" the latter's prestige by consciously renaming their area or by redefining boundaries so as to include themselves within it. Residents of the higher-status communities, however, often would not reciprocate, and were themselves likely to differentiate smaller higher-status neighborhoods within the larger community. For example, the community area of Beverly ranks very high in status among Chicago's local communities, but to the residents of Beverly itself there are important status distinctions between North and South Beverly. These observations were supported by the survey finding that class distinctions were the most frequently mentioned criterion for differentiating smaller neighborhoods within larger community areas. Above all, these results point out that local communities are themselves objects of status ranking and that the multiple levels of status differentiation closely parallel the "hierarchy of community" defined by residents.

Cognition of local areas varied with the different statuses occupied by residents, and statuses implying heightened integration into the local social structure apparently lead to increased clarity in the cognitive perception of the local area. For example, the longer a person has lived in the area, the clearer is his image of it. Also, those under twenty and those in their sixties have the clearest image of the local area, whereas those who are in their productive years and are most mobile, especially those in their twenties, have the least clear cognitive image. Similarly, participation in and "awareness of" local voluntary organizations increases the clarity of the cognitive image of the local community. However, a few findings suggested that integration in only the local social structure may lead to too local an orientation and that greater cognitive clarity will be expressed by those who journey outside the narrow social and spatial confines of the local community, thereby becoming more aware of the local area's spatial and social limits.[10] For example, those with most friends inside the local area have the least clear cognitive image, those with most friends outside the local area have a clearer cognitive image, and those with friends *both* inside and outside the area have the clearest image. Furthermore, males, suggested as being less locally oriented and more mobile, are slightly more likely to have a clear cognitive image of the local area than females.

In looking at the "general" social statuses of race and class, I found that the higher the class the clearer the cognitive image of the local community, and that whites were generally better able than blacks to name and delimit the boundaries of their local areas. Similarly, residents of higher economic status areas and white areas had a clearer cognitive image than residents of lower economic status areas and black areas. Also, the higher the family status of the community the clearer was the cognitive image expressed by residents. However, closer analysis of the responses suggests that blacks operate at a different conceptual level of community than do whites. Blacks are more likely to delimit a small "social block" immediately surrounding their home, whereas whites are more likely to delimit a larger neighborhood or community area. Given that primary relations and primary groups are the basic unit of social organization at this smaller level of symbolic community, then a distinctive area name and a clear set of larger area boundaries may simply be less important in black residents' cognitive organization of their social and spatial milieu.[11]

Evaluation of the local area appears to be highly dependent upon *general* social statuses occupied by residents (race and class) and upon the characteristics *of the area*. For example, those who have a higher occupation, are white, and live in higher economic status, higher family status, and predominantly white areas are more likely to evaluate their areas positively. This is undoubtedly due in part to the differential distribution of amenities within these areas based upon areal characteristics and individual statuses. We should remember that the previous section showed that these dimensions or statuses are the most significant bases of ecological segregation in today's urban setting.[12]

Attachment to the local area, however, appears much more dependent upon *local* social statuses and the degree to which the individual is integrated into the social structure of the local area itself. General social statuses and characteristics of the area are relatively unimportant in explaining variations in local affect or sentiment. For example, those with friends living in the area, those with children, those belonging to local organizations, and those utilizing local facilities for work, shopping, worship, and recreation are much more likely to express attachment to the local area. However, attachment varies little by class, race, or characteristics of the area.[13]

The findings which point out these relationships most dramatically, perhaps, are those relating race to evaluation of and attachment to the local community. Although blacks are slightly less likely to express attachment to the local area than whites, they are much less likely to evaluate the area positively. When one controls for economic status *of the area* in which they reside, however, the relationship between race and attachment disappears while the relationship between race and evaluation persists. The need to consider both statuses of the individual and characteristics of the community is also shown in the findings relating family status to local evaluation. In general, the findings showed that those with children now at home are less likely to evaluate the area positively than are those without children. However, when we control for family status of the area, one finds that in high family status areas those with children living at home are *more* likely to evaluate the area positively than those without children, whereas in low family status areas those with children living at home are *less* likely to evaluate the area positively than those without children.[14]

The sizes of the areas defined by residents summarize best, perhaps, the relationships between residents' orientations toward their local communities and the different symbolic levels or hierarchies of communities resulting from the urban increase in scale. Relating size of area to types of central locations as a measure of "functional image" of the area, I found, for example, that residents defining smaller areas are less likely to define a central location; that the larger the area defined the more likely it is that a shopping center will be named as a central location; and that parks and schools are more likely to be mentioned as central locations by residents defining an intermediate size of community. This shows that the different levels of symbolic communities defined by residents correspond to the different scales at which different functions operate. In short, the hypothesized impact of the urban "increase in scale" is not generalized and uniform for all functions and all institutions. For example, children's playgrounds and schools are still organized on the scale of the "social block" and the "neighborhood," while shopping may be done on a larger scale of "community" and employment is considered on a still larger "regional" scale. The result has not been a "loss of function" for the local urban community; instead, differentiated "hierarchies of community" have emerged as a symbolic reorganization of the urban environment to match this functional differentiation in scale. Therefore a person will define a "symbolic community" consonant with his functional needs and interests.

Variations in a person's general and local social statuses are also related to size of area defined, and many of the relationships are direct and as expected from our previous findings. For example, larger areas were defined by those who were white, had higher-level occupations, had lived in an area longer, belonged to local organizations, knew of local organizations, and had children.

Family and economic characteristics *of the area*, however, show a more complex, curvilinear relationship, with the smallest and largest "symbolic" areas being defined by people from the same type of community. For example, those from low family status communities and those from low economic status areas are more likely to define the smallest or the largest areas, whereas those from high family status and high economic status areas are more likely to define an intermediate-sized community. It appears that within these communities of higher family status and higher economic status there is a stronger local culture, which on the one hand pulls individuals out of the small "egocentric" conception of community immediately surrounding the home and on the other hand more effectively limits this conception to a symbolic definition of community maintained in viable institutions operating at this local scale.

Attachment to the local area shows a supporting curvilinear relationship to size of area. Those defining the smallest areas are slightly less likely to express attachment to *only* their area, but are most likely to express attachment to *both* their area and another in the city.

Relating size of area defined to evaluation of the local area shows the importance of the "exclusive-inclusive" function of boundaries and area size, which enables residents to cognitively manipulate the size, the composition, and therefore the evaluation of their symbolic communities. For example, the larger the area defined the more likely residents are to say the area is racially mixed, and the more likely they are to give it an "ambivalent" (good *and* bad) evaluation. People defining a smaller area, however, are more likely to see it as either good *or* bad and to say that it is all white or all black. Also, the smaller the area defined the more positive is the evaluation about people living in the area, which reinforces the importance of primary ties at the smaller level of symbolic community.

These findings may be seen in part as a fuller explication of the theory of "the community of limited liability." The three symbolic-cultural dimensions of local orientation outlined above—cognition, evaluation, and attachment—are found to be varied and limited depending upon the needs and interests associated with the different social statuses occupied by residents, and depending upon characteristics of the area and the capacity of the local community to satisfy these demands.

Furthermore, my findings more fully specify the hypothesized impact of the urban "increase in scale" upon the symbolic order of Chicago's local communities. The forces of ecological and social change have resulted in a complex symbolic reorganization of local communities, which includes overlapping and changing boundaries and a series of levels of "hierarchies of community." Although we may have "lost" the unique natural urban community of the past, with its strong local culture containing a common name rich in connotations and a distinct set of shared "natural boundaries," we have "found" in its place a dynamic system of "symbolic communities" that meaningfully organizes the complex and rapidly changing social and spatial milieu of today's urban resident.

COMMUNITY SOCIAL STRUCTURE AND CHANGE

To explore the social structure of Chicago's local communities, I analyzed local community voluntary organizations, asking: Who joins these organizations? and What are the organizations' characteristics?

The concept of increasing scale includes a spatial dimension and an organizational dimension, both of which have been hypothesized to be destructive to local community social structure. Aspatial and exclusive membership groups based upon interest would become more important than the spatially defined inclusive membership groups found in local urban communities. Furthermore, the ascriptive ties of kinship and ethnicity would decrease in importance as societies' distributive systems rely increasingly upon individually achieved statuses, reflected primarily in occupation, income, or class.

The previous sections of this study have shown that in fact ecological segregation based on economic status is more powerful than the decreasing segregation based on family status and ethnicity.

Scott Greer, however, in discussing the community of limited liability, suggests that such locally defined inclusive spatial groups are still to be found in the urban setting, since they represent a framework for the varying types of involvement centering on the home and family, however limited this involvement may be.[15] He therefore sees these groups as fulfilling a different function than the aspatial membership groups based upon interest, with the former providing integration into the social structure of the local community and the latter providing integration into the wider society.

The purpose of this section, therefore, was to assess the consequences and correlates of participation in local community organizations, and, second, to explore in greater detail the goals and structures of the local organizations themselves.

In general, my findings agree with those of other studies which have looked at correlates of participation in local voluntary associations. For example, those with children are more likely to participate than those without, those with friends in the area participate more often than those whose friends live elsewhere, and the higher a person's class and the longer his length of residence the more likely he is to participate. In the light of previous research, it was somewhat surprising to find that blacks are just as likely as whites to participate in local community organizations.[16] This result may have been obtained because I considered as local organizations the "block clubs" which appear to be more prevalent within the black communities of Chicago. Furthermore, when economic status of the area was controlled, blacks from the highest economic status areas were more likely to participate in local organizations than whites living in such areas. Perhaps the same norms of participation govern both groups, but blacks do not have the same opportunities for participation outside of their local communities as whites and so their involvement in the organized social life of the local community is greater.

Membership in local community organizations increases the clarity of the cognitive image of the local area, results in a more positive evaluation of the area, and increases attachment to the local community. Local community organizations may increase local orientation in two primary ways. First, such organizations are a framework for social interaction, thus increasing the primary bonds with fellow residents in the area. For example, informal and formal interaction at the local level are positively related, and primary or informal interaction appears to be very significant in creating attachment to the local community. Second, local community voluntary organizations operate as communication systems, increasing cognitive knowledge of the area, and—usually by providing selective knowledge—they heighten the positive evaluation of the community.

This communication function extends beyond an organization's members. Individuals who were aware of local organizations but did not belong were more likely to have a clear cognitive image of the community and to evaluate it positively than those who .were unaware of such organizations. Furthermore, awareness of such organizations is as widespread as actual membership, for although fewer than a third are members, almost two-thirds either are aware of or belong to such local organizations. Therefore a study of the role of local community organizations in heightening local orientations should not be confined to analysis of membership.

Analysis of the goals and structures of these organizations showed that they are not all small independent groups oriented only to narrow activities in the local area. Well over half are formally affiliated with other community organizations. Furthermore, these federations extend through several hierarchical levels, going from small block clubs to large regional organizations like the Roseland Area Planning Association.

This federated structure appears to be a community organizational response to the "collective benefits" (as opposed to previous "individual benefits"), provided by the increased scope and more extensive impact of decisions by citywide and predominantly governmental bureaucracies. As such, then, these federated organizations need to be understood in terms of the political context in which they operate, and they should be seen as a community response to the organizational component of the urban increase in scale.

The goals and structures of the different levels reflect entirely different orientations, but they are mutually supporting. The smaller local organizations which make up the larger federated ones generally provide through their basic structural property—the primary group—a normative motivation for continued voluntary participation as well as closer social control and public surveillance of the local area and its residents. The goals of these smaller units are generally oriented to individuals within the community. On the other hand, the larger federated organizations are generally oriented to groups outside the community, and through their larger size, professional, paid full-time staff, and greater organizational effectiveness they are better able to represent the needs of the community and to protect the community's interests in relationships with external agencies.

In contrast, then, to Greer's discussion of the rather limited functions of spatially defined inclusive membership groups operating at the level of the local community, my findings suggest that these groups not only operate as mechanisms of social control and social integration at the local level, but through their hierarchical federations also serve to integrate the individual into the wider social structure. The formal organizational structure which is more typical of aspatial membership groups based upon interest has been "borrowed" and transformed by spatially defined membership groups in local communities, thus serving to maintain and enhance local orientations while at the same time integrating "the periphery" with "the center."[17] This is not to suggest that such contacts between the periphery and the center did not exist previously; precinct captains and ward committeemen have long exercised local social control while dispensing "individual benefits" on a highly personal basis. However, with the increasing scale and scope of "collective benefits" distributed through increasingly bureaucratized governmental agencies, the federated and hierarchical organizations have come to be a community response on the same level and in the same form. This structure does not portend the decline of the local community, but it points to a reorganization of local social structure that serves to integrate residents into both the local community and the city as a whole.

TOWARD A RECONCEPTION OF LOCAL COMMUNITIES
AS A SYMBOLIC ORDER

This study has explored empirically the ecology, symbolic culture, and social structures of Chicago's local urban communities and has assessed changes brought about by the urban increase in scale during the past half century. To a large extent, and in a very literal sense, I have retraced the steps of Burgess and his students as they went about the streets of Chicago attempting to delimit its "natural areas," or local communities. On the other hand, this research has also addressed several theories of community structure and change and assessed their validity by drawing on a variety of data and research strategies appropriate to the multiple theoretical dimensions of "community" under study.

There are no radically new findings here, but rather further specifications of theories of local urban communities and community change. In large part the research specifies the consequences for local communities of an urban increase in scale. It also specifies and elaborates upon the theory of "the community of limited liability," which stresses the persistence, the transformation, and the variability of local orientations and community solidarity in a modern urban setting. Finally, it attempts to integrate these theories with the Chicago school's traditional ecological theories of urban structure and change and to further specify these latter theories.

In conclusion, my findings suggest that a number of reconceptions are required to describe, analyze, and understand local communities in the highly urbanized, industrialized setting of the late twentieth century. These reconceptions emphasize points that have often been slighted or ignored in previous theory and research. I advance them as a partial synthesis of my findings and as a guide to further research. The first reconception was my starting point and dictated the form and content of my investigation; namely, that community should be defined and analyzed as a multidimensional rather than a single-dimensional concept. The different dimensions of community raise different questions and concerns and require different data, methods, and research strategies. The dimensions I have highlighted are the ecological, the social structural, and the cultural symbolic. The first is explicitly concerned with space and territoriality, and with the structure and dynamics exhibited by local communities as subunits occupying different "functional niches" in the ecological structure of a city. The second dimension involves normative patterns of social interaction—the statuses and roles, forms of social organization, and social institutions that develop within each local community. The third dimension involves the local customs, traditions, symbols, and sentiments of community. Robert Park could also have been referring to local communities when he wrote, "The city is . . . à state of mind, a body of customs and traditions, and of the organized attitudes and sentiments that inhere in these customs and are transmitted with this tradition."[18]

It is important to recognize that the dimensions of community are interrelated, and future research should attempt to further explain the nature of these relationships. Such relationships are exemplified by my finding that economic status is the most significant basis of ecological segregation and is also significant in explaining residents' evaluations of their local areas. On the other hand, it is equally important to realize that the three dimensions are somewhat independent —that changes in ecology, or in social organization, may not lead directly to comparable changes in symbols and sentiments of community. There may in fact be a "cultural lag." Furthermore, we should recognize the possibility that there is multi-causation between the three dimensions, instead of a "hierarchy of orders" with implicit causation running from the ecological substructure to the moral superstructure.[19] For example, the social organization and sentiments of community may alter ecological processes, just as ecological processes like racial invasion may result in new evaluations and sentiments of community.

A second reconception requires a full appreciation of local communities as social objects. In Durkheim's terms they are "social facts" or "collective representations" which are experienced in varying degrees by their residents as mutually defined external entities that constrain and pattern collective sentiment and behavior.[20] Therefore there is a need not only to develop sociological types of communities, but also to determine social types as these are perceived and defined by residents.[21] I have taken one approach to this "definition of the situation" by relying on the three orientations for social action outlined by Parsons: cognition, evaluation, and affect. I have related variations in these local orientations to variations in the social structure and ecology of communities as the objects of orientation.

My findings about residents' orientations lead me to conclude that local areas cannot be conceptualized solely on a two-dimensional plane, but instead that there are various "levels of community" or "community hierarchies." Such levels form a continuum which runs from small "social blocks" of primary relations through homogeneous "residential neighborhoods" and more institutionally and functionally complete "communities" to large "regions" encompassing whole sectors of a city. Symbols and sentiments, social structure, and ecological composition were found to vary systematically from level to level.

This conception of "community hierarchies" has important implications for the distinction between "inclusive" membership groups based on shared space and "exclusive" membership groups based on common interest. This study has shown that definitions of community names and boundaries serve both inclusive and exclusive functions, as when residents of a higher-status community consciously or unconsciously drew sharp boundaries that excluded residents of an adjacent lower-status area, while the latter "blurred" these boundaries to include themselves within the higher-status community. The dynamics of inclusion versus exclusion result in structural and symbolic fusion and differentiation of communities that is closely linked to the concept of "community hierarchies." At one level "my area" and "your area" may be sharply delimited and mutually exclusive, but on a higher level they may be joined in a larger, more inclusive community known as "our area."[22]

A related reconception is to recognize that a city's local areas are not necessarily mutually exclusive and exhaustive; instead they may overlap or their residents simply may not perceive and symbolically define them as collective social units. In short, a city cannot be neatly carved up like a jigsaw puzzle, for some of the pieces will not fit and others may be missing. There is variation in the clarity of local names and boundaries, and such symbolic ambiguity has important consequences—positive and negative—for the social and psychological life of the community and its residents.[23] Such ambiguity also means that maps outlining local areas, such as this research has produced, are only reifications, although sometimes "useful" ones, of the complexity and diffuseness of local areas as objects and settings for social life.[24]

These reconceptions also imply that local urban communities should not be viewed as immutable, static social units whose names, boundaries, and other defining characteristics may be permanently and authoritatively fixed. The "mapping" of local areas will inevitably be "wrong," because of historical change and because of the different criteria that observers or participants may use in "their" definitions of community. Instead, the defining elements of community must be seen as variable and subject to "phylogenetic," "ontogenetic," and "sociogenetic" change. Phylogenetically a community's "natural history," as Park called it, may be expected to bring about changes in local population, institutions, and culture as ecological change takes place within a city. By ontogenetic change I mean that as individuals pass through the life-cycle their life-space shifts, and symbolic definitions of local communities may be expected to reflect changes in individual biographies and resulting changes in patterns of local social interaction, utilization, and orientation. The social world or symbolic community of an individual who as a child is not allowed to cross the street will change when he begins school, learns to drive a car, gets a job, raises a family, and retires.

By "sociogenetic" change I mean that as individuals go about the routine of satisfying their daily needs they come to occupy different social positions or statuses, or that in different situations some statuses will be more salient than others. As individuals move from one status to another, from one institutional area to another, from one collectivity to another, the operating "reference community" is also likely to shift.[25] The requirements and expectations of different statuses and roles may heighten the salience of different levels of symbolic community in different settings and at different times. In the

morning I am more aware of my "metropolitan community"
as I journey from home to work and associate with colleagues
in the office. In the evening while playing touch football in
the street, I am more aware of the "social block" of my children and their friends.

The symbols of community not only represent the community as an object but are also symbols used in communication,[26] and the various "levels" or "hierarchies" of community
may be thought of as various levels of symbolic abstraction.
Therefore they share properties of abstraction characteristic
of all symbols used in communication. My answer to the
question of where I am from—in short, the establishment of
my status as "citizen"—will vary from setting to setting. While
walking the streets of Paris, I am an American; in the streets
of New York City, a Rochesterian; in Rochester, a Nineteenth
Warder; and in the Nineteenth Ward, a resident of the
Heights. Which level of symbolic community one defines as
one's "reference community," which abstract level of citizen-
ship one claims, depends in part upon what people know—or
think they know—about one another and upon the use to
which such knowledge will be put. Within cities, the level
of symbolic community defined will be geared to a certain
level of abstraction appropriate to the goals and purposes of
the interaction. Too general a level is too obvious; it does
not convey enough about social and physical position. Too
specific a level is unlikely to be widely known and therefore
is often meaningless.[27]

Another major reconception is to recognize that although
the local urban community is an external object, a "social
fact," nonetheless it arises from a process of social interaction.
In short, it is a social product. The symbolic definition and
identification of local communities, like the individual identity formation of Mead and Cooley, is a process of symbolic
interaction. Names and boundaries used as identifying symbols of social units require shared definitions that are often
worked out in the communication and interaction of residents from juxtaposed areas.[28] The "looking-glass self" has its
parallel in the "looking-glass community."

The development of community identity means that communities come to be defined comparatively as objects that

occupy different positions or statuses within the overall social and symbolic order of the city. This is the symbolic analogue to what human ecologists call a community's "functional niche" in the ecological order. Furthermore, the differences in the spatial distribution of social and demographic variables which human ecologists analyze are often central components of a local community's symbolic position.

The degree to which a local community's position within the symbolic order corresponds to a resident's own social positions has important social and psychological implications. Socially, the degree of correspondence will affect a resident's behavioral commitment and general orientation to the local community. We have seen, for example, that a resident whose individual family status is inconsistent with his community's "family status" is more likely to evaluate his local community negatively. This relationship between individual status and community status may be thought of as a problem of "status inconsistency." Among the multiple statuses an individual occupies are those he acquires by being a member of a given community which itself occupies particular positions in the social and symbolic order of the city.[29]

Psychologically, the relationship between individual and community statuses means we should consider the community as an internal component of individual identity rather than merely as an external entity or setting. Just as reference groups generally provide normative and comparative standards for individuals, so too symbolic communities operate as mechanisms for identifying individuals in physical and social space. How individuals perceive and define local communities, and how others perceive and define them, will undoubtedly affect self-conceptions. Individuals whose self-identity does not fit the symbolic identification of their local area might exhibit signs of psychic and social withdrawal, or they might manipulate the symbolic definitions of the area or even move to a new area to bring about consistency between self-identity and community identity.[30]

The possibility that symbols of community might be consciously or unconsciously manipulated is also derived from the perspective that community identity is a product of social and symbolic interaction. Drawing upon a distinction which

Peter Blau makes for formal organizations, we may speak of crescive versus created communities.[31] The usual conception is that local urban communities are crescive entities springing up spontaneously from the "grass roots." However, we have seen that there is often a very conscious and frequently external attempt to manipulate and even to create desired symbols of community.[32] Since local urban communities are often ambiguously defined, residents may turn to "authoritative" external sources. This would help explain the persistence of the seventy-five community areas delimited by Burgess in the *Local Community Fact Book.*

Local community organizations are one of the more authoritative internal sources for the definition and manipulation of local community symbols. All the organizations I studied have distinct area names and operate within clearly delimited sets of community boundaries. And many of the organizations were actively and consciously engaged in manipulating the symbols of their local area—by changing boundaries, by changing the area's name, or by more subtle attempts to change the connotation of the name. Such consciously created and often external sources of local community definition should not necessarily be viewed as "unnatural." The development of local community identity inevitably requires some external and conscious inputs. The recent community action programs of the federal government are examples of this conscious external attempt to foster a "sense of community" and local commitment by creating and supporting local organizations. The difficulties many of these programs encountered may be traced in part to the inherent contradiction between the reality of how community was being created and the rhetoric that fostered an unrealistic conception of the "autonomous," "grass-roots," "natural" community exercising "local community control."[33]

The significance of conscious inputs from external institutions also requires a reconception of the "functional basis" of community. The argument has been advanced by some that the local community, like that other primordial unit, the family, is a unit of social structure that has lost functions as other forms and levels of social organization have developed to satisfy the needs it previously met.[34] However, institutional differentiation is not uniform and not all functions exhibit comparable increases in scale; some, such as schools, may retain a more local scale while others, such as the employment market, may exist on a metropolitan scale.

My findings showed that both the definition of local areas by residents and the structure of local voluntary associations exhibit hierarchical levels of symbolic and social organization comparable in scale to these different functions. Therefore it appears that functional differentiation has not necessarily meant "functional loss" for local areas, but rather has meant a more differentiated conception of community comparable to this functional differentiation. Such a symbolic and social redefinition does not spell the "decline" of local communities, but rather indicates their persisting ability, in the words of Edward Shils, to integrate the "periphery" with the "center." It is a social and symbolic organization of the urban environment which can provide meaningful channels of collective sentiment and collective social action.

These conclusions are purposely incomplete and "open ended." Much more could be written on any of the above points, but I feel I have extended my data as far as they will go—some might think too far. I do hope, however, that these extensions will stimulate further empirical and theoretical efforts. Let me close with two cautions to thinking about "community" in today's urban setting. First, when one empirically focuses on this or that dimension or this or that variable, one should not lose sight of the many and diverse theoretical meanings of the concept of community. Second, when one begins to theoretically abstract the important meanings of the concept, one should avoid reification and should continue to consider its diversity of meanings in the social and symbolic life of local community residents. Community should neither be overspecified as representing this or that reality nor abstracted into oblivion.

Appendix I   *The Interviews*

The data on residents' perceptions of their local communities were collected in 1966 and 1967, and the procedures reflect the dilemma of attempting to do both exploratory field observation and systematic survey research. The research reflects the strengths of both approaches, but it also combines their faults and is therefore subject to criticism from both perspectives.[1]

The interview instrument was designed to explore by open-ended questions how residents throughout the city viewed their local communities. The original plan was to get approximately ten interviews from each of the seventy-five community areas initially delimited by Burgess, and a total of 801 were obtained, with a minimum of five and a maximum of eighteen for each area. Interviews were conducted with available residents at locations chosen to give a broad geographical coverage of each community area. The interviews were meant to quickly supply a composite picture of how the local neighborhoods and communities of the city were defined. The validity of the short interview technique (each interview took only about ten to fifteen minutes) was partially confirmed by more intensive research conducted in two areas, South Shore and South Chicago; this produced very similar neighborhood and community definitions.[2] Consequently, this purpose of the research appears to have been fulfilled.

However, the eight hundred interviews contained additional data that could be analyzed to see what light they might throw upon variations in residents' perceptions of their local communities. Although the analysis of these data relies extensively upon cross-tabulation, the reader should constantly bear in mind that given the sampling procedures used the findings reported have a higher probability than usual of being wrong when generalized to the resident population of Chicago as a universe. Consequently, tests of significance are not utilized, because the sampling procedures do not justify such concreteness, and the rhetoric of "significance" is noticeably absent.[3]

Furthermore, some items were added at different points in the interviewing procedure, causing large deviations in sample size. For example, the question about family structure (whether there were children in the home) was asked only midway through the interviewing period, and so the sample size on this item is only 349. Large deviations in sample size are also found for the items on class (occupation of head of household), location of work, and previous residence. The item on previous residence was also inserted after the interviewing had begun, and the small size of the sample on the other two items was due to uncodable responses. For other items the loss of cases is for the most part due to nonresponse.

The information collected by the interview instrument can be categorized into four broad areas (the numbers of questions tapping each area are in parentheses):

1 Background data—age, sex, race, occupation of family head, years living in present area, previous areas of Chicago lived in, and children at home
   (Items 18, 19, 20, 21)

2 Cognitive perception of the local area—ability to name the area, give boundaries, name central locations, define neighborhoods, and describe changes and problems in the area, and knowledge of organizations
   (Items 1, 2, 3, 4, 7, 12, 13)

3 Sentiments about the area—how they evaluated the area and its people, and what attachment they felt to the local area or others and why
   (Items 5, 6, 16)

4 Local activity or utilization and participation within the local area—shopping for both food and clothing, church attendance, location of friends and recreation, and membership in voluntary associations
   (Items 7, 8, 9, 10, 11, 17)

"Sample" Characteristics

The following characteristics of the sample (gathered in 1966–67) are compared with 1960 census data for the city of Chicago (NA = no answer).

Characteristic	Sample	Census (1960)
Sex ratio	64.2	94.7
Race		
Percentage white	72.3	76.4
Percentage nonwhite	25.6	23.6
	97.9	100.0
	NA = (2.1)	
Occupation		
Professional, technical	4.5	9.7
Managerial, clerical, sales	35.5	27.4
Craftsmen, operatives, laborers	37.3	53.2
Service, household	7.0	9.7
NA or could not classify, no occupation	15.7	
	100.0	100.0

Some major deviations of the sample distributions from those of the census should be noted, especially where these variables are not controlled in the analysis. The sample includes many more females, older people, and residentially stable persons than does the Chicago population. Occupationally overrepresented are managers and clerical and sales workers, and underrepresented are professionals, craftsmen and laborers, and service workers. The sample corresponds more closely to the census with respect to race, with nonwhites being only slightly overrepresented.

Center for Social Organizations Studies   University of Chicago

COMMUNITY AREA STUDY QUESTIONNAIRE

1. What is the name of this part of Chicago?
2. What are its boundaries?
3. Does _____ [name of area] have any central location or thing? Where?
   [Probes: shopping areas, parks, monuments, etc.]
4. Is _____ all pretty much the same or are there any distinct sections or neighborhoods in it? Name and locate.
5. When you think of _____ what feelings come to mind?
6. What kind of people live in _____?
7. Do you belong to any organizations in _____? Do your neighbors? Which ones?
8. Do you go to church in _____? Do your neighbors?

9. Do most of your friends live in _____ or in other areas of the city?

10. Do you do most of your shopping in _____? Does that include shopping for clothing as well as for food?

11. Where do you usually go when you go someplace for recreation?

12. Have there been any changes in _____ in the last several years?

13. Are there any problems which concern people around here? What?

14. On this blank sheet of paper could you please sketch a map of this particular area.

15. [If respondent has not already done so] Could you also please mark any particular sections or neighborhoods within the area.

16. What areas of Chicago do you personally feel any attachment to?

17. What area of Chicago do you live in? Work in?

18. Occupation?

19. Interviewer estimate of respondent's age _____ sex _____ race _____

20. How long have you lived in this area? Have you lived in any other areas of Chicago?

21. Do you have any children living at home? Their ages?

Appendix II

A Partial List of the Larger Federated Local Community Voluntary Organizations Operating in Chicago in 1967-68

Allied North Side Community Organization (ANSCO)
  1. Edgewater Community Council
  2. North Town Community Council
     1. West Rogers Park Community
     2. North Town Civic League
     3. North Town Improvement Association
     4. North Boundary Homeowner's League
  3. Rogers Park Community Council

Beverly Area Planning Association (BAPA)
  1. Beverly Improvement Association
  2. Beverly Manor Home Owners Association
  3. Beverly Ridge Homeowners Association
  4. Beverly Woods–Kennedy Park Improvement Association
  5. East Beverly Association
  6. Morgan Park Manor Improvement Association
  7. Ridge Homes Improvement Association
  8. Southwest Beverly Improvement Association
  9. Vanderpool Improvement Association

Committee on Community Organization (COCO)
  1. Near North Areas Council
  2. Sandburg and East Area Council
  3. Tenants Action Council
  4. The United Friends
     1. Olivette Neighbors
     2. Wheland Area Association

Greater Lawndale Conservation Commission
  —Four district councils
     —Each district council has from two to four block club councils
        —Each block club council has from three to twenty-three block clubs

Lincoln Park Conservation Commission (LPCC)
1. Lincoln Central Association
2. Mid-North Association
3. Old Town Triangle Association
4. Park West Community Association
5. Ranch Triangle Association
6. Sheffield Neighbors Association
7. Wrightwood Neighborhood Association

North River Commission
1. Albany Park Action Conference
2. Hollywood North Park Civic Association
3. Peterson Park Improvement Association
4. Ravenswood Manor Improvement Association

Northwest Community Organization (NCO)
1. Emerson Community Council
2. Erie-Eckhart Property Owners Association
3. Humboldt Park Homeowners Protective Association
4. Organization of Palmer Square
5. PROS Neighborhood Organization
6. Smith Park Conservation Council
7. Wicker Park Neighborhood Council
8. COPA
9. St. Fideles Group
10. Northwest Clergy Association
11. Trinity Lutheran Improvement Group

Northwest Federation of Improvement Clubs
1. Big Oaks Improvement Club
2. Bryn Mawr–Higgins Community Club
3. Cragin Improvement Council
4. Edgewood Community Council
5. Edison Park Community Council
6. Foreman Community Association
7. Foster-Harlem Property Owners' Association
8. Glen Edens Homeowner's Association
9. Hollywood–North Park Civic Association
10. Homeowners Association of Belmont Heights
11. Jefferson Park Improvement Club
12. Kedzie–Bryn Mawr Improvement Association
13. Kilbourn Park Improvement Club
14. Krim Civic Association

15. Logan Square Homeowners' Association
16. Merimac Gardens Community Club
17. North Austin Improvement Club
18. North Mayfair Improvement Association
19. North Portage Park Community Association
20. Parkview Citizens' Association
21. Parkview Improvement Citizens Club
22. Portage Park West End
23. Progressive Community Club
24. West Big Oaks Community Association

Organization for a Better Austin
1. Austin Tenants and Owners Association
2. Columbus Community Council
3. North Austin Community Council

Organization of the Southwest Community
1. Altgeld Civic Organization
2. Auburn Improvement Association
3. Auburn Park Neighborhood Civic Organization
4. Bogan Area Community Relations Council
5. Co-operative Organization of Fernwood
6. Euclid Park Improvement Association
7. Foster Park Community Council
8. Greenview Park Community Council
9. Gresham Community Council
10. Longwood Manor Civic Association
11. Maple Park Homeowners Association
12. Morgan Park Civic League
13. Morgan Park Planning Organization
14. Oakdale Civic Association
15. West Chatham Improvement Association
16. West Englewood Improvement Association
17. West Hamilton Civic Association
18. Westchester Highland Improvement Association
19. Winneconda Lakes Improvement Association

Ravenswood Conservation Commission
1. Ravenswood Civic League
2. Ravenswood Garden Home Owners Association
3. Ravenswood Rockwell Improvement Association

Roseland Area Planning Association (RAPA)
1. Central Roseland Improvement Association

2. Colonial Village Improvement Association
3. Fairview Civic Association
4. Fernwood-Bellevue Civic Association
5. Gano Civic League
6. Kensington Improvement Association
7. North Central Roseland Improvement Association
8. North Pullman Civic Association
9. Palmer Park Civic Association
10. Placerdale Civic Association
11. Pullman Civic Association
12. Rosegrove Improvement Association
13. Roselawn Civic Association
14. Rosemoor Community Association
15. Sheldon Heights Civic Association
16. Sheldon Park Civic Association
17. South Roseland Civic Association
18. Victory Heights Civic League
19. Washington Heights Civic League
20. West Pullman Civic Club

Southwest Community Organization (SECO)

1. Manors Community Assembly
2. Marynook Homeowners Association
3. Marionette Manor
4. North Avalon Community Organization
5. South Avalon Community Organization
6. South Shore Gardens Betterment Association
7. South Shore Valley Community Organization
8. Stony Island Heights Civic Association
9. Stony Island Park Civic Association
10. West Avalon Community Association

South Shore Commission

1. Bryn Mawr East
2. Bryn Mawr West
3. Central South Shore Commission
4. Jeffery Yates Neighbors
5. O'Keefe Area Council
6. Parkside Area Council
7. South East South Shore Community Organization
8. South End West Area Council

Notes

INTRODUCTION

1. There are numerous definitions of the concept of "community" within the sociological literature. For a review and synthesis of many of them the reader should consult George A. Hillery, Jr., "Definitions of Community: Areas of Agreement," *Rural Sociology* 20 (June 1955): 111–23.

2. Ernest W. Burgess, "Can Neighborhood Work Have a Scientific Basis?" in *The City*, ed. Robert E. Park, Ernest W. Burgess, and Roderick D. McKenzie, pp. 142–55 (Chicago: University of Chicago Press, 1967).

3. The results of Robert Park's and Ernest Burgess's collaborative efforts are to be found in many writings, but perhaps the most significant product was their *Introduction to the Science of Sociology*, 3d ed. (Chicago: University of Chicago Press, 1969; originally published in 1921). For the purposes of this research one should see especially chapter 3, "Society and the Group," pp. 161–225, which begins with the heading "Society, the Community, and the Group."

4. The work of Herbert Spencer drew heavily on a biological and evolutionary perspective, and of his many writings one should consult *The Study of Sociology* (Ann Arbor: University of Michigan Press, 1961). Examples of Weber's and Simmel's influence are to be found in Max Weber, *The City*, trans. and ed. Don Martindale and Gertrud Neuwirth (New York: Free Press, 1958); and Georg Simmel, "The Metropolis and Mental Life," in *The Sociology of Georg Simmel*, ed. Kurt H. Wolff, trans. H. H. Gerth and C. Wright Mills, pp. 409–24 (New York: Free Press, 1950).

5. Ernest W. Burgess, "The Growth of the City," in Park, *The City*, pp. 47–62.

6. Robert Park's ideas on "social and spatial distance" are succinctly stated in the following paragraph. "Human ecology, as sociologists conceive it, seeks to emphasize not so much geography as space. In society we not only live together, but at the same time we live apart, and human relations can always be reckoned, with more or less accuracy, in terms of distance. Insofar as social structure can be defined in terms of position, social changes may be described in terms of movement; and society exhibits, in one of its aspects, characters that can be measured and described in mathematical formulas" ("The Urban Community as a Spatial Pattern and a Moral Order," in

Robert E. Park, *Human Communities*, pp. 165–77 [New York: Free Press, 1952]). More recent studies relating social and physical space include Beverly Duncan and Otis D. Duncan, "Residential Distribution and Occupational Stratification," *American Journal of Sociology* 60 (March 1955): 493–503; Arnold S. Feldman and Charles Tilly, "The Interaction of Social and Physical Space," *American Sociological Review* 25 (December 1960): 877–84; Stanley Lieberson, *Ethnic Patterns in American Cities* (New York: Free Press, 1962); Edward O. Lauman, *Prestige and Association in an Urban Community* (Indianapolis: Bobbs–Merrill, 1966); and Gerald Suttles, *The Social Order of the Slum* (Chicago: University of Chicago Press, 1968).

7. William H. Form, et al., "The Compatibility of Alternative Approaches to the Delimitation of Urban Sub-Areas," *American Sociological Review* 19 (August 1954): 434–40. Paul K. Hatt, "The Concept of Natural Area," in *Studies in Human Ecology*, ed. George A. Theodorson, pp. 104–8 (Evanston, Ill.: Harper and Row, 1961).

8. Eshref Shevky and Wendell Bell, *Social Area Analysis* (Stanford: Stanford University Press, 1955). Eshref Shevky and Marilyn Williams, *The Social Areas of Los Angeles* (Berkeley and Los Angeles: University of California Press, 1949).

9. Theodore R. Anderson and Janice A. Egeland, "Spatial Aspects of Social Area Analysis," *American Sociological Review* 26 (June 1961): 392–98. Brian J. L. Berry and Philip H. Rees, "The Factorial Ecology of Calcutta," *American Journal of Sociology* 74 (March 1969): 445–91.

10. Ferdinand Toennies, *Community and Society (Gemeinschaft und Gesellschaft)*, trans. Charles P. Loomis (East Lansing, Michigan: Michigan State University Press, 1957). Emile Durkheim, *The Division of Labor in Society*, trans. George Simpson (New York: Free Press, 1949).

11. Park, "Spatial Pattern and Moral Order."

12. Suttles, *Social Order of the Slum*.

13. Kevin Lynch, *The Image of the City* (Cambridge: Massachusetts Institute of Technology Press, 1960).

14. Walter Firey, *Land Use in Central Boston* (Cambridge: Harvard University Press, 1947).

15. Examples of "holistic" studies of communities include Robert Lynd and Helen Lynd, *Middletown* (New York: Harcourt, Brace and World, 1929); W. Lloyd Warner, *Yankee City* (New Haven: Yale University Press, 1963); and Arthur J. Vidich and Joseph Bensman, *Small Town in Mass Society* (Princeton: Princeton University Press, 1958).

16. Morris Janowitz, *The Community Press in an Urban Setting* (Chicago: University of Chicago Press, 1967).

17. Basil G. Zimmer and Amos H. Hawley, "The Significance of Membership in Associations," *American Journal of Sociology* 65 (September 1959): 190–201; Morris Axelrod, "Urban Structure and

Social Participation," *American Sociological Review* 21 (February 1956): 14–18.

18. Scott Greer, *The Emerging City* (New York: Free Press, 1962).

19. Harry Harman, *Modern Factor Analysis* (Chicago: University of Chicago Press, 1960).

20. The results of Burgess's work have become "institutionalized" in the *Local Community Fact Book for Chicago* (see bibliography), from which the data for this analysis were taken.

21. Here we use factor analysis with a different logic than has been employed in many previous studies. The factor scores represent the relative position of a given community on one of the three factors at a single point in time. Since the position is relative to the distribution of the variables throughout the city as a whole, a change in position may take place without the local community's *necessarily* experiencing any intrinsic change in composition. In short, this is an analysis of positional shifts of communities within the ecological structure of the city as a whole, and as such it is much closer to a functional analysis than to an analysis of change in community composition. Furthermore, this approach is similar in perspective to many of the earlier case studies of Chicago's communities which emphasized their functional position or functional "niche" within the total ecological structure of the city.

22. Recent studies have once again begun to test the propositions contained in Burgess's "concentric zone" model of urban growth and decentralization. See Avery M. Guest, "Retesting the Burgess Zonal Hypothesis: The Location of White Collar Workers," *American Journal of Sociology* 76 (May 1971) : 1094–1108; Lee J. Haggerty, "Another Look at the Burgess Hypothesis: Time as an Important Variable," *American Journal of Sociology* 76 (May 1971): 1084–93.

23. See Appendix 1 for a brief discussion of the methods.

24. These distinctions draw directly from the work of Parsons and Shils, who say, "Thus the cognitive mapping of the situation, or relevant parts of it, is one essential aspect of any actor's orientation to it. nor can there be cognition without any associated cathexis" (p. 69). "The third of the three basic modes of motivational orientation is evaluation. The evaluative mode is essentially the organizational or integrative aspect of a given actor's system of action and hence it is directly relevant to the act of choice" (Talcott Parsons and Edward A. Shils, eds., *Toward a General Theory of Action* [New York: Harper and Row, 1951], p. 70) .

25. The distinction between "general" and "local" social statuses is similar to the distinction between "locals" and "cosmopolitans" advanced by Merton. However, where Merton sees these distinctions as applying to different "individuals," I see the distinction applying also to different "statuses." The content and normative expectations of some statuses are more generalized throughout a society (cosmopolitan); other statuses are rooted in their content and normative

expectations to a particular more specific locality (local). In this sense one may think of a local-cosmopolitan continuum depending upon the degree of specificity or generality of the norms associated with a given status. Robert K. Merton, *Social Theory and Social Structure*, enlarged edition (New York: Free Press, 1968); see especially chapter 12, "Patterns of Influence: Local and Cosmopolitan Influentials," pp. 441–74.

26. On structural effects see Peter M. Blau, "Structural Effects," *American Sociological Review* 25 (April 1960): 178–93; and James A. Davis, Joe Spaeth, and Carolyn Huston, "A Technique for Analyzing the Effects of Group Composition," *American Sociological Review* 26 (1961): 215–26.

27. Greer, *Emerging City*; and Suzanne Keller, *The Urban Neighborhood* (New York: Random House, 1968).

28. See Appendix 2 for a partial list of the larger federated community organizations.

29. For a comprehensive discussion and review of the literature, see Peter M. Blau and W. Richard Scott, *Formal Organizations* (San Francisco: Chandler, 1962). For a specific discussion of organizational goals see Mayer Zald, "Sociology and Community Organization Practice," in *Organizing for Community Welfare*, ed. Mayer Zald (Chicago: Quadrangle Books, 1967), pp. 27–61; and for a specific look at community voluntary associations see Nicholas Babchuk and C. Wayne Gordon, *The Voluntary Association in the Slum* (Lincoln: University of Nebraska Press, 1962).

30. Burgess, "Neighborhood Work," p. 148.

31. For discussion of "increase in scale" one should see Shevky and Bell, *Social Area Analysis*; Greer, *Emerging City*; and Godfrey Wilson and Monica Wilson, *The Analysis of Social Change* (Cambridge: Cambridge University Press, 1954).

32. Donald J. Bogue, *The Structure of the Metropolitan Community* (Ann Arbor: University of Michigan Press, 1949).

33. For an older work emphasizing the negative aspects of "mass society" see Gustav Le Bon, *The Crowd* (New York: Ballantine Books, 1969). For a focus on "mass culture" see Bernard Rosenberg and David Manning White, eds., *Mass Culture: The Popular Arts in America* (New York: Free Press, 1957); and for more general discussions see Daniel Bell, *The End of Ideology* (New York: Free Press, 1960); and William Kornhauser, *The Politics of Mass Society* (New York: Free Press, 1959).

34. The views of Edward Shils are presented in a number of writings, but one should see "Daydreams and Nightmares: Reflections on the Criticism of Mass Culture," *Sewanee Review* 65 (1957).

35. Louis Wirth, "Urbanism as a Way of Life," in *Cities and Society*, ed. Paul Hatt and Albert Reiss, Jr., pp. 46–63 (New York: Free Press, 1957), p. 54.

36. Keller, *Urban Neighborhood.*

37. The "loss of community" refers to all three dimensions, ecological and spatial, normative and social, and cultural and symbolic. One might also add its social-psychological implications for "anomie" and "alienation." See Maurice Stein, *The Eclipse of Community* (New York: Harper and Row, 1960); and Robert A. Nisbet, *The Quest for Community* (New York: Oxford University Press, 1953).

CHAPTER ONE

1. On the subject of human ecology as "holistic," macrosociological perspective, see Leo Schnore, *The Urban Scene* (New York: Free Press, 1965), pp. 29–43, "The Myth of Human Ecology." On the perspective of viewing cities as "organisms" see Leo Schnore, "The City as a Social Organism," *Urban Affairs Quarterly* 1 (March 1966): 58–69.

2. As Park says of the significance of "space" to social life, "geographical barriers and physical distances are significant for sociology only when and where they define the conditions under which communication and social life are actually maintained. . . . It is because communication is fundamental to the existence of society that geography and all the other factors that limit or facilitate communication may be said to enter into its structure and organization at all" (Robert Park, *Human Communities* [New York: Free Press, 1952], p. 174).

3. Harvey M. Zorbaugh, *The Gold Coast and the Slum* (Chicago: University of Chicago Press, 1929).

4. The significance of economic land values is indicated by Burgess in the following paragraph. "Land values, since they reflect movement, afford one of the most sensitive indexes of mobility. The highest land values in Chicago are at the point of greatest mobility in the city, at the corner of State and Madison streets, in the Loop. . . . Our investigations so far seem to indicate that variations in land values, especially where correlated with differences in rents, offer perhaps the best single measure of mobility, and so of all the changes taking place in the expansion and growth of the city" (Burgess, "The Growth of the City," p. 61). It was precisely such variation in "rents" which led Homer Hoyt to propose his "sector theory" of city structure and growth. See Homer Hoyt, *The Structure and Growth of Residential Neighborhoods in American Cities* (Washington, D.C.: U.S. Federal Housing Administration, 1939).

5. On the development of "functional niche" in human ecology, see Amos Hawley, *Human Ecology* (New York: Ronald Press, 1950). Burgess states it in the following way: "This differentiation into natural economic and cultural groupings gives form and character to the city. For segregation offers the group, and thereby the individuals who compose the group, a place and a role in the total organization of city life" (Burgess, "Growth of the City," p. 56).

6. Hoyt, *Structure and Growth of Neighborhoods.*

7. Berry and Rees, "Factorial Ecology of Calcutta."

8. Chauncy D. Harris and Edward L. Ullman, "The Nature of Cities," *Annals* 242 (November 1945): 7–17.

9. Shevky and Bell, *Social Area Analysis.*

10. Anderson and Egeland, "Spatial Aspects of Social Area Analysis."

11. Berry and Rees, "Factorial Ecology of Calcutta."

12. Wendell Bell, "The City, the Suburb, and a Theory of Social Choice," in *The New Urbanization,* ed. Scott Greer et al., pp. 132–68. (New York: St. Martin's Press, 1968).

13. William H. Form, "The Place of Social Structure in the Determination of Land Use: Some Implications for a Theory of Urban Ecology," *Social Forces* 32 (May 1954): 317–23.

14. Evelyn M. Kitagawa and Karl E. Taeuber, *Local Community Fact Book for Chicago Metropolitan Area, 1960* (Chicago: Chicago Community Inventory, University of Chicago, 1963), p. xiii.

15. Duncan and Duncan, "Residential Distribution."

16. Feldman and Tilly, "Social and Physical Space."

17. Ernest R. Mowrer, *Family Disorganization* (Chicago: University of Chicago Press, 1927).

18. Michael Young and Peter Wilmott, *Family and Kinship in East London* (London: Routledge, and Kegan Paul, 1957). Bert N. Adams, *Kinship in an Urban Setting* (Chicago: Markham, 1968).

19. E. Franklin Frazier, "The Negro Family in Chicago," in *Contributions to Urban Sociology,* ed. Ernest W. Burgess and Donald J. Bogue, pp. 404–18 (Chicago: University of Chicago Press, 1964); St. Clair Drake and Horace R. Cayton, *Black Metropolis* (Evanston, Ill.: Harper and Row, 1945); Otis Dudley Duncan and Beverly Duncan, *The Negro Population of Chicago: A Study of Residential Succession* (Chicago: University of Chicago Press, 1957); Karl E. Taeuber, "The Effect of Income Redistribution on Racial Residential Segregation," *Urban Affairs Quarterly* 4 (September 1968): 5–14.

20. Harman, *Modern Factor Analysis.*

21. There are other approaches that utilize correlation analysis in the study of urban change. One method is the "correlation of deviational changes" used by Myers in a comparative study of Rochester and Seattle. George C. Myers, "Variations in Urban Population Structure," *Demography* 1: 156–63.

22. James Coleman, *Mathematical Sociology* (New York: Free Press, 1964). See especially chapter 5, "Relations between Attributes: Over-Time Data," pp. 132–88.

23. Berry and Rees, "Factorial Ecology of Calcutta"; and Janet Abu-Lughod, "Testing the Theory of Social Area Analysis: The Ecology of Cairo, Egypt," *American Sociological Review* 34 (April 1969): 198–212.

24. Philip H. Rees, "The Factorial Ecology of Metropolitan Chicago," in *Geographic Perspectives on Urban Systems,* ed. Brian J. L.

Berry and Frank E. Horton (Englewood Cliffs, N.J.: Prentice–Hall, 1969).

25. Louis Wirth, *The Ghetto* (Chicago: University of Chicago Press, 1928). Stanley Lieberson, *Ethnic Patterns in American Cities* (New York: Free Press, 1962).

26. Peter H. Rossi and Robert A. Dentler, *The Politics of Urban Renewal* (New York: Free Press, 1961).

27. Helena Znaniecki Lopata, "The Function of Voluntary Associations in an Ethnic Community: 'Polonia,'" in *Contributions to Urban Sociology*, ed. Ernest W. Burgess and Donald J. Bogue, pp. 203–23 (Chicago: University of Chicago Press, 1964).

28. Brian J. L. Berry, "Internal Structure of the City," in *Internal Structure of the City*, ed. Larry S. Bourne, pp. 97–103 (New York: Oxford University Press, 1971), p. 101.

29. Edgar M. Hoover and Raymond Vernon, *Anatomy of a Metropolis* (Garden City, N.Y.: Doubleday, 1962), pp. 183–98.

30. Coleman, *Mathematical Sociology*.

31. Hoover and Vernon in *Anatomy of a Metropolis* note that "Since bottom income groups necessarily have but little choice in where they can live within the Region, we do not find them split into widely separated and radically different areas, as the top income group is split, nor do we find them spread over virtually all the Region as the middle income groups are" (p. 168).

32. Peter Rossi, *Why Families Move* (New York: Free Press, 1955).

33. The following articles develop the thesis of an "evolutionary" sequence of city-suburban status differences: Leo Schnore and James R. Pinkerton, "Residential Distribution of Socioeconomic Strata in Metropolitan Areas," *Demography* 3 (1966): 491–99; Leo Schnore, "Measuring City-Suburban Status Differences," *Urban Affairs Quarterly* 3 (September 1967): 95–108; and Leo Schnore and Joy K. O. Jones, "The Evolution of City-Suburban Types in the Course of a Decade," *Urban Affairs Quarterly* 4 (June 1969): 421–42.

34. Karl E. Taeuber and Alma F. Taeuber, *Negroes in Cities: Residential Segregation and Neighborhood Change* (Chicago: Aldine, 1965), p. 7.

35. North Center, the one area not following the sequence, is one of the more aberrant and rapidly changing communities in the city in terms of the indexes of this study. In the thirties it experienced a stage IV transition from low economic and low family status to low economic and high family status. Then in the forties it made an aberrant shift from low economic and high family status to high economic and low family status; that is, it shifted both its economic and its family status. Finally, in the fifties it made the stage III transition from high economic/low family status to low economic/low family status. In short, in 1960 North Center had the same economic and family status it had had thirty years before.

36. Harvey Molotch, *Managed Integration* (Berkeley and Los Angeles: University of California Press, 1972).

CHAPTER TWO

1. As Max Weber says, "Of those cultural elements that represent the most important positive basis for the formation of national sentiment everywhere, a common language takes first place" (*From Max Weber*, trans. and ed. H. H. Gerth and C. Wright Mills [New York: Oxford University Press, 1958], pp. 177–78).

2. A number of studies have explored local neighborhood names and boundaries, among them H. Laurence Ross, "The Local Community: A Survey Approach," *American Sociological Review* 27 (February 1962): 127–34; Donald L. Foley, "The Use of Local Facilities in a Metropolis," in *Cities and Society*, ed. Paul Hatt and Albert Reiss, Jr., pp. 607–16 (New York: Free Press, 1959); Form et al., "Compatibility of Alternative Approaches"; Walter T. Firey, "Sentiment and Symbolism as Ecological Variables," *American Sociological Review* 10 (April 1945): 140–48. For a summary of a number of studies see Keller, *Urban Neighborhood*.

3. Status and role changes as a function of movement through space are the central theme of Simmel's essay "The Stranger": "If wandering is the liberation from every given point in space, and thus the conceptional opposite to fixation at such a point, the sociological form of the 'stranger' presents the unity, as it were, of these two characteristics. This phenomenon, too, however, reveals that spatial relations are only the condition, on the one hand, and the symbol, on the other, of human relations." Suttles uses a similar argument in his discussion of the "segmental order" based on ethnicity and territory on Chicago's West Side. *The Sociology of Georg Simmel*, ed. Kurt H. Wolff, trans. H. H. Gerth and C. Wright Mills (New York: Free Press, 1950), p. 402. Suttles, *Social Order of the Slum*, chap. 2, "The Ecological Basis of Ordered Segmentation," pp. 13–38.

4. See Appendix 1.

5. Ross, "Local Community"; Foley, "Use of Local Facilities"; Svend Riemer, "Villagers in Metropolis," *British Journal of Sociology* 11 (March 1951): 31–43.

6. As Keller says in *The Urban Neighborhood*, "Subjective demarcations are likewise unreliable guides—when people are asked to draw the boundaries of their neighborhoods, few of them draw identical ones. And when asked to state the name of their neighborhood, they often do not use the one officially used by outsiders for the area or district" (p. 98).

7. This is, of course, a paraphrase of what has come to be called "the Thomas Dictum"—"If men define situations as real, they are real in their consequences" (W. I. Thomas, *On Social Organization and Social Personality*, edited and with an introduction by Morris Janowitz [Chicago: University of Chicago Press, 1966], p. xl).

8. For one of the stronger critiques of planners' attempts to "construct" urban neighborhoods see Reginald Isaacs, "Are Urban Neighborhoods Possible?" *Journal of Housing*, July 1948, pp. 177–80; and

"The Neighborhood Theory," *Journal of the American Institute of Planners* 14 (spring 1948): 15–23. For a good summary of this discussion see Richard Dewey, "The Neighborhood, Urban Ecology and City Planners," in *Cities and Society*, edited by Paul Hatt and Albert Reiss, Jr., pp. 783–90. New York: Free Press, 1957.

9. Janowitz, *Community Press*; Svend Riemer, "Hidden Dimensions of Neighborhood Planning," *Land Economics* 26 (May 1950): 197–201.

10. Hatt, "Concept of Natural Area."

11. Herbert Gans, *The Urban Villagers* (New York: Free Press, 1962).

12. The Burgess papers are currently being collected and cataloged in Regenstein Library at the University of Chicago and should provide a useful accounting of the urban life of the period and as well serve as a basis of historical comparative analysis for future researchers.

13. The community names and boundaries necessarily represent an "abstraction" from both resident interviews and community organizations. They are abstract because of residents' lack of knowledge or consensus in naming and bounding certain areas. The map does not depict this "variation" in cognitive consensus from one community area to another. It should be noted that the delimiting of community areas by Burgess was similarly "abstract" as he attempted to reconcile a number of different criteria used in defining the communities. Kitagawa and Taeuber, *Fact Book . . . 1960*, p. xiii.

14. The importance of dimensions of social stratification in selectively segregating populations in space has of course been widely studied and is the focus of part 1 of this book. However, there has been no systematic study of the "status ranking" of communities as units of analysis, and the secondary acquisition of these communal status characteristics by virtue of "membership" in the community has not received thorough investigation. For a number of studies that refer to similar phenomena see Keller, *Urban Neighborhood*; William H. Whyte, Jr., *The Organization Man* (Garden City, N.Y.: Doubleday-Anchor, 1957); Firey, *Land Use in Central Boston*; and Bernard Barber, "Family Status, Local-Community Status, and Social Stratification: Three Types of Social Ranking," *Pacific Sociological Review* 4 (Spring 1961): 3–10.

15. Drake and Cayton, *Black Metropolis*; and Alan Spear, *Black Chicago* (Chicago: University of Chicago Press, 1967).

16. Suttles, *Social Order of the Slum*.

17. The "natural barriers" were seen to result in the delimiting of "natural areas"—as such these barriers restricted communication between "social groups" and also served as geographical symbols of such social differentation. See Park, *Human Communities*, pp. 168–72.

18. Warner, *Yankee City*; Richard Centers, *The Psychology of Social Classes* (Princeton: Princeton University Press, 1949).

19. W. Lloyd Warner, Marcia Meeker, and Kenneth Eells, *Social Class in America* (New York: Harper and Row, 1960), pp. 39–42.

20. On the distinction between individual and structural mobility see Bernard Barber, *Social Stratification* (New York: Harcourt, Brace and World, 1957), pp. 412–18.

21. The relationship between an individual's status characteristics and the status characteristic of his community may be conceptualized as a problem of "status inconsistency" and might be fruitfully analyzed by use of "structural effects." Gerhard Lenski, "Status Crystallization," *American Sociological Review* 19 (1954): 405–13. Blau, "Structural Effects."

22. Bell, "City, Suburb, and Social Choice."

23. Albert J. Reiss, Jr., *A Review and Evaluation of Research on Community*, a working memorandum prepared for the Committee on Social Behavior of the Social Science Research Council, Nashville, Tennessee (1954), p. 32.

24. This point is especially relevant, since an increasing number of municipalities are beginning to define "authoritative" local community administrative and political districts. Such "formal boundaries" may reduce the local community's adaptability to change.

25. A similar typology of physical and functional elements in the urban environment is developed by Kevin Lynch in *The Image of the City.*

26. Burgess, "Neighborhood Work," p. 149.

27. Park, "Spatial Pattern and Moral Order," p. 174.

CHAPTER THREE

1. Merton, *Social Theory and Social Structure.*

2. It would be nearly impossible to list all the studies which have included "length of residence" as a variable. Its commonness as a "face sheet" datum attests its importance as an independent variable, though its full meaning and implications have yet to be systematically explored.

3. Whyte says of Park Forest, the Chicago suburb he studied, "It begins with the children. There are so many of them and they are so dictatorial in effect that a term like 'filiarchy' would not be entirely facetious" (Whyte, *Organization Man*, p. 378).

4. Charles Horton Cooley, "Primary Groups," in *Sociological Analysis*, ed. Logan Wilson and William L. Kolb, pp. 278–89. (New York: Harcourt, Brace and World, 1949).

5. As Keller says, "These small 'natural' neighborhoods find their limits where personal relations stop. This makes their boundaries fluid, though still recognizable to those familiar with local customs" Keller, *Urban Neighborhood*, p. 100.

6. Gans, *Urban Villagers*, p. 11.

7. Elizabeth Bott, *Family and Social Network* (London: Tavistock Publications, 1957); Gans, *Urban Villagers*; Elliot Liebow, *Tally's Corner* (Boston: Little, Brown, 1967); Ulf Hannerz, *Soulside* (New

York: Columbia University Press, 1969). The last author says, "Since ghetto dwellers are not much involved with one another in relationships of power and livelihood, the social structure of the ghetto community is made up primarily of a multitude of connecting personal networks of kinsmen, peers, and neighbors" (p. 34).

8. Whyte, *Organization Man*; Herbert Gans, *The Levittowners* (New York: Random House–Vintage, 1967).

9. On neighborhood utilization, see Foley, "Use of Local Facilities"; and Keller, *Urban Neighborhood*, "Use of Neighborhoods," pp. 103–6.

10. Numerous studies have noted variations in sizes of neighborhoods defined by residents, even residents of the same area. See Ross, "The Local Community"; Riemer, "Villagers in Metropolis"; Joel Smith, William H. Form, and Gregory P. Stone, "Local Intimacy in a Middle-Sized City," *American Journal of Sociology* 60 (November 1954): 276–84; and especially Roderick McKenzie, *The Neighborhood: A Study of Local Life in the City of Columbus, Ohio* (Chicago: University of Chicago Press, 1923).

11. This argument of "cognitive overload" is similar to Simmel's argument of the blasé urban attitude: "If so many inner reactions were responses to the continuous external contacts with innumerable people as are those in the small town, where one knows almost everybody one meets and where one has a positive relation to almost everyone, one would be completely atomized internally and come to an unimaginable psychic state" (Georg Simmel, "The Metropolis and Mental Life," in Wolff, *Sociology of Georg Simmel*, p. 415).

12. Greer, *Emerging City*.

13 This finding has important implications for the distinction between "locals" and "cosmopolitans" and further supports the previous argument that perhaps this should be conceptualized as a continuum applying to statuses. Therefore an individual occupying a number of different statuses may at the same time, depending upon which status is salient, be categorized as both a local and a cosmopolitan. See Merton, *Social Theory and Social Structure*.

14. The use of "reference group theory" as developed by Hyman and elaborated by Merton has not been fully utilized in analysis of community-related behavior. For one example see Eugene Litwak, "Reference Group Theory, Bureaucratic Career, and Neighborhood Primary Group Cohesion," *Sociometry* 23 (March 1960): 72–84. See also the original work of Herbert Hyman, "The Social Psychology of Status" (Ph.D. diss. Columbia University, 1942) and its elaboration by Merton, *Social Theory and Social Structure*.

15. In short, the formation of "community identity" may be similar in process to Mead's conception of individual identity formation as a function of social interaction. For the community (as for the individual) this "external" interaction may be both horizontal, with individuals and institutions from other areas, and vertical, in the form of "authoritative" definitions promulgated "on high."

George Herbert Mead, *On Social Psychology*, edited by Anselm Strauss (Chicago: University of Chicago Press, 1964).

CHAPTER FOUR

1. Parsons and Shils, *Toward a General Theory of Action.*

2. "Evaluation" of the local community involves a much more complex process than I was able to pursue in this research. First, evaluating an area as "good" or "bad" implies some standard or desired goal of action—"Good or bad for what?" Second, evaluation implies a comparative reference—"Good or bad compared with what?"—which may vary from individual to individual. For some it may be a previous area of residence; for others, some other known area; and for some, an "idealized" sense of community. Third, the final evaluation is a complex summation of ratings on a number of different criteria—e.g., density, facilities, people. There exist a number of studies which have touched on one or more of these points and the reader should consult: Marc Fried and Peggy Gleicher, "Some Sources of Residential Satisfaction in an Urban Slum," in *Neighborhood, City, and Metropolis*, ed. Robert Gutman and David Popenoe, pp. 730–45 (New York: Random House, 1970); John B. Lansing, Robert W. Marans, and Robert B. Zehner, *Planned Residential Environments* (Ann Arbor, Mich.: Survey Research Center, Institute for Social Research, 1970); and Alvin L. Schorr, *Slums and Social Insecurity* (Washington, D.C.: U.S. Government Printing Office, 1963).

3. Cooley, "Primary Groups." Weber says, "The routinized economic cosmos, and thus the rationally highest form of the provision of material goods which is indispensable for all worldly culture, has been a structure to which the absence of love is attached from the very root" (*From Max Weber*, p. 355).

4. Stein, *Eclipse of Community*; Warner, *Yankee City*; Robert O. Schulze, "The Bifurcation of Power in a Satellite City," in *Community Political Systems*, ed. Morris Janowitz, pp. 19–30 (New York: Free Press, 1961); and Fried and Gleicher, "Sources of Residential Satisfaction."

5. The "valued community hypothesis" may be thought of as an extension of Janowitz's concept of "the community of limited liability" coupled with "exchange theory" as developed by Blau and Homans. In short, receiving "benefits" from the community may increase the "indebtedness" of individuals to the community, thereby heightening local commitment and attachment as a function of the "norm of reciprocity." See Janowitz, *Community Press*, George C. Homans, *Social Behavior: Its Elementary Forms* (New York: Harcourt, Brace and World, 1961); and Peter M. Blau, *Exchange and Power in Social Life* (New York: Wiley, 1964).

6. This confirms but qualifies the suggestion of Fried and Gleicher, in "Sources of Residential Satisfaction," that for middle-class residents, "Distances are very readily transgressed; friends are dispersed

in many directions; preferred places are frequently quite idiosyncratic. . . . This orientation to the use of space is the very antithesis of that localism so widely found in the working class" (p. 738).

7. The lack of relationships between sex and local orientations might highlight the possibility that cognition, evaluation, and attachment are orientations worked out within the context of the family as a consensual unit. See Rossi, *Why Families Move.*

8. The significance of physical space for the symbolic retention of past social relationships and sentiments applies to individual biographies as well as to "historical" events. See Firey, *Land Use in Central Boston.*

9. This "structural effect" may be thought of as a problem of "status inconsistency" between individual and collective statuses. See Blau, "Structural Effects"; and Lenski, "Status Crystallization."

10. This suggests that by choosing to move, and by deciding where to locate, individuals will bring about greater consistency between individual and community statuses, or between the reality of their community and their "standards." See Bell, "City, Suburb, and Social Choice"; Berry and Rees, "Factorial Ecology of Calcutta"; and Lenski, "Status Crystallization."

11. The finding that increased interaction within the local community leads to increased attachment to it is a variation of one of Homans's central propositions. Here, however, the increased interaction and the positive sentiments generated by it are generalized to the setting in which they occur. See George C. Homans, *The Human Group* (New York: Harcourt, Brace and World, 1950).

12. The implication that increased size leads to greater heterogeneity and in turn to a greater ambivalence is of course closely related to the thesis presented by Wirth in "Urbanism as a Way of Life."

13. Greer, *Emerging City.*

14. These results are similar to those of Smith, Form, and Stone in "Local Intimacy"; they found that for the lower economic groups "friendships in this stratum of the urban population tend to be dispersed more widely through the city's space than friendships among urbanites in higher strata" (p. 283).

CHAPTER FIVE

1. For a review of the "community organizing" literature a standard text is Murray Ross, *Community Organization* (New York: Harper and Row, 1967). A more recent volume is Robert Perlman and Arnold Gurin, *Community Organization and Social Planning* (New York: John Wiley, 1972). For a recent reader in the field see Ralph M. Kramer and Harry Specht, eds., *Readings in Community Organization Practice* (Englewood Cliffs, N.J.: Prentice-Hall, 1969).

2. Kornhauser, *Politics of Mass Society*; and James Coleman, *Community Conflict* (New York: Free Press, 1957).

3. Wirth, "Urbanism as a Way of Life."

4. Charles R. Wright and Herbert Hyman, "Voluntary Association Membership of American Adults," *American Sociological Review* 23 (June 1958): 284–94; and the same authors' replication, "Trends in Voluntary Association Memberships of American Adults," *American Sociological Review* 36 (April 1971): 191–206.

5. For recent studies on voluntary association membership of blacks which essentially confirm my findings see A. M. Orum, "A Reappraisal of the Social and Political Participation of Negroes," *American Journal of Sociology* 72 (July 1966): 32–46; M. E. Olson, "Social and Political Participation of Blacks," *American Sociological Review* 35 (August 1970): 682–97; and Nicholas Babchuk and J. Edwards, "Voluntary Associations and the Integration Hypothesis," *Sociological Inquiry* 35 (spring 1965): 149–62.

6. E. Franklin Frazier says, "The great significance which 'social' life has for Negroes has been due to their exclusion from participation in American life. The numerous 'social' clubs and other forms of voluntary associations which have existed among them provided a form of participation that compensated for their rejection by the white community" (*Black Bourgeoisie* [New York: Free Press, 1957], p. 204).

7. Basil G. Zimmer, "Participation of Migrants in Urban Structures," *American Sociological Review* 20 (April 1953): 218–24.

8. Axelrod, "Urban Structure and Social Participation."

9. Although this statement emphasizes reasons for *commitment*, it is closely related to the *compliance* typology developed by Etzioni. The commitment of members at the local level most closely corresponds to "normative compliance" in Etzioni's typology, while commitment at the federated level involves a more utilitarian orientation. Overall, these community organizations exemplify this hybrid type, utilitarian-normative. See Amitai Etzioni, *A Comparative Analysis of Complex Organizations* (New York: Free Press, 1961), pp. 66–67.

10. I thank Gerald Suttles for suggesting this latter point.

11. Park, "Spatial Pattern and Moral Order."

12. Janowitz, *Community Press.*

13. This boundary has also become a source of debate in the literature. See Harvey Molotch, "Racial Change in a Stable Community," *American Journal of Sociology* 75 (September 1969): 226–38; Avery M. Guest and James J. Zuickes, "Another Look at Residential Turnover in Urban Neighborhoods," *American Journal of Sociology* 77 (November 1971): 457–67; and Molotch's "Reply" in the same issue, pp. 468–71.

14. A national survey report by Norman M. Bradburn, Seymour Sudman, and Galen L. Gockel suggests that such groups are for the most part unsuccessful in stemming such invasion and operate more importantly as transitional structures easing the changeover in population and reducing conflict. See *Racial Integration in American Neighborhoods* (Chicago: National Opinion Research Center, 1970).

15. Zorita Wise Mikva, "The Neighborhood Improvement Association: A Counter-Force to the Expansion of Chicago's Negro Population" (M.A. thesis, Department of Sociology, University of Chicago, 1951).

16. Molotch, *Managed Integration.*

17. Perlman and Gurin, *Community Organization and Social Planning.*

18. See Weber, *From Wax Weber;* and Blau and Scott, *Formal Organizations.*

19. Alvin N. Gouldner, "Organizational Analysis," in *Sociology Today,* ed. Robert K. Merton, Leonard Broom, and Leonard S. Cottrell, Jr., pp. 400–428 (New York: Harper and Row, 1959).

20. See the typology of organizational goals developed in Zald, "Sociology and Community Organization Practice."

21. Mikva, "Neighborhood Improvement Association."

22. Rossi and Dentler, *Politics of Urban Renewal.*

23. See Amitai Etzioni and Eva Etzioni, eds., *Theories of Social Change* (New York: Basic Books, 1964).

24. Zald, "Sociology and Community Organization Practice."

25. Robert A. Dahl, *Who Governs?* (New Haven: Yale University Press, 1961).

26. This information was taken from the newsletter of the Northwest Community Organization, the *Observer,* n.d .

27. Daniel Patrick Moynihan, *Maximum Feasible Misunderstanding* (New York: Free Press, 1969).

28. Cooley, "Primary Group." On the significance of primary groups in organizations see Homans, *Human Group,* chap. 3, "The Bank Wiring Observation Room, pp. 48–80, which is based on the research of F. J. Roethlesberger and W. J. Dickson, *Management and the Worker* (Cambridge: Harvard University Press, 1939).

29. Etzioni, *Comparative Analysis of Complex Organizations .*

30. For a recent article analyzing the significance of formal and informal interaction at the local level, see Claude S. Fischer, "Urban Alienation and Anomie," *American Sociological Review* 38 (June 1973): 311–16.

31. Albert Hunter and Gerald Suttles, "The Expanding Community of Limited Liability," in Gerald Suttles, *The Social Construction of Communities* (Chicago: University of Chicago Press, 1972), pp. 44–81.

CHAPTER SIX

1. For a fascinating brief history of the Chicago school see Robert E. L. Faris, *Chicago Sociology, 1920–1932* (San Francisco: Chandler, 1967).

2. On the use of "triangulation" or multiple methods in social research see Eugene J. Webb, et al., *Unobtrusive Measures* (Chicago: Rand McNally, 1966).

3. Wirth, "Urbanism as a Way of Life"; Berry and Rees, "Factorial Ecology of Calcutta."

4. Stein, *Eclipse of Community*; Nisbet, *Quest for Community*.

5. Greer, *Emerging City*.

6. Form, "Place of Social Structure in Land Use." See also James Q. Wilson, ed., *Urban Renewal* (Cambridge: Massachusetts Institute of Technology Press, 1966), for the effect of "organizations," both governmental from the top and citizen from the bottom, upon urban land use.

7. Janowitz, *Community Press*, p. 212.

8. The various concepts I have used to analyze the symbolic culture of local communities—"the definition of the situation," "the city as a state of mind," "natural areas as spatial and moral orders," and "collective representations" emphasize only one perspective, which I would call "urban imagery" but which is referred to by Martindale as "the urban mentality." Although Martindale criticizes both this approach and the "ecological" approach and favors Weber's "institutional" approach, this research attempts to explore local urban communities from all three perspectives. See Anselm Strauss, *Images of American Cities* (New York: Free Press, 1961), and Max Weber, *The City*, trans. and ed. Don Martindale and Gertrud Neuwirth (New York: Free Press, 1958).

9. In their debate with Molotch Guest and Zuiches passingly comment, "It appears that residents of South Shore psychologically 'de-annexed' the black areas when they described the community to Molotch" (p. 459). To counter the suggestion that this is somehow "inappropriate" compared with the use of other "authoritative" sources, Molotch responds, "Communities are in the minds of men, not in forty-year-old tomes created on the basis of census data gathered from people who are mostly dead" (p. 470). It is precisely these dynamics of relationship of the symbols of community to organizational-structural definitions, and to ecological definitions of community that result not only in sociological debate but also in social conflict and competition in the local community.

10. These findings have implications for the study of "alienation" and "social integration" in urban life—from a psychological, social, and political perspective. It is important to ask at which "level of community" or social structure integration (or alienation) occurs. Some writers emphasize a zero-sum conception of the problem—increased integration at one level (usually higher) implies less integration at another level (usually lower). Martindale typifies many writers when he says, "The modern city is losing its external and formal structure. Internally it is in a state of decay while the new community represented by the nation everywhere grows *at its expense.* The age of the city seems to be at an end" (p. 67 in Weber, *The City*; italics added).

Other writers emphasize what might be called a "multiplier effect," with increased integration at lower levels leading to increased integration at higher levels. Thus, for example, my findings and those of others show that "informal" and "formal" interactions vary positively together, in contrast to Wirth's assertion in "Urbanism as a Way of Life" that the latter increase at the expense of the former.

In a different perspective the "higher level" may attempt to foster "integration" at the lower level so as to increase overall social integration and commitment. This is one reading of the Community Action Program of the federal government during the sixties. Moynihan, *Maximum Feasible Misunderstanding*. See also, Fischer, "Urban Alienation and Anomie."

11. Gans, *Urban Villagers*; Hannerz, *Soulside*.

12. This agrees with Berry and Rees's conception that the decision-making process of where to "live" is an attempt to locate oneself in social space—the space defined by the three dimensions of social area analysis—by finding a corresponding physical space. See "Factorial Ecology of Calcutta."

13. Again, this emphasizes the significance of personal interaction in generating collective as well as individual sentiments. Homans, *Human Group*.

14. See Blau, "Structural Effects"; Lenski, "Status Crystallization."

15. Greer also suggests, metaphorically, another reason for the persistence of local groups: "Spatial collocation produces problems of order and a need for common facilities, strengthening the local role system and resulting in a coercive power over the actions of each exclusive membership group. The corporation or state bureaucracy must come to earth in order to work, and wherever it does it finds neighbors" (*Emerging City*, p. 52).

16. Similar results were found in Orum, "Reappraisal of the Participation of Negroes"; and Olson, "Social Participation of Blacks."

17. Edward Shils, *The Logic of Personal Knowledge* (London: Routledge and Kegan Paul, 1961), "Centre and Periphery."

18. Park, "The City," p. 1.

19. This "hierarchy of orders" is found in Park's essay "Human Ecology" in *Human Communities*, where he says, "It is interesting also that these divergent social orders seem to arrange themselves in a kind of hierarchy. In fact they may be said to form a pyramid of which the ecological order constitutes the base and the moral order the apex. Upon each succeeding one of these levels, the ecological, economic, political and moral, the individual finds himself more completely incorporated into and subordinated to the social order of which he is a part than upon the preceding" (p. 157).

20. Conrad M. Arensberg and Solon T. Kimball, *Culture and Community* (New York: Harcourt, Brace and World, 1965), p. 8.

21. Suttles, *Social Construction of Communities*.

22. Mead also considered the tendency toward "universalism" of ever-enlarging communities, as well as a social reconstruction uniting previously distinct and perhaps conflicting social wholes. "And the way in which any such social reconstruction is actually effected by the minds of the individuals involved is by a more or less abstract intellectual extension of the boundaries of the given society to

which these individuals all belong and which is undergoing the reconstruction—an extension resulting in a larger social whole in terms of which the social conflicts that necessitate the reconstruction of the given society are harmonized or reconciled, and by reference to which, accordingly, these conflicts can be solved or eliminated" (*On Social Psychology*, p. 269). See also Gerald D. Suttles, *The Social Construction of Communities* (Chicago: University of Chicago Press, 1972).

23. Suttles emphasizes the importance of clear and distinguishable boundaries in maintaining "the segmental social order" in Chicago's West Side slum community (*Social Order of the Slum*). However, ambiguity of boundaries may be more generally indicative of the urbanites' characteristic blasé, tolerant attitude. Wirth, "Urbanism as a Way of Life."

24. The map of Chicago's communities, as was previously noted, is an abstraction from resident interviews and the local community organization data. Given this reason and the inherent dynamics of local communities in their symbolic culture, ecology, and social organization, it is expected that portions of the map are already "history."

25. Hyman, *Psychology of Status*; Merton, *Social Theory and Social Structure*.

26. Although they are "abstract" referents for "other entities," symbols too become objects capable of evoking sentiment and action in and of themselves, and also have important implications in defining the self. Roger Brown, *Social Psychology* (New York: Free Press, 1965).

27. The idea of varying levels of community was well stated by Robert MacIver over half a century ago. "It is a question of the degree and intensity of the common life. The one extreme is the whole world of men, one great but vague and incoherent common life. The other extreme is the small intense community within which the life of an ordinary individual is lived, a tiny nucleus of common life with a sometimes larger, sometimes smaller and always varying fringe" (*Community* [London: Macmillan, 1957], p. 7).

28. Mead often used as a metaphor for the development of the social self and "the generalized other" members of a baseball team anticipating and reacting to the behavior of others on the team. "The illustration used was of a person playing baseball. Each one of his own acts is determined by his assumption of the action of the others who are playing the game" (*On Social Psychology*, p. 218). In a more abstract vein, he speaks of an individual's social identity as arising from relationships with the "social community." How that social community itself becomes defined is a question he does not pursue. I suggest that the same interaction process applied to the individual can be applied to the community as a unit of analysis. More concretely, a baseball game usually involves two teams.

29. Given that statuses or positions may be applied to individuals

as well as communities as two distinct units of analysis, one might think of those statuses acquired by an individual by virtue of his membership in a community as "secondary statuses," and of the former as "primary statuses."

30. From the perspective of "the community of limited liability" the psychological "costs" of status inconsistency may result in "shopping" for a new home and neighborhood that would bring greater consistency and rewards equal to costs, if not "profit."

31. Blau and Scott, *Formal Organizations.*

32. Wirth himself was fully aware of the possibility of symbolic manipulation in the urban context: "It follows, too, that the masses of men in the city are subject to manipulation by symbols and stereotypes managed by individuals working from afar or operating invisibly behind the scenes through their control of the instruments of communication" ("Urbanism as a Way of Life," p. 62).

33. Moynihan, *Maximum Feasible Misunderstanding.* Louis Wirth anticipated by two decades the major criticism of the federal government's Community Action Program of the sixties: "Self-government either in the economic, the political, or the cultural realm is under these circumstances reduced to a mere figure of speech, or, at best, is subject to the unstable equilibrium of pressure groups." ("Urbanism as a Way of Life," p. 62).

34. As Wirth says, "The distinctive features of the urban mode of life have often been described sociologically as consisting of the substitution of secondary for primary contacts, the weakening of bonds of kinship, and the declining social significance of the family, the disappearance of the neighborhood, and the undermining of the traditional basis of social solidarity. . . . Such functions as the maintenance of health, the methods of alleviating the hardships associated with personal and social insecurity, the provisions for education, recreation, and cultural advancement have given rise to highly specialized institutions on a community-wide, statewide or even national basis ("Urbanism as a Way of Life," p. 60).

APPENDIX I

1. For a discussion of "multiple methods" or "triangulation," see Webb, *Unobtrusive Measures*; see also a recent article by Sam D. Sieber, "The Integration of Fieldwork and Survey Methods," *American Journal of Sociology* 78 (May 1973); 1335–59. The attempt to combine various research methods was itself one of the strengths of the old Chicago school; as Burgess relates a conversation with a student, "I recall Nels Anderson telling me he was greatly bored by his landlady in the roominghouse district where he was studying the homeless man, telling him her life history. I told him, 'Why, this is valuable, you must get it down on paper.' . . . Out of this one document you get more insight into how life moves in the roominghouse area, and especially from the standpoint of the roominghouse keeper, than you do from a mountain of statistics that might have

been gathered. So what we get from the life history, of course, also enables us to pose more questions to the statistician, to get to the other answers" (*Contributions to Urban Sociology*, p. 9).

2. This project has had many participants, all fellows of the Center for Social Organization Studies. Those who have contributed papers on this or related topics include Charles Derber, Charles Goldsmid, Harvey Molotch, and Daniel Willick.

3. On tests of significance see Hanan C. Selvin, "A Critique of Tests of Significance in Survey Research," *American Sociological Review* 22 (October 1957): 522–23.

Bibliography

Abu-Lughod, Janet. "Testing the Theory of Social Area Analysis: The Ecology of Cairo, Egypt." *American Sociological Review* 34 (April 1969): 198–212.

Adams, Bert N. *Kinship in an Urban Setting*. Chicago: Markham, 1968.

Alihan, Milla A. *Social Ecology*. New York: Columbia University Press, 1938.

Anderson, Theodore R., and Egeland, Janice A. "Spatial Aspects of Social Area Analysis." *American Sociological Review* 26 (1961): 392–98.

Arensberg, Conrad M., and Kimball, Solon T. *Culture and Community*. New York: Harcourt, Brace and World, 1965.

Axelrod, Morris. "Urban Structure and Social Participation." *American Sociological Review* 21 (February 1956): 14–18.

Babchuk, Nicholas, and Edwards, J. "Voluntary Associations and the Integration Hypothesis." *Sociological Inquiry* 35 (spring 1965): 149–62.

Babchuk, Nicholas, and Gordon, C. Wayne. *The Voluntary Association in the Slum*. Lincoln: University of Nebraska Press, 1962.

Banfield, Edward C. *Political Influence*. New York: Free Press, 1961.

Barber, Bernard. "Family Status, Local-Community Status, and Social Stratification: Three Types of Social Ranking." *Pacific Sociological Review* 4 (spring 1961): 3–10.

———. *Social Stratification*. New York: Harcourt, Brace and World, 1957.

Barlow, Carrie Mae. "Auburn–Gresham: The Survey of a Local Community." M.A. thesis, University of Chicago, Department of Sociology, August 1934.

Bell, Daniel. *The End of Ideology*. New York: Free Press, 1960.

Bell, Wendell. "The City, the Suburb, and a Theory of Social Choice." In *The New Urbanization*, ed. Scott Greer et al., pp. 132–68. New York: St. Martin's Press, 1968.

———. "The Utility of the Shevky Typology for the Design of Urban Sub-Area Field Studies." In *Studies in Human Ecology*, ed. George A. Theodorson, pp. 244–52. New York: Harper and Row, 1961.

Bell, Wendell, and Boat, Marion D. "Urban Neighborhoods and Informal Social Relations." *American Journal of Sociology* 62 (January 1957): 391–98.

227

Berry, Brian J. L. "Internal Structure of the City." In *Internal Structure of the City*, ed. Larry S. Bourne, pp. 97–103. New York: Oxford University Press, 1971.

Berry, Brian J. L., and Rees, Philip H. "The Factorial Ecology of Calcutta." *American Journal of Sociology* 74 (March 1969): 445–91.

Beshers, James M. *Urban Social Structure*. New York: Free Press, 1962.

———. "Urban Social Structure as a Single Hierarchy." *Social Forces* 51 (March 1963): 233–29.

Blau, Peter M. *Exchange and Power in Social Life*. New York: Wiley, 1964.

———. "Structural Effects." *American Sociological Review* 25 (April 1960): 178–93.

Blau, Peter M., and Scott, W. Richard. *Formal Organizations*. San Francisco: Chandler, 1962.

Bloch, Donald S.; Gable, George A.; Schrag, Delbert J.; and Vajda, Emil H. "Identification and Participation in Urban Neighborhoods." M.A. thesis, University of Chicago, Department of Sociology, June 1952.

Bogue, Donald J. *Population Growth in Standard Metropolitan Areas, 1900–1950, with an exploratory Analysis of Urbanized Areas*. Washington, D.C.: U.S. Housing and Home Finance Agency, 1953.

———. *The Structure of the Metropolitan Community*. Ann Arbor: University of Michigan Press, 1949.

———. "Urbanism in the United States, 1950." In *Cities and Society*, ed. Paul K. Hatt and Albert J. Reiss, pp. 83–102. New York: Free Press, 1957.

Booth, Charles. *On the City: Physical Pattern and Social Structure*. Edited by Harold W. Pfautz. Chicago: University of Chicago Press, 1967.

Bott, Elizabeth. *Family and Social Network*. London: Tavistock Publications, 1957 .

Bradburn, Norman M.; Sudman, Seymour; and Gockel, Galen L. *Racial Integration in American Neighborhoods*. Chicago: National Opinion Research Center, 1970.

Brown, Roger. *Social Psychology*. New York: Free Press, 1965.

Burgess, Ernest W. "Can Neighborhood Work Have a Scientific Basis?" In *The City*, ed. Robert E. Park, Ernest W. Burgess, and Roderick D. McKenzie, pp. 142–55. Chicago: University of Chicago Press, 1967.

———. "The Growth of the City." In *The City*, ed. Robert E. Park, Ernest W. Burgess, and Roderick D. McKenzie, pp. 47–62. Chicago: University of Chicago Press, 1967.

———, ed. *The Urban Community*. Chicago: University of Chicago Press, 1926.

Burgess, Ernest W., and Bogue, Donald J., eds. *Contributions to Urban Sociology*. Chicago: University of Chicago Press, 1964.

Burgess, Ernest W., and Newcomb, Charles, eds. *Census Data of the City of Chicago*, 1920. Chicago: University of Chicago Press, 1931.
———. *Census Data of the City of Chicago*, 1930. Chicago: University of Chicago Press, 1933.
Caplow, Theodore; Stryker, Sheldon; and Wallace, Samuel E. *The Urban Ambiance*. Totowa, N.J.: Bedminster Press, 1964.
Centers, Richard. *The Psychology of Social Classes*. Princeton: Princeton University Press, 1949.
Coleman, James. *Community Conflict*. New York: Free Press, 1957.
———. *Mathematical Sociology*. New York: Free Press, 1964.
Cooley, Charles Horton. "Primary Groups." In *Sociological Analysis*, ed. Logan Wilson and William L. Kolb, pp. 287–89. New York: Harcourt, Brace and World.
Dahl, Robert A. *Who Governs?* New Haven: Yale University Press, 1961.
Davis, James A.; Spaeth, Joe L.; and Huston, Carolyn. "A Technique for Analyzing the Effects of Group Composition." *American Sociological Review* 26 (1961): 215–26.
Dewey, Richard. "The Neighborhood, Urban Ecology and City Planners." In *Cities and Society*, ed. Paul Hatt and Albert Reiss, Jr., pp. 783–90. New York: Free Press, 1957.
Drake, St. Clair, and Cayton, Horace R. *Black Metropolis*. Evanston, Ill.: Harper and Row, 1945.
Duncan, Beverly, and Hauser, Philip M. *Housing a Metropolis*. Glencoe, Ill.: Free Press, 1960.
Duncan, Otis Dudley, and Duncan, Beverly. *The Negro Population of Chicago: A Study of Residential Succession*. Chicago: University of Chicago Press, 1957.
———. "Residential Distribution and Occupational Stratification." *American Journal of Sociology* 60 (March 1955): 493–503.
Duncan, Otis Dudley, and Lieberson, Stanley. "Ethnic Segregation and Assimilation." *American Journal of Sociology* 64 (January 1959): 364–74.
Duncan, Otis Dudley, and Schnore, Leo F. "Cultural, Behavioral, and Ecological Perspectives in the Study of Social Organization." *American Journal of Sociology* 65 (September 1959): 196–201.
Durkheim, Emile. *The Division of Labor in Society*. Translated by George Simpson. New York: Free Press, 1949.
Etzioni, Amitai. *A Comparative Analysis of Complex Organizations*. New York: Free Press, 1961.
Etzioni, Amitai, and Etzioni, Eva, eds. *Theories of Social Change*. New York: Basic Books, 1964.
Faris, Robert E. L. *Chicago Sociology 1920–1932*. San Francisco: Chandler, 1967.
Feldman, Arnold S., and Tilly, Charles. "The Interaction of Social and Physical Space." *American Sociological Review* 25 (December 1960): 877–84.
Fellin, Philip, and Litwak, Eugene. "Neighborhood Cohesion under

Conditions of Mobility." *American Sociological Review* 28 (June 1963): 364–77.

Firey, Walter T. *Land Use in Central Boston.* Cambridge: Harvard University Press, 1947.

———. "Sentiment and Symbolism as Ecological Variables." *American Sociological Review* 10 (April 1945): 140–48.

Fischer, Claud S. "Urban Alienation and Anomie." *American Sociological Review* 38 (June 1973): 311–16.

Foley, Donald L. *Neighbors or Urbanites.* Rochester: University of Rochester, 1952.

———. "The Use of Local Facilities in a Metropolis." In *Cities and Society,* ed. Paul Hatt and Albert Reiss, Jr., pp. 607–16. New York: Free Press, 1959.

Form, William H. "The Place of Social Structure in the Determination of Land Use: Some Implications for a Theory of Urban Ecology." *Social Forces* 32 (May 1954): 317–23.

Form, William H.; Smith, Joel; Stone, Gregory P.; and Cowhig, James. "The Compatibility of Alternative Approaches to the Delimitation of Urban Sub-Areas." *American Sociological Review* 19 (August 1954): 434–40.

Fortune (editors). *The Exploding Metropolis.* Garden City, N.Y.: Doubleday, 1958.

Frazier, E. Franklin. *Black Bourgeoisie.* New York: Free Press, 1957.

———. "The Negro Family in Chicago." In *Contributions to Urban Sociology,* ed. Ernest W. Burgess and Donald J. Bogue, pp. 404–18. Chicago: University of Chicago Press, 1964.

Fried, Marc, and Gleicher, Peggy. "Some Sources of Residential Satisfaction in an Urban Slum." In *Neighborhood, City, and Metropolis,* ed. Robert Gutman and David Popenoe, pp. 730–45. New York: Random House, 1970.

Galpin, C. J. *The Social Anatomy of an Agricultural Community.* Madison: University of Wisconsin Agricultural Experiment Station, Research Bulletin no. 34, May 1915.

Gans, Herbert. *The Levittowners.* New York: Random House–Vintage, 1967.

———. *The Urban Villagers.* New York: Free Press, 1962.

Gibbs, Jack P., ed. *Urban Research Methods.* Princeton, N.J.: Van Nostrand, 1961.

Gibbs, Raymond Lee. "The Life Cycle of Oakland Community." M. A. thesis, University of Chicago, Department of Sociology, June 1937.

Goodman, Leo A. "Statistical Methods for Analyzing Processes of Change." *American Journal of Sociology* 68 (July 1962): 57–78.

Gouldner, Alvin W. "Organizational Analysis." In *Sociology Today,* ed. Robert K. Merton et al., chap. 18. New York: Harper and Row, 1959.

Greer, Scott. *The Emerging City.* New York: Free Press, 1962.

———. "Urbanism Reconsidered: A Comparative Study of Local Areas in a Metropolis." *American Sociological Review* 21 (February 1956): 19–25.

Guest, Avery M. "Retesting the Burgess Zonal Hypothesis: The Location of White Collar Workers." *American Journal of Sociology* 76 (May 1971): 1094–1108.

Guest, Avery M., and Zuickes, James J. "Another Look at Residential Turnover in Urban Neighborhoods." *Americal Journal of Sociology* 77 (November 1971): 457–67.

Haggerty, Lee J. "Another Look at the Burgess Hypothesis: Time as an Important Variable." *American Journal of Sociology* 76 (May 1971): 1084–93.

Hannerz, Ulf. *Soulside*. New York: Columbia University Press, 1969.

Harman, Harry. *Modern Factor Analysis*. Chicago: University of Chicago Press, 1960.

Harris, Chauncy D., and Ullman, Edward L. "The Nature of Cities." *Annals* 242 (November 1945): 7–17.

Hatt, Paul K. "The Concept of Natural Area." In *Studies in Human Ecology*, ed. George A. Theodorson, pp. 104–8. Evanston, Ill.: Harper and Row, 1961.

Hatt, Paul, and Reiss, Albert J., Jr., eds. *Cities and Society*. New York: Free Press, 1957.

Hauser, Philip M., and Kitagawa, Evelyn M., eds. *Local Community Fact Book for Chicago, 1950*. Chicago: Chicago Community Inventory, University of Chicago, 1953.

Hawley, Amos H. *Human Ecology*. New York: Ronald Press, 1950.

Hawley, Amos H., and Duncan, Otis Dudley. "Social Area Analysis: A Critical Appraisal." *Land Economics*, November 1957, pp. 337–45.

Henderson, C. R. "The Place and Functions of Voluntary Associations." *American Journal of Sociology* 1 (November 1895): 327–34.

Hillery, George A. "Definitions of Community: Areas of Agreement." *Rural Sociology* 20 (June 1955): 111–23.

Homans, George C. *The Human Group*. New York: Harcourt, Brace and World, 1950.

———. *Social Behavior: Its Elementary Forms*. New York: Harcourt, Brace and World, 1961.

Hoover, Edgar M., and Vernon, Raymond. *Anatomy of a Metropolis*. Garden City, N.Y.: Doubleday, 1962.

Hoyt Homer. *The Structure and Growth of Residential Neighborhoods in American Cities*. Washington, D.C.: U.S. Federal Housing Administration, 1939.

Hunter, Albert. "Community Change." *American Journal of Sociology* 79 (January 1974)) 923–47.

———. "The Ecology of Chicago: Persistence and Change, 1930–60." *American Journal of Sociology* 77 (November 1971): 425–44.

Hunter, Albert, and Suttles, Gerald. "The Expanding Community of

Limited Liability." In *The Social Construction of Communities*, ed. Gerald Suttles, pp. 44–81. Chicago: University of Chicago Press, 1972.

Hyman, Herbert, "The Psychology of Status." Ph.D. dissertation, Columbia University, 1942.

Hyman, Herbert, and Singer, Eleanor, eds. *Readings in Reference Group Theory*. New York: Free Press, 1968.

Isaacs, Reginald. "The Neighborhood Theory." *Journal of the American Institute of Planners* 14 (spring 1948): 15–23.

––––. "Are Urban Neighborhoods Possible?" *Journal of Housing*, July 1948, pp. 177–80.

Jacobs, Jane. *The Death and Life of Great American Cities*. New York: Vintage Books, 1961.

Janowitz, Morris, ed. *Community Political Systems*. New York: Free Press, 1961.

––––.*The Community Press in an Urban Setting*. Chicago: University of Chicago Press, 1967.

Keller, Suzanne. *The Urban Neighborhood*. New York: Random House, 1968.

Kemeny, John G.; Snell, J. Laurie; and Thompson, Gerald L. *Introduction to Finite Mathematics*. Englewood Cliffs, N.J.: Prentice-Hall, 1956.

Kish, Leslie. "Differentiation in Metropolitan Areas." *American Sociological Review* 19 (August 1954): 388–98.

Kitagawa, Evelyn M., and Taeuber, Karl E., eds. *Local Community Fact Book for Chicago Metropolitan Area, 1960*. Chicago: Chicago Community Inventory, University of Chicago, 1963.

Kornhauser, William. *The Politics of Mass Society*. New York: Free Press, 1959.

Kramer, Ralph M., and Specht, Harry, eds. *Readings in Community Organization Practice*. Englewood Cliffs, N.J.: Prentice Hall, 1969.

Lansing, John B.; Marans, Robert W.; and Zehner, Robert B. *Planned Residential Environments*. Ann Arbor, Mich.: Survey Research Center, Institute for Social Research, 1970.

Laumann, Edward O. *Prestige and Association in an Urban Community*. Indianapolis: Bobbs-Merrill, 1966.

LeBon, Gustav. *The Crowd*. New York: Ballantine Books, 1969.

Lenski, Gerhard. "Status Crystallization." *American Sociological Review* 19 (1954): 405–13.

Levine, Sol, and White, Paul E. "Exchange as a Conceptual Framework for the Study of Interorganizational Relationships." *Administrative Science Quarterly* 5 (March 1961): 583–601.

Lewis, Oscar. *Five Families: Mexican Case Studies in the Culture of Poverty*. New York: Basic Books, 1959.

Lieberson, Stanley. *Ethnic Patterns in American Cities*. New York: Free Press, 1962.

Liebow, Elliot. *Tally's Corner*. Boston: Little, Brown, 1967.

Litwak, Eugene. "Reference Group Theory, Bureaucratic Career, and Neighborhood Primary Group Cohesion." *Sociometry* 23 (March 1960): 72–84.

Litwak, Eugene, and Meyer, Henry J. "A Balance Theory of Coordination between Bureaucratic Organizations and Community Primary Groups." *Administrative Science Quarterly* 2 (June 1966): 31–58.

Local Community Fact Book for Chicago, 1930. Edited by Louis Wirth and Margaret Furez. Chicago: Chicago Recreation Commission, 1938.

Local Community Fact Book for Chicago, 1940. Edited by Louis Wirth and Eleanor Bernert. Chicago: Chicago Community Inventory, University of Chicago, 1949.

Local Community Fact Book for Chicago, 1950. Edited by Philip M. Hauser and Evelyn M. Kitagawa. Chicago: Chicago Community Inventory, University of Chicago, 1953.

Local Community Fact Book for Chicago Metropolitan Area, 1960. Edited by Evelyn M. Kitagawa and Karl E. Taeuber. Chicago: Chicago Community Inventory, University of Chicago, 1963.

Lopata, Helena Znaniecki. "The Function of Voluntary Associations in an Ethnic Community: 'Polonia.' " In *Contributions to Urban Sociology,* ed. Ernest W. Burgess and Donald J. Bogue, pp. 203–23. Chicago: University of Chicago Press, 1964.

Lynch, Kevin. *The Image of the City.* Cambridge: Massachusetts Institute of Technology Press, 1960.

Lynd, Robert, and Lynd, Helen. *Middletown.* New York: Harcourt, Brace and World, 1929.

———. *Middletown in Transition.* New York: Harcourt, Brace and World, 1937.

McGough, Donna M. "Social Factor Analysis." City of Philadelphia Community Renewal Program, Technical Report no. 11. Philadelphia, October 1964.

MacIver, Robert M. *Community.* London: Macmillan, 1957.

McKenzie, Roderick. *The Neighborhood: A Study of Local Life in the City of Columbus, Ohio.* Chicago: University of Chicago Press, 1923.

———. "The Scope of Human Ecology." In *Studies in Human Ecology,* ed. George A. Theodorson, pp. 30–36. Evanston, Ill.: Harper and Row, 1961.

Mann, Peter H. "The Concept of Neighborliness." *American Journal of Sociology* 60 (September 1954): 163–68.

Mead, George Herbert. *On Social Psychology.* Ed. Anselm Strauss. Chicago: University of Chicago Press, 1964.

Merton, Robert K. *Social Theory and Social Structure.* Enlarged ed. New York: Free Press, 1968.

Meyerson, Martin, and Banfield, Edward C. *Politics, Planning and the Public Interest: The Case of Public Housing in Chicago.* Glencoe, Ill.: Free Press, 1955.

Mikva, Zorita Wise. "The Neighborhood Improvement Association:

A Counter-Force to the Expansion of Chicago's Negro Population." M.A. thesis, Department of Sociology, University of Chicago, 1951.

Molotch, Harvey. *Managed Integration.* Berkeley and Los Angeles: University of California Press, 1972.

———. "Racial Change in a Stable Community." *American Journal of Sociology* 75 (September 1969): 226–38.

———. "Urban Community Boundaries: A Case Study." Center for Social Organization Studies, Working Paper no. 60. Chicago: University of Chicago, 1966.

Mowrer, Ernest R. *Family Disorganization.* Chicago: University of Chicago Press, 1927.

Moynihan, Daniel Patrick. *Maximum Feasible Misunderstanding.* New York: Free Press, 1969.

Myers, George C. "Variations in Urban Population Structure." *Demography* 1, no. 1 (1964): 157–63.

National Association of Social Workers. *Community Development and Community Organization: An International Workshop.* New York: National Association of Social Workers, 1961.

Nisbet, Robert A. *Community and Power.* New York: Oxford University Press, 1962.

———. *The Quest for Community* (New York: Oxford University Press), 1953.

Olson, M. E. "Social and Political Participation of Blacks." *American Sociological Review* 35 (August 1970): 682–97.

Orleans, Peter. "Robert Park and Social Area Analysis." *Urban Affairs Quarterly* 1 (June 1966): 5–19.

Orum, A. M. "A Reappraisal of the Social and Political Participation of Negroes." *American Journal of Sociology* 72 (July 1966): 32:46.

Palmer, Vivian Marie. "The Primary Settlement Area as a Unit of Urban Growth and Organization." Ph.D. dissertation, Department of Sociology, University of Chicago, 1932.

Park, Robert E. "The City: Suggestions for the Investigation of Human Behavior in the Urban Environment." In *The City,* ed. Robert E. Park, Ernest W. Burgess, and Roderick D. McKenzie, pp. 1–46. Chicago: University of Chicago Press, 1967.

———. *Human Communities.* New York: Free Press, 1952.

———. "The Urban Community as a Spatial Pattern and a Moral Order." In *Human Communities,* pp. 165–77. New York: Free Press, 1952.

Park, Robert E., and Burgess, Ernest W. *Introduction to the Science of Sociology.* 3d ed. Chicago: University of Chicago Press, 1969.

Park, Robert E.; Burgess, Ernest W.; and McKenzie, Roderick D., eds. *The City.* Chicago: University of Chicago Press, 1925.

Parsons, Talcott, and Shils, Edward A., eds. *Toward a General Theory of Action.* New York: Harper and Row, 1951.

Perlman, Robert, and Gurin, Arnold. *Community Organization and Social Planning.* New York: Wiley, 1972.

Quinn, James A. "Ecological versus Social Interaction." *Sociology and Social Research* 18 (July-August 1934): 565–70.

Redfield, Robert. *The Little Community.* Chicago: University of Chicago Press, 1960.

Rees, Philip H. "The Factorial Ecology of Metropolitan Chicago." In *Geographic Perspectives on Urban Systems,* ed. Brian J. L. Berry and Frank E. Horton. Englewood Cliffs, N.J.: Prentice-Hall, 1969.

Reiss, Albert J., Jr. *A Review and Evaluation of Research on Community.* A working memorandum for the Committee on Social Behavior of the Social Science Research Council, Nashville, Tennessee, 1954.

Riemer, Svend. "Hidden Dimensions of Neighborhood Planning." *Land Economics* 26 (May 1950): 197–201.

———. "Villagers in Metropolis." *British Journal of Sociology* 11 (March 1951): 31–43.

Roethlesber, F. J., and Dickson, W. J. *Management and the Worker.* Cambridge: Harvard University Press, 1939.

Rosenberg, Bernard, and White, David Manning, eds. *Mass Culture: The Popular Arts in America.* New York: Free Press, 1957.

Ross, H. Laurence. "The Local Community: A Survey Approach." *American Sociological Review* 27 (February 1962): 127–34.

Ross, Murray G. *Community Organization.* New York: Harper and Row, 1967.

Rossi, Peter H. *Why Families Move.* New York: Free Press, 1955.

Rossi, Peter H., and Dentler, Robert A. *The Politics of Urban Renewal.* New York: Free Press, 1961.

Schnore, Leo F. "The City as a Social Organism" *Urban Affairs Quarterly* 1 (March 1966): 58–69.

———. "Measuring City-Suburban Status Differences." *Urban Affairs Quarterly* 3 (September 1967): 95–108.

———. *The Urban Scene.* New York: Free Press, 1965.

Schnore, Leo, and Jones, Joy K. O. "The Evolution of City-Suburban Types in the Course of a Decade." *Urban Affairs Quarterly* 4 (June 1969): 421–42.

Schnore, Leo, and Pinkerton, James R. "Residential Distribution of Socioeconomic Strata in Metropolitan Areas." *Demography* 3 (1966): 491–99.

Schorr, Alvin L. *Slums and Social Insecurity.* Washington, D.C.: U.S. Government Printing Office, 1963.

Schulze, Robert O. "The Bifurcation of Power in a Satellite City." In *Community Political Systems,* ed. Morris Janowitz, pp. 19–30. New York: Free Press, 1961.

Selvin, Hanan C. "A Critique of Tests of Significance in Survey Research." *American Sociological Review* 22 (October 1957): 522–23.

Sheldon, Eleanor B., and Moore, Wilbert E., eds. *Indicators of Social Change.* New York: Russell Sage Foundation, 1968.

Shevky, Eshref, and Bell, Wendell. *Social Area Analysis.* Stanford: Stanford University Press, 1955.

Shevky, Eshref, and Williams, Marilyn. *The Social Areas of Los Angeles.* Berkeley and Los Angeles: University of California Press, 1949.

Shils, Edward A. "Daydreams and Nightmares: Reflections on the Criticism of Mass Culture." *Sewanee Review* 65 (1957).

———. *The Logic of Personal Knowledge.* London: Routledge and Kegan Paul, 1961.

———. *Political Development in the New States.* The Hague: Mouton, 1966.

Sieber, Sam D. "The Integration of Fieldwork and Survey Methods." *American Journal of Sociology* 78 (May 1973): 1335–59.

Simmel, Georg. "The Metropolis and Mental Life." In *The Sociology of Georg Simmel,* ed. Kurt H. Wolff, trans, H. H. Gerth and C. Wright Mills, pp. 409–24. New York: Free Press, 1950.

———. *The Sociology of Georg Simmel.* Edited by Kurt H. Wolff, translated by H. H. Gerth and C. Wright Mills. New York: Free Press, 1950.

Sinclair, Upton. *The Jungle.* Upton Sinclair, 1920.

Sjoberg, Gideon. *The Preindustrial City.* New York: Free Press, 1960.

Smith, Joel; Form, William H.; and Stone, Gregory P. "Local Intimacy in a Middle-Sized City." *American Journal of Sociology* 60 (November 1954): 276–84.

Spear, Alan. *Black Chicago.* Chicago: University of Chicago Press, 1967.

Spencer, Herbert. *The Study of Sociology.* Ann Arbor: University of Michigan Press, 1961.

Stein, Maurice R. *The Eclipse of Community.* New York: Harper and Row, 1960.

Strauss, Anselm. *Images of American Cities.* New York: Free Press, 1961.

Sudman, Seymour; Bradburn, Norman M.; and Gockel, Galen. "The Extent and Charasteristics of Racially Integrated Housing in the United States." *Journal of Business* 42 (January 1969): 50–92.

Sussman, Marvin B., ed. *Sourcebook on Marriage and the Family.* Boston: Houghton Mifflin, 1955.

Suttles, Gerald D. *The Social Construction of Communities.* Chicago: University of Chicago Press, 1972.

———. *The Social Order of the Slum.* Chicago: University of Chicago Press, 1968.

Sweetser, Frank L. "Factorial Ecology: Helsinki, 1960." *Demography* 2, no. 1 (1965): 372–85.

Sykes, Gresham M. "The Differential Distribution of Community Knowledge." In *Cities and Society,* ed. Paul K. Hatt and Albert J. Reiss, Jr., pp. 711–21. New York: Free Press, 1957.

Taeuber, Karl E. "The Effect of Income Redistribution on Racial Residential Segregation." *Urban Affairs Quarterly* 4 (September 1968): 5–14.

Taeuber, Karl E., and Taeuber, Alma F. *Negroes in Cities: Residential Segregation and Neighborhood Change.* Chicago: Aldine, 1965.

Theodorsen, George A., ed. *Studies in Human Ecology.* Evanston: Harper and Row, 1961.

Thomas, W. I. *On Social Organization and Social Personality.* Edited and with an introduction by Morris Janowitz. Chicago: University of Chicago Press, 1966.

Toennies, Ferdinand. *Community and Society (Gemeinshaft und Gesellschaft).* Translated by Charles P. Loomis. East Lansing: Michigan State University Press, 1957.

Udry, J. Richard. "Increasing Scale and Spatial Differentiation: New Tests of Two Theories from Shevky and Bell." *Social Forces* 42 (May 1964): 403–13.

Van Arsdol, Maurice D., Jr.; Camilleri, Santo F.; and Schmid, Calvin F. "The Generality of Urban Social Area Indexes." *American Sociological Review* 23 (June 1958): 277–84.

Vidich, Arthur J., and Bensman, Joseph. *Small Town in Mass Society.* Princeton: Princeton University Press, 1958.

Warner, W. Lloyd. *Yankee City.* New Haven: Yale University Press, 1963.

Warner, W. Lloyd; Meeker, Marcia; and Eels, Kenneth. *Social Class in America.* New York: Harper and Row, 1960.

Warren, Roland L. *The Community in America.* Chicago: Rand McNally, 1963.

Webb, Eugene J., et al. *Unobtrusive Measures.* Chicago: Rand McNally, 1966.

Weber, Max. *The City.* Trans. and ed. Don Martingale and Gertrude Neuwirth (New York: Free Press, 1958).

———. *From Max Weber.* Translated and edited by H. H. Gerth and C. Wright Mills. New York: Oxford University Press, 1958.

Whyte, William Foote. *Street Corner Society.* Chicago: University of Chicago Press, 1955.

Whyte, William H., Jr. *The Organization Man.* Garden City, N.Y.: Doubleday-Anchor, 1957.

Wilson, Godfrey, and Wilson, Monica. *The Analysis of Social Change.* Cambridge: Cambridge University Press, 1954.

Wilson, James Q., ed. *Urban Renewal.* Cambridge, Mass.: Massachusetts Institute of Technology Press, 1966.

Wirth, Louis. *On Cities and Social Life.* Edited by Albert J. Reiss, Jr. Chicago: University of Chicago Press, 1964.

———. *The Ghetto.* Chicago: University of Chicago Press, 1928.

———. "Urbanism as a Way of Life." In *Cities and Society,* ed. Paul Hatt and Albert Reiss, Jr., pp. 46–63. New York: Free Press, 1957.

Wirth, Louis, and Bernert, Eleanor H., eds. *Local Community Fact*

Book for Chicago, 1940. Chicago: Chicago Community Inventory, University of Chicago, 1949.

Wirth, Louis, and Furez, Margaret, eds. *Local Community Fact Book for Chicago Metropolitan Area, 1960.* Chicago: Chicago Community Recreation Commission, 1938.

Wright, Charles R., and Hyman, Herbert. "Trends in Voluntary Association Memberships of American Adults." *American Sociological Review* 36 (April 1971): 191–206.

————. "Voluntary Association Memberships of American Adults: Evidence from National Sample Surveys." *American Sociological Review* 23 (June 1958): 284–94.

Young, Michael, and Wilmott, Peter. *Family and Kinship in East London.* London: Routledge and Kegan Paul, 1957.

Zald, Mayer. "Sociology and Community Organization Practice." In *Organizing for Community Welfare,* ed. Mayer Zald. Chicago: Quadrangle Books, 1967.

Zimmer, Basil G. "Participation of Migrants in Urban Structures." *American Sociological Review* 20 (April 1953): 218–24.

Zimmer, Basil G., and Hawley, Amos H. "The Significance of Membership in Associations." *American Journal of Sociology* 65 (September 1959): 190–201.

Zollschan, George K., and Hirsch, Walter, eds. *Explorations in Social Change.* Boston: Houghton Mifflin, 1964.

Zorbaugh, Harvey M. *The Gold Coast and the Slum.* Chicago: University of Chicago Press, 1929.

Index